AF678669

An Introduction to the THERAPEUTIC RELATIONSHIP in Counselling and Psychotherapy

SAGE | 50 YEARS

SAGE was founded in 1965 by Sara Miller McCune to support the dissemination of usable knowledge by publishing innovative and high-quality research and teaching content. Today, we publish more than 750 journals, including those of more than 300 learned societies, more than 800 new books per year, and a growing range of library products including archives, data, case studies, reports, conference highlights, and video. SAGE remains majority-owned by our founder, and on her passing will become owned by a charitable trust that secures our continued independence.

Los Angeles | London | Washington DC | New Delhi | Singapore

An Introduction to the THERAPEUTIC RELATIONSHIP in Counselling and Psychotherapy

Stephen Paul
Divine Charura

SAGE

Los Angeles | London | New Delhi
Singapore | Washington DC

SAGE

Los Angeles | London | New Delhi
Singapore | Washington DC

SAGE Publications Ltd
1 Oliver's Yard
55 City Road
London EC1Y 1SP

SAGE Publications Inc.
2455 Teller Road
Thousand Oaks, California 91320

SAGE Publications India Pvt Ltd
B 1/I 1 Mohan Cooperative Industrial Area
Mathura Road
New Delhi 110 044

SAGE Publications Asia-Pacific Pte Ltd
3 Church Street
#10-04 Samsung Hub
Singapore 049483

Editor: Kate Wharton
Assistant editor: Laura Walmsley
Production editor: Rachel Burrows
Marketing manager: Camille Richmond
Cover design: Shaun Mercier
Typeset by: C&M Digitals (P) Ltd, Chennai, India
Printed and bound by CPI Group (UK) Ltd,
Croydon, CR0 4YY

MIX
Paper from responsible sources
FSC® C013604

© Stephen Paul and Divine Charura 2015
First published 2015

Apart from any fair dealing for the purposes of research or private study, or criticism or review, as permitted under the Copyright, Designs and Patents Act, 1988, this publication may be reproduced, stored or transmitted in any form, or by any means, only with the prior permission in writing of the publishers, or in the case of reprographic reproduction, in accordance with the terms of licences issued by the Copyright Licensing Agency. Enquiries concerning reproduction outside those terms should be sent to the publishers.

Library of Congress Control Number: 2014936186

British Library Cataloguing in Publication data

A catalogue record for this book is available from the British Library

ISBN 978–1–4462–5663–3
ISBN 978–1–4462–5664–0 (pbk)

At SAGE we take sustainability seriously. Most of our products are printed in the UK using FSC papers and boards. When we print overseas we ensure sustainable papers are used as measured by the Egmont grading system. We undertake an annual audit to monitor our sustainability.

To our clients, supervisees, and students
Whose narratives helped make this book

Contents

About the authors

Stephen Paul has recently retired as Director of The Centre for Psychological Therapies at Leeds Metropolitan University after 20 years of service. He is a client-centred psychotherapist. He is co-editor of *The Therapeutic Relationship: Themes and Perspectives* (PCCS, 2008) and *The Therapeutic Relationship Handbook: Theory and Practice* (McGraw-Hill/Open University Press, 2014). Stephen was instrumental in developing a relational approach to therapy with Geoff Pelham (1999). He has worked extensively in both adult and child and adolescent psychiatry. He has been head of a therapeutic school and was Director of the VSO programme in Bhutan. Stephen now writes, practises therapy, undertakes supervision and coaching, and provides training.

I have practised as a therapist in a wide range of settings since the mid-1970s. I worked in a psychiatric hospital in Liverpool where there were no strategies in place for working psychologically with patients. The therapeutic ethos was focused around drugs, ECT (electro convulsive therapy) and what was loosely called at the time 'basket weaving'. In the late 1970s I set up a counselling centre in Bradford, one of the first in the UK, and met my first client. I had no formal training in counselling, there was little around in those days in Yorkshire. We just sat and I tried to be fully present to her and offer her a helping environment. I had no techniques to use, just myself. To this day I remember that first session. In the 1980s I trained and took courses in psychodynamic, humanistic and existential modalities to help me become fully equipped as a therapist. I ran groups in a London NHS Unit using what we would now call CBT for about eight years.

I found that the different models helped me to understand and work with my clients, but as time went by none worked exclusively for me. It became clear to me that while techniques might work well for some people, they did not for others, even those with very similar life issues. I found that it was something in the relationship that was helpful. I later trained as a client-centred psychotherapist.

In the 1990s, while developing counsellor training in Leeds and working with colleagues from very different modalities, we discovered that so much of what we did was very similar although we conceptualized it very differently. We thus formulated a relational paradigm and an approach that focused explicitly on what happened in the session.

Divine Charura is a Senior Lecturer at Leeds Metropolitan University in Counselling and Psychotherapy. He is an Adult Psychotherapist who works in the NHS, the voluntary sector and in private practice. He has published various papers and contributed to various books.

I started working in mental health settings in the late 1990s. I commenced psychiatric nurse training in Leeds and I worked in the old psychiatric asylums, including St James Hospital, Roundhay Wing and High Royds Mental Hospital, which was one of the oldest asylums in the UK and was opened in 1888 as the West Riding Pauper Lunatic Asylum. In these setting I worked with clients who were experiencing acute mental ill-health. Many of them were there against their will and had been detained under the Mental Health Act for assessment or treatment. The therapeutic interventions in these settings were often giving medication to clients, and supporting clients with activities of daily living. At times, when patients became agitated or violent, they were restrained, injected, then secluded and monitored through a small window in what was called a seclusion/de-escalation room. In worst case scenarios, I escorted patients many times to the electroconvulsive therapy (ECT) suite, where electric shock treatment was administered to them. These interventions made me question the therapeutic relationship that was being offered to those experiencing mental distress.

I decided that, as I was dissatisfied with the practice, I would train further in counselling and psychotherapy. I spent eight years training in different psychotherapy modalities. In that time I met Steve Paul, who had co-developed with colleagues a relational paradigm that focused explicitly on the relationship as being central to change. This hugely impacted on my learning and practice.

Since I have worked as a psychotherapist, I have learnt that a good therapeutic relationship is the most central and key ingredient to client therapeutic change.

Contact details
Stephen Paul: www.stephen-paul.co.uk
Divine Charura: psychotherapyinleeds@gmail.com

Acknowledgments

SP

With my thanks to

Alice Oven, who invited me to write this book, and later to Kate Wharton, whose encouragement kept it on track

Other members of the team at SAGE including Laura Walmsley, Rachel Burrows, Camille Richmond, and Shaun Mercier, plus Sarah Bury our copyeditor and Bryan Campbell our proofreader

Jacqui Gray from BACP

Divine who came on board at the half-way mark and helped bring it to fruition

Colleagues, whose advice and information helped craft both content and design: Brian Charlesworth, Joy Cullwick, Tracey Hitchcock, Geoff Pelham and Pete Sanders

Colleagues at Leeds Met University, including, Kay McFarlane, Paul Nicholson and Jayne Godward

Joyce Cramond, Judith Dryhurst and Nina Wright

Kathy Paul, who read the book through and gave a layperson's advice and guidance

Joan Dexter and Rosie Paul who were always there in the writing of the book

Sheila Haugh, whose guidance and insights helped sow the seeds that are evident here

DC

With my thanks to

Steve Paul, a great mentor and teacher, for inviting me to help write this book and spending many hours working on it with me

Professor Colin Lago, a wise mentor and colleague, for your inspiration and encouragement

My parents Alois and Letisia, my wife Helen, and my siblings David, Tatenda, Talent, Elizabeth and Enock, for all your love and for always being there

Colleagues, students at Leeds Met University and at St Anne's community services who continually teach me so much

Inspiring colleagues, Lynne Fordyce, Misha Fell, Anne Burghgraef, Jonathan Philpot, Anne Sunter, Stuart Gore and Andrew Hawkins

With thanks for health, strength, faith and love, which make all things possible

Thanks to all who have helped and inspired us whose names we may have omitted here: You know who you are

Acronyms

ACT	Acceptance and Commitment Therapy
BT	Behavioural Therapy
CBT	Cognitive Behavioural Therapy
CORE	Clinical Outcome in Routine Evaluation
CT	Cognitive Therapy
EBPs	Evidence-based Practices
ECT	Electro Convulsive Therapy
GD	Guided Discovery
IAPT	Improving Access to Psychological Therapies
MBCBT	Mindfulness-based Cognitive Behavioural Therapy
MBSR	Mindfulness-based Stress Reduction Practice
MRI	Magnetic Resonance Imaging
NHS	National Health Service
NICE	National Institute for Health and Care Excellence
RA	Relational Approach
RCT	Randomized Control Trial
RFT	Relational Frame Theory
TR	Therapeutic Relationship
UPR	Unconditional Positive Regard

Introduction

The therapeutic relationship in counselling and psychotherapy

Welcome to this book. In this book you will be introduced to all aspects of the therapeutic relationship in the practice of counselling and psychotherapy and when working in a wider range of health, social care and helping relationships.

This book offers a clear practical and evidenced-based guide to what works in therapy grounded in the latest research. It breaks down the elements of the relationship and provides a non-school/modality-based guide. Historically, the psychological therapies have been developed, taught, practised and evidenced by their theoretical *school*, *model* or *modality* (e.g. psychodynamic, humanistic, cognitive-behavioural, transpersonal, and associated versions thereof).

The importance of the relationship in therapy has become a key factor in recent years, mainly as a result of research which indicates common factors in therapy. It is acknowledged by most academic researchers now that the model or school of practice is not the central agent in change.

This book draws on the latest approaches to the practice of therapy from the different models and is written in such a way that practitioners and trainers across modalities will be able to develop both their understanding and practice.

The authors believe that twenty-first-century practice needs to be based on what is effective and grounded in evidence. This evidence points to the therapeutic relationship (TR) as the most important factor that the therapist can influence in therapy: it is significantly more important than model, school, modality or theory. The training and continuing professional development of therapists needs to reflect modern developments and not be rooted in a non-evidenced theoretical paradigm (see Haugh and Paul, 2008a: 247–54).

The TR is core to all counselling and psychotherapy training and implicit in a range of associated professional trainings, yet there is little written that explores the issues impacting on the development of the TR across modalities.

Modern trainees are encouraged to practise what is proven to work in therapy and to be aware of their effectiveness. This book provides a modern guide that *transcends* the school or modality. Furthermore, it is not a generic guide based on skills.

Most practitioners develop their own way of working after their core training. This book invites the practitioner, both experienced and the trainee, to consider and develop what works and how it can be applied in practice. It offers a radical new approach to the training of therapists and to continuing professional practice.

The book achieves its aim by:

- Being grounded in the evidence
- Identifying and illustrating practice across models of practice
- Using research, theory, practice and case studies to guide the reader
- Being written and presented in a clear format with material given in a range of informative ways to assist the reader.

Broadly, the place and practice of the relationship is at the centre of the book. This is contextualized and developed to include the following content: the history and development of the relationship in therapy, the different modalities and the place of the relationship in therapy, research, practice and the process of therapy, therapeutic skills, challenges, context, power and anti-oppressive practice, working with diversity, the self and personal development, and looks at new developments.

The book is arranged in three sections:

Part I Introducing the Therapeutic Relationship introduces the reader to the history and development of the relationship in therapy and to the different models of practice.

Part II Establishing and Maintaining the Relationship draws out the key concepts and skills, taking the reader through the process from Beginnings to Endings and exploring the challenges along the way and the use of self in the relationship.

Part III The Relationship in Context covers the therapeutic setting, the use of the relationship in a range of therapeutic practices and the application of the relationship to a range of professional roles. Issues of diversity are further developed. In the final chapter areas for developing practice and a critique of the relational approach are discussed.

WHO IS THIS BOOK FOR?

- This book is written for all practitioners and trainee practitioners in health, social care and related professions, such as teaching.

- All trainee practitioners in the UK taking counselling and psychotherapy training courses, i.e. Therapeutic Counselling, Counselling Psychology, Psychotherapeutic Counselling and Psychotherapy.
- Trainers and practitioners in Counselling, Counselling Psychology, Psychotherapy and the Psychological Therapies and for Continuing Professional Development courses. The book will also help meet the curriculum needs of BACP accredited courses and the typical curricula of UKCP courses.
- Practitioners and trainees in mental health nursing, clinical psychology, occupational therapy, social work, and specialist education, for whom the therapeutic relationship is part of their work.

CORE MODELS

Most practitioners ground their work in an integrated theoretical model and accredited therapy trainings are underpinned with a **core model**. This book is intended for trainees and practitioners who may use different theoretical models. Much of the theory we use comes from psychodynamic and **humanistic** practice.

This book focuses on the therapeutic relationship and will be equally of use to practitioners of different orientations who wish to deepen their understanding of the relationship and what works in therapy, as well as those for whom a **relational approach** is central to their training and/or practice.

A relational approach draws on the practice from different models in a complementary manner. Each modality is considered as throwing light on a different dynamic of the relationship. It is quite possible, therefore, that a practitioner may work from a relational core model or that a psychodynamic, existential-humanistic, cognitive or transpersonal therapist may use the concepts and material in this book to illustrate their own practice.

HOW TO USE THIS BOOK

The book is written in a style and format that enables you to access it in a number of ways:

1. For in-depth reading
2. Key points and summaries
3. Background and illustrative information

This is achieved by the text of each chapter being contextualized thus:

- Chapter introductions, summaries and linking boxes
- Client Clips

- Practitioner Clips
- Theory Clips
- Research Clips
- Figures – illustrations and diagrams
- Resource Boxes – giving background material for further exploration
- Reflection Points – with key points for discussion and consideration
- A list of acronyms at the front of the book
- Tables – for example, comparing and contrasting different modality approaches/debates/concepts regarding the relationship
- A glossary of key terms at the end of the book

The Clips, which aim to be bite-sized for easy assimilation, help you make further sense of what is being explained and may in themselves be useful for further exploration, discussion and study.

Client and Practitioner Clips are drawn from the experience of practice. They are anonymized and do not describe or refer to any one client. However, all the examples describe real-life situations. Pseudonyms are used in all the Clips in this book.

You are signposted through the book via the chapter introduction and summaries, and there are linking sections throughout. These help you to see the material in its context. These linking sections have a grey background.

Key terms, written in **bold**, are explained in the glossary at the end of the book.

Each acronym (e.g. RA for relational approach) is used for simplicity and ease of reading. It is spelt out in full when first introduced and is included in the List of Acronyms at the front of the book.

Competencies

We introduce relational competencies for good practice which help the reader to consider how to work effectively. Some readers may choose to work with these to develop their proficiency. They are a guide to good practice.

A note on style

We present the material in this book to you, the reader, in an informative accessible style and format. This helps both trainees and practitioners to be guided through the relevant theoretical and practice knowledge and to identify the kinds of skills or qualities that are key to the helping relationship. It aims to go to the heart of therapy and focus on what works and how to be an effective practitioner.

Wherever possible we present the material in an easily readable format. At times, some of the concepts may be difficult to understand and we hope that the relevant Clips and reflection points are helpful.

Terms and concepts

For the purposes of this book, the terms counsellor, psychotherapist, counselling or clinical psychologist and, to some extent, psychological therapist may be considered interchangeable and indicate a practitioner whose primary role is therapeutic. What the therapist does may differ, but this may have as much to do with the context, the setting and the relationship itself. For the purposes of this book, therefore, the terms therapy and counselling or psychotherapy may be considered interchangeable unless explicitly differentiated. In the main, we use the word *therapist* to include all of these.

The word *practitioner* is used to describe therapists and health, social care and related professionals who use the relationship as part of their work.

In some studies and practice the term *patient* or *service user* may be used. In this book, the authors predominantly use the term *client* unless there is specific reason to do otherwise.

We refer to clients and therapists as 'they', except where we are discussing a particular client.

We use CE (Common Era) for dates in place of the more traditional AD (Anno Domino) to acknowledge and respect the cultures and religions of the world.

EUROCENTRICISM

The health and social care professions globally have tended to develop in a philosophy of practice based on the cultures of Europe, North America and Australasia. Much of the content of this book is taken from ways of understanding human nature and therapeutic practice founded in these approaches. Clearly, when human relationships, which are living, dynamic processes, are explored, professionals need to work in the best way possible for their clients. Where this conflicts with models that are clearly Eurocentric, tensions may occur.

In this book many of the theories and studies explored are from this Eurocentric perspective. This signifies the prevalence of theories as defined and studied by Eurocentric authors and researchers. To ensure a balanced book, however, we give examples in our case and Practitioner Clips that take into consideration wider cross-cultural perspectives.

Therapists must be very careful to understand that the cultural and social context of the client impacts on their experience and ways of relating. This in turn influences how they relate to the therapist in the relationship.

Our intention, therefore, is to provide a text which supports practice that is applicable in the widest range of cultures and contexts. We are committed to an approach which is facilitative and not dominated by the therapist, their model and their culture. The client is the expert. We demonstrate the importance of this from theoretical, practical and socio-cultural perspectives.

LASTLY...

We hope you find the content of this book useful. We believe it covers much of what a therapist in the twenty-first century needs – to practise in a way which honours the relationship and the client's potential to find their own answers. We have tried to introduce the material in a way which respects the different bodies of theory and practice. We invite you to draw out what helps and informs you and to put aside that which does not. The additional resources we recommend will help you to further equip yourself to work successfully in the way that maximizes your effectiveness.

Part I

Introducing the Therapeutic Relationship

This part sets out for the reader the history and development of the relationship in therapy and the different models of practice.

1

Introducing the therapeutic relationship

The aims of this chapter are for the reader to develop an understanding of:

- The development of psychiatry, psychology and the talking therapies.
- The development of modalities and differing perspectives.
- The importance of the therapeutic relationship in counselling and psychotherapy.

In this chapter the development of counselling and psychotherapy are explained. We give an overview of how the different modalities of therapy evolved in their historical and socio-cultural contexts. We introduce the basic elements of the therapeutic relationship (TR) and their place in the philosophy, psychology, practice and evaluation of therapy. This is done from the perspective of both modality and practice, introducing the reader to a multi-dimensional picture of the therapeutic encounter. The reader is brought up to date with recent developments and research in practice.

PSYCHIATRIC AND PSYCHOLOGICAL FOUNDATIONS

In this section we detail the development of the talking therapies from medical practice, psychiatry and psychology. The field of counselling and psychotherapy mushroomed in growth in the twentieth century. With roots going back through hundreds of years in philosophy and religion, it was in the twentieth century that the professions were founded. Counselling and psychotherapy are therefore very new professions

Psychiatry

From ancient times mental health problems were often thought to have supernatural or spiritual causes and mentally ill people were considered to be in some way possessed by bad spirits. Treatments were often made using magic or sorcery and exorcism was a commonly considered 'cure'.

Hospitals for those with mental health problems are thought to have been established in medieval Islamic society in Baghdad. In 1247 the first mental institution was opened in Europe – the Bethlehem Royal Hospital, later shortened to 'Bedlam'. There were no real treatments for people who were admitted to these institutions.

The word 'psychiatry' has its roots in the Greek words *psyche*, meaning soul or mind, and *iatros*, meaning physician. It was not until 1808 that the term was coined by the physician Johann Christian Reil. Mental health institutions developed more humane treatment methods in the nineteenth century (for example, William Tuke, a Quaker who founded the York Retreat in 1796) and psychiatry was then considered to be a recognized, specialized discipline.

As psychiatry continued to evolve, in the 1930s specialized drugs were developed. Electroconvulsive therapy (ECT) started being widely used from 1938. Drugs such as lithium, which was used for treating mania, were developed in 1948 and antipsychotic drugs were introduced from 1951.

In the 1960s leading writers such as Laing, Szasz, Lacan and Michael Foucault offered critiques of psychiatry. This led to the anti-psychiatry movement which, in essence, was a criticism of certain practices rather than opposing all that psychiatry did. In the UK, the 1959 Mental Health Act encouraged a change towards community care. In the 1970s the development of selective serotonin reuptake inhibitors (SSRIs), typically used in the treatment of depression and anxiety disorders, further facilitated possibilities of community care. Drugs with lesser side-effects, such as Prozac, were developed in the late 1980s.

P

PRACTITIONER CLIP 1.1 BARS ON THE WINDOWS OF THE MIND

I (Steve) was told by the Senior Nursing Officer of a mental hospital in the north of England in 1975 that with the advent of drug treatments 'We have taken the bars off the windows of the mental hospitals and put them in the minds of the patients'.

In the UK in the late 1980s and the 1990s legislation for community care set out the basis for psychiatric support in the community. The large psychiatric asylums closed down and more patients started to live in less institutionalized settings.

The twentieth century brought with it further understanding of the biology behind many mental disorders and the development of new drugs for the treatment of many psychiatric conditions. In current psychiatry, the focus is on a medicalized approach, with referral for psychological treatments or talking therapies where government guidelines recommend.

Psychology

Psychology also has its roots in the great civilizations of Egypt, Greece, China and India. The first psychological therapy was performed by Islamic physicians on those with mental illness in a psychiatric hospital built in Fez, Morocco, in the eighth century CE.

Ahmed ibn Sahl al-Balkhi (850–934) proposed that 'if the *nafs* (psyche) gets sick, the body may also find no joy in life and may eventually develop a physical illness'. He stated that the body and the soul can be healthy or sick, or 'balanced or imbalanced', and that imbalance of the body can result in fever, headaches and bodily illnesses, while imbalance of the soul can result in anger, anxiety and sadness, which could be treated psychologically (Deuraseh and Talib, 2005).

Psychology was considered a branch of **philosophy** until the mid-nineteenth century when it was developed as a scientific discipline in Germany and then, in the USA, with the focus on the structure of mind. Wundt (1896) wrote the first textbook on the subject and his perspective was from empirical experimentation. The development of psychology as a natural science was in some way counterbalanced by the work of Freud, who has remained influential into the twenty-first century. In the twentieth century, the development of behaviourism and cognitivism were central to mainstream psychology and its empirical focus. Psychology as a new human science flourished.

Freud is regarded as the founder of **psychoanalysis**, the precursor to psychotherapy. Freud's original work was with the 'unconscious' and working with 'hysterical' patients. Traditionally, the therapist analysed the client and there was little emphasis on the interpersonal relationship.

His ideas greatly influenced the work of Jung, Adler, Assagioli, Rank and a host of others who went on to form diverse schools of therapy. Parsons (1909) coined the term 'counselling' in relation to vocational guidance, but it was Carl Rogers who developed counselling as a disciplined therapeutic practice, as distinct from psychotherapy. This was primarily because the practice of psychotherapy was restricted to physicians.

Table 1.1 outlines a brief history of psychiatry, psychology and counselling and psychotherapy. The information here can be followed up with further reading.

TABLE 1.1 Timeline: The development of talking therapies through psychiatry and psychology

705 – The first psychiatric hospital was built in Baghdad
circa 900 – The concept of mental health was introduced by Ahmed ibn Sahl al-Balkhi. He recognized that illnesses can have psychological causes
circa 900 – al-Razi documented the concept of psychotherapy (*al-'ilaj al-nafs*)
1247 – Bethlehem Royal Hospital was founded as a priory; later known as Bedlam Hospital
1758 – William Battie published a *Treatise on Madness*, calling for all people with mental health problems to be treated in asylums
1793 – Phillipe Pinel developed the idea of 'moral treatment'. In 1809, he first documented dementia praecox
1796 – The York Retreat is founded by William Tuke, a Quaker, who developed humane treatments
1870 – Jean Charcot began clinical research into hysteria (conversion disorder) in Paris using hypnosis
1893 – Emil Kraepelin defined 'dementia praecox', later to be called Schizophrenia
1890 – William James published *The Principles of Psychology*. His more spiritual views on human nature were superseded by the development of a scientific psychology
1895 – Sigmund Freud and Josef Breuer published *Studies on Hysteria*, based on the case of Anna O. and initiated the talking therapies
1892 – Foundation of the American Psychological Association
1906 – Ivan Pavlov published the first studies on behavioural conditioning
1908 – The term 'Schizophrenia' was introduced by Swiss psychiatrist Paul Bleuler
1900 – Freud published *Interpretation of Dreams*
1910 – Freud founded the International Psychoanalytical Association with Carl Jung and Otto Rank
1911 – Alfred Adler left Freud's Psychoanalytic Group, refuting Freud's focus on sexuality and developed his theory on childhood and social forces
1913 – The British Psychoanalytical Society was founded by Ernest Jones, who became Freud's biographer; Jung split with Freud, disputing Freud's inability to acknowledge religion and spirituality, and founded Analytical Psychology; Jacob Moreno developed Psychodrama in Vienna
1933 – Wilhelm Reich published *Character Analysis*, proposing that a person's character, rather than individual symptoms, should be treated
1936 – Karen Horney published *Feminine Psychology*, a critique of Freudian theory
1938 – Electroconvulsive therapy (ECT) was developed
1942 – Ludwig Binswanger founded Existential Therapy; rupture between Freud's daughter Anna Freud and Melanie Klein, key founder of Object Relations Theory, caused the British Psychoanalytical Society to split into three camps; Carl Rogers published *Counseling and Psychotherapy*; the World Psychiatric Association was founded
1950s – Fritz Perls develops Gestalt therapy; Transactional Analysis developed by Eric Berne
1952 – Carl Rogers publishes *Client-Centered Therapy*; first clinical trial of chlorpromazine (major antipsychotic); publication of *The Diagnostic and Statistical Manual of Mental Disorders* (*DSM*)
1953 – B.F. Skinner introduced behavioural therapy
1954 – Abraham Maslow established humanistic psychology
1956 – Gregory Bateson and others introduced the double bind theory of schizophrenia, which locates its causes as interpersonal and as often being linked in the family
1957 – Albert Ellis introduced Rational Emotive Behaviour Therapy

1960 – Ronald Laing published *Sanity, Madness and the Family*, proposing that the roots of schizophrenia lie in the family; Thomas Szasz published *The Myth of Mental Illness*, which led to the anti-psychiatry movement; Stanislav Grof developed LSD therapy and later holotropic breath work

1967 – Aaron Beck proposed a psychological model of depression and developed Cognitive Therapy

1969 – Maslow, Grof and Anthony Sutich published the *Journal of Transpersonal Psychology*

1980 – David Burns published *Feeling Good*, which led to the upsurge in Cognitive Behavioural Therapy

1988 – Stephen Mitchell published *Relational Concepts in Psychoanalysis*, considered to be the first significant relational text

1996 – Transpersonal Psychology Section of the British Psychological Society established

1990s – Meta-research studies indicate that no model of therapy is any better and the relationship is central to change

2000 – Ken Wilber published *Integral Psychology*, a new transpersonal model of the human psyche

The talking therapies are historically a relatively new phenomenon. Until the Freudian era, working with mental health had been the domain of doctors, who applied a medical approach. The development of psychology in the nineteenth century led to an objective approach to understanding the structure and functions of the human mind. From the early work of Freud, four forces or traditions which aim to work psychotherapeutically with human distress have developed.

THE FOUR FORCES OF PSYCHOLOGY

The **psychodynamic/psychoanalytic** modality focuses on the dynamics between the conscious and the unconscious parts of the self and relations with the outer/social world. A Freudian therapist typically analysed the patient and functioned in an expert role. Adler, Ferenczi, Abraham, Rank, Jung, Fairbairn, Guntrip, Klein and others were all influenced by Freud's work and were instrumental in different ways in developing analytic approaches to therapy. In recent years, there has been an increasing emphasis on interpersonal relations in the therapeutic process.

Behaviourism developed out of social learning theory influenced by the work of Skinner, Watson and others. The focus here was on changing behaviour. Beck, Ellis and others have developed a range of approaches in this area. In the last 30 years there has been an emphasis on cognition and its effect on behaviour. Specific approaches, such as cognitive therapy and cognitive behavioural therapy, were developed. The therapist here is seen more as a trainer and their role is more of an educator.

The **existential-humanistic** modality has developed from divergent roots, focusing on individual responsibility and self-determination. Fromm, Laing, Maslow,

Rogers, Perls and others contributed to the development of widely differing approaches. Bugental, Laing and others were key in the development of existential therapy, as distinct from a newer area of humanistic psychology which included client-centred therapy, Gestalt and other approaches. The existential-humanistic therapist is typically engaged in helping the client take responsibility for their situation and acts as a facilitator for growth.

Transpersonal therapy, the most recently developed modality, focuses specifically on the development of *being*, spirituality and a holistic view of the individual. Assagioli, Jung and others have all contributed to this approach. A transpersonal therapist is mainly concerned as a guide or catalyst for the holistic development of the client.

In the last 25 years, a range of interpersonal approaches have developed which have focused more on the TR. There has been a growth in eclectic and integrative ways of working. Many practitioners train in one modality and further develop their own practice from a wide range of sources.

There is now a multitude of diverse approaches to counselling and psychotherapy. Corsini and Wedding (2010) count over 400. Those within established schools are often characterized by slight nuances that differentiate them from each other.

Current research (Lambert, 2004; Cooper, 2008) reflects that there is no clear evidence that any one approach is better than any other. Research has also

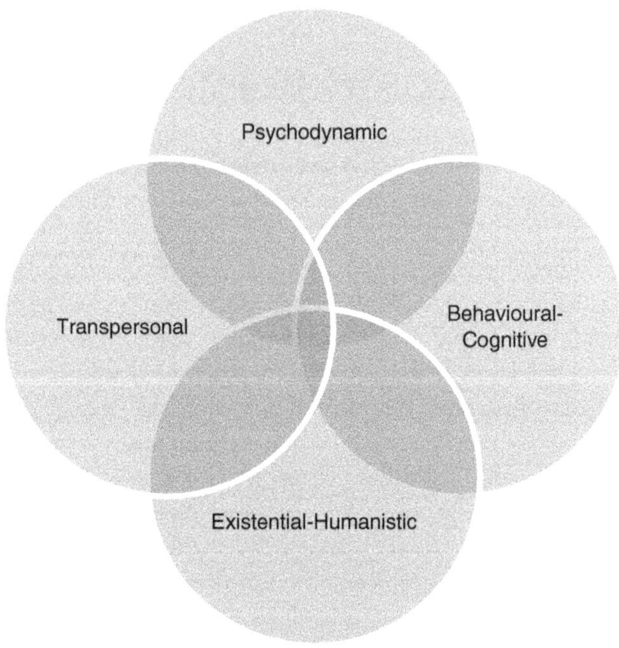

FIGURE 1.1 The traditional 'forces' of psychology

indicated that the relationship itself in therapy can be considered as more instrumental to the change process than any model of therapy or use of techniques or interventions.

Another psychological model could be called 'integral' or 'integrative'. This approach attempts to honour and integrate the complex and diverse aspects of our being, incorporating elements of the human psyche. Many therapists conceptualize and practise from an integrative perspective. However, this is likely to mean different things for different practitioners.

PHILOSOPHY AND PSYCHOLOGY

Psychology is a relatively new discipline which developed in the latter nineteenth century. Before then philosophy had been the domain for the exploration of human nature. With the development of human sciences, the new field of Psychology was introduced as an attempt to understand human mentality through objective science (using the methods of the natural sciences, such as medicine, biology, etc.). It is worth clarifying the difference between the two disciplines (Figure 1.2).

In the past 130 years the focus has moved from questions of human nature to how the mind works. We consider both philosophy and psychology to be central to understanding the human condition and individual problems.

The field of psychology developed as an attempt to map out and understand the human psyche. These first psychologists were informed by their own views of human nature and these views influenced how they attempted to structure and explain the psyche.

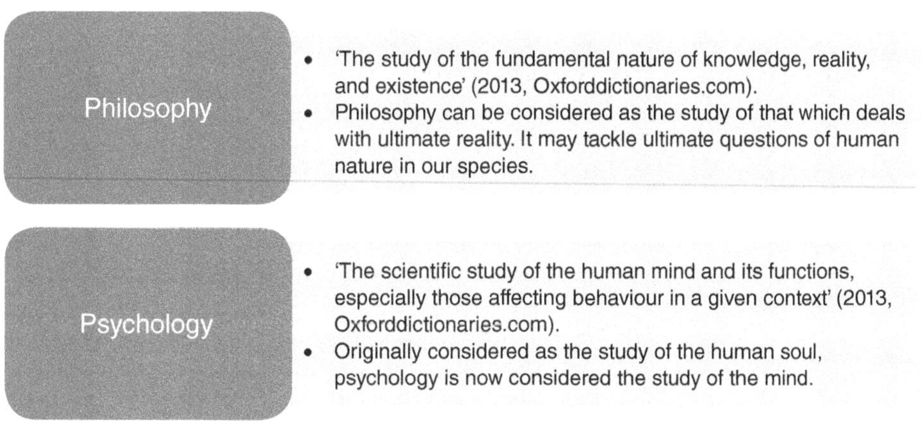

FIGURE 1.2 Philosophy and Psychology

Many people enter training in counselling and psychotherapy choosing a local course or one that has a good reputation, or perhaps one that has a model of therapy they know something about. If we consider that the different modalities of therapy are informed by different views on human nature, then it is important for individuals to reflect on their own philosophy in choosing a modality to train and practise in. An individual who has a strong religious worldview *may* find training in psychodynamic therapy does not sit well, and conversely an atheist *may* struggle with the theory and practice of psychosynthesis, a transpersonal therapy.

It is important to note that philosophy, and hence all psychology, is located within its sociocultural and historical setting. The birth of psychology was significantly influenced by the mechanistic nature of science in the nineteenth century. Wundt was concerned with experimental psychology. These influences led to a psychology which was more concerned with the *structure* of the psyche as opposed to the *function* of the psyche, i.e. how it worked.

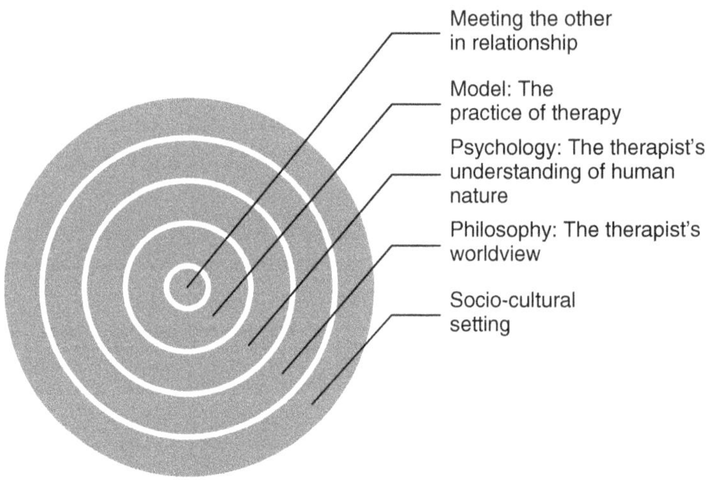

FIGURE 1.3 The context of the TR

As it has grown, psychology has become more inclusive to the different worldviews and has incorporated the four main approaches acknowledged today.

> A great deal of contemporary psychology [is] alarmingly ignorant of social and cultural history. It made assumptions about identity, purposes and methodology without considering the basis of these assumptions and what alternatives existed. It presupposed a body of knowledge, skill and a capacity for objectivity which it did not possess. (Howard, 2000: 8)

TABLE 1.2 The traditional four forces of psychology

	Philosophical foundations	**Some European influences**	**Psychological theorists**	**Examples of practice**
Psychoanalysis	Mechanistic view of the psyche; we are biologically determined	Monotheistic 'psychology' Schopenhauer Greek Myths	Freud Jung Harry Stack Sullivan Klein Winnicott Bowlby Kohut	Psychoanalysis Psychodynamic therapy
Behaviourism and later cognitive therapy	Our outcomes determine our behaviours The mind seeks to understand and make sense of reality	Aristotle Descartes Locke/Hume	Pavlov Watson Skinner Wolpe Beck Kelly Ellis	Behaviour therapy Cognitive behaviour therapy
Existential-humanistic	We have the potential to reach inner potential The mind seeks to understand and make sense of Reality	Descartes Kierkegaard Nietzsche	Maslow Sartre Kierkegaard Rogers Laing Perls Berne Yalom	Cognitive therapy Person-centred counselling Existential therapy Transactional Analysis Gestalt therapy
Transpersonal	We are part of a greater whole and seek to transcend our individual selves	Plato Schopenhauer James	William James Maslow Jung Wilber Assagioli	Psychosynthesis Integral therapy

Through the latter part of the twentieth century, from these diverging fields of theory and practice 'core models' developed. Practitioners were trained in and practised through the philosophical worldview of a particular model, often excluding any input from other approaches.

As society changed from the 1960s onwards, and with the advent of computer technology and a more empirical approach to the psychological therapies, there were a number of developments:

- Many different approaches to therapy were developed, often growing out of a particular model.
- Eclecticism developed whereby practitioners used interventions and approaches from and across a range of modalities.
- Research found that:
    - there are common factors across approaches that are universally effective.
    - no approach per se is better than any other.
- Consideration of socio-cultural factors and new ways of conceptualizing human distress developed. The development of **Postmodern Psychology** questioned whether there is an ultimate or singular version of the truth. Reality is considered as multi-dimensional and practitioners sought to avoid reducing human experiencing to a model based on past social perspectives.

The 1980s were therefore a rich period in the development of different approaches. Interest in relational factors grew as practitioners explored what worked in therapy.

We have seen how the fields of counselling and psychotherapy have developed out of Psychiatry and Psychology. Divergent philosophical models developed which were often exclusive and formed their own unique concepts and language. In recent years social changes and research have led to an interest in what actually works in therapy and this has resulted in an interest in the relationship at the heart of therapy.

THE IMPORTANCE OF THE RELATIONSHIP

In a review of the literature, Paul and Haugh (2008) identified key themes which led to a developing attention to the place of the relationship.

THEORY CLIP 1.1 KEY THEMES IN THERAPY

1. The therapeutic relationship is central to all therapy and the relationship has many different dimensions (or different levels).
2. Evidence points to the relationship, not the theory, as being fundamental.
3. Much training, practice and theorizing is focused on a particular body of theory with little cross-over of ideas.
4. Many practitioners view themselves as trans-theoretical /integrative as they develop years of practice.

5. The need to focus on the client not the theory.
6. Therapists often marginalize issues of power and culture.
7. The therapeutic relationship is expressed in a myriad of ways, verbally and non-verbally, and takes place in a myriad of settings.
8. Increasingly, much current training now focuses more extensively on the relationship itself.

Paul and Haugh (2008 4–6)

Now let us explore this in more detail:

- The therapeutic relationship is central to all therapy

The theme common to all therapeutic practice is the two-way interaction between client and therapist. This interaction is the context for all that happens in the therapeutic meeting. While the different models or approaches make sense of and work with this relationship in different ways, all to varying degrees have come to accept the centrality of relationship and that the client and therapist together create this relationship.

- Evidence points to the relationship not the model as fundamental

Research has evidenced that the **core model** of the therapist has much less influence on the outcome of therapy than previously thought. It is now considered that the therapeutic relationship itself is the most important element that the therapist can affect in therapy. Research has further identified **common factors** in the relationship that work across all approaches and all helping relationships.

- Much writing around training has been focused on a body of theory with little cross-over of ideas

Traditional schools or modalities in the past have operated within their own **frame of reference**. This included distinctive philosophies, languages and concepts. With increasing evidence of generic therapeutic factors, a common understanding of theory and practice is helpful for all. In this book we consider the philosophy, theory and practice of different modalities through the medium of the TR. Training is moving towards a more relationally-oriented approach. The emphasis for practice and review is on the relationship and what works in the relationship.

- Many practitioners view themselves as transtheoretical/integrative as they develop years of practice

Feltham, in his paper 'Challenging the core model' (1997), among others, has noted the trend for practitioners to train in one model and then to develop a wide range of expertise that fits their own needs. Many counsellors, for example, do further training in CBT, which they incorporate into their own way of working. An approach rooted in the TR can accommodate different methods and develop understanding.

- Focus on the client not the theory

The focus for change is now clearly in the client. A theoretical model helps understanding in the processes in therapy.

- Issues of power and culture are often marginalized by therapists

Issues of diversity and power and anti-oppressive practice have not historically been considered central to practice. Courses may have *added in* sessions on diversity. However, all aspects of difference are present in every therapeutic encounter. It could be considered blinkered to presume otherwise. In the modern era approaches to practice which ignore such dimensions are limited and perhaps counterproductive.

- Much current training now focuses more extensively on the relationship itself

Research findings over the past 60 years have increasingly pointed to the importance of the relationship and, consequently, there has been an increasing focus on the place of the relationship in the training of therapists, regardless of model.

THE RELATIONAL PARADIGM

A combination of social factors and research findings has led to the development of more holistic approaches to the theory and practice of therapy. Over the past few decades, since the 1980s, a new therapeutic **paradigm** has emerged that takes the relationship as the key concept in the theory and practice of therapy. This paradigm has crystallized into approaches that are called relational, but also, more broadly, the concept of relationship has come to be regarded as central in therapy, largely as a result of research. By 'paradigm', we mean a framework through which to work. There will be different formulations of working relationally. Some may be embedded in psychoanalytic theory and some in humanistic theory, and so on. We therefore maintain *a* relational approach as opposed to *the* relational approach.

The **relational approach** (RA) was the name given to a new core model for a professional training course in counselling in Leeds in the mid-1990s, an approach developed by the staff from a variety of therapeutic traditions which sought to find a common approach that all could sign up to.

The key principles of this approach are expressed in the following:

1. Relations between people are the basis of social and individual life and relational concepts are used to understand human life in all its complexity.
2. Relationships are of fundamental importance in:
   - The development of personality and a sense of self
   - The difficulties clients bring to therapy (relations with the self and relations with other people)
   - The therapeutic process (the therapy relationship is the heart of the process) (Paul and Pelham, 2000: 110)

A RA is therefore perhaps best considered as a paradigm, or framework, rather than a model in itself, as relational factors are central to virtually all approaches. For some, they are pivotal to change, while for others they are the medium for forming a good working relationship in therapy. As a framework, the relationship is central to the therapeutic encounter. All models of therapy work through the relationship and make sense of it from different perspectives. What matters is that the relationship is the central agent for change.

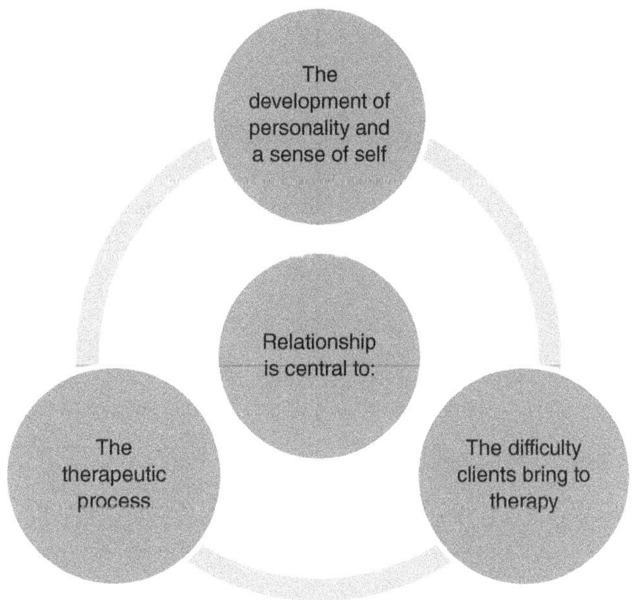

FIGURE 1.4 The centrality of relationship in a RA

Relational approaches draw from a basic given: *we are motivated by a need to relate*. From the moment of birth our phenomenological (subjective) worldview is grounded in and developed through our relationship with others. This can be illustrated in Object Relations theory, humanistic views of human development, Gestalt and cognitive psychologies (the 'object' refers to the personal target of the need to relate).

Most importantly, our sense of self forms in the context of our relationships. In relational approaches this is central, as the interaction between client and therapist is considered as the main instrument for change.

RESOURCE BOX 1

Gask, L. (2004) *A Short Introduction to Psychiatry*. London: Sage.
Shorter, E. (1997) *A History of Psychiatry: From the Era of the Asylum to the Age of Prozac*. New York: John Wiley & Sons.
Two introductions to the development of psychiatry.

Deuraseh, Nurdeen and Talib, Mansor Abu (2005) 'Mental health in Islamic medical tradition', *The International Medical Journal* 4(2): 76–79.
Syed, Ibrahim B. (2002). 'Islamic Medicine: 1000 years ahead of its times', *Journal of the International Society for the History of Islamic Medicine*, (2): 2–9 (7–8).
Traditional Islamic perspectives on mental health.

Chung, M.C. and Hyland, M.E. (2011) *History and Philosophy of Psychology*. London: John Wiley & Sons.

Philosophical foundations of psychology and mental health.
Howard, A. (2000) *Philosophy for Counselling & Psychotherapy*. London: Palgrave.
Overview of philosophers and their impact on therapy.

FILMS

One Flew Over the Cuckoo's Nest (1975)

Based on a novel by Ken Kesey (1959), the film critiques psychiatric approaches to mental illness and the institution as a method of social control in the US context.

Girl Interrupted (1999)

Based on the memoirs of Susanna Kaiser, the film tells the story of a young woman in a psychiatric hospital in the 1960s after she was diagnosed with borderline personality disorder.

A Dangerous Method (2011)

Based on the relationship between Sigmund Freud, founder of psychoanalysis, and Carl Jung, initially his 'Crown Prince', the film details the developing split between the two.

Family Life (1971)

A teenage girl gets pregnant and the domination of her parents leads to a breakdown and her eventual treatment for catatonic schizophrenia. This film makes a strong case for the social causes of psychological disturbance.

WEBSITE WITH FILM

www.rcpsych.ac.uk/training/studentassociates/historyofpsychiatry/psychiatrytimeline.aspx

WEBSITE

http://webspace.ship.edu/cgboer/historyofpsych.html

CHAPTER SUMMARY

In this chapter, to introduce the reader to the therapeutic relationship, we presented and discussed the following:

- Counselling and psychotherapy have rapidly developed over less than 120 years.
- Four forces, or schools of therapy, have developed out of different modalities of psychology.
- There are now many diverse models of therapy.
- The therapeutic relationship is recognized as central to all therapy.
- Evidence points to the relationship not the model as being fundamental to change.
- Much writing around training has been focused on a body of theory with little cross-over of ideas.
- Many practitioners view themselves as being transtheoretical/integrative as they develop years of practice.
- The focus needs to be on the client not the theory.
- Issues of power and culture are often marginalized by therapists.
- A relational paradigm has been developed which crosses the traditional models.

2

What the research tells us

The aims of this chapter are for the reader to develop an understanding of:

- The key evidence for what works in therapy.
- The skills and attitudes that form the basis of effective practice.
- A critique of the research methods used in therapy research.
- Important developments in therapy from neuroscience, attachment and their centrality to a reparative relationship.
- The 'evidence base' for the concepts, theory and practice that follow.

Many funding and commissioning bodies as well as consumer groups and the media require evidence as to the effectiveness of different approaches. Similarly, individuals may seek informed information as to what type of therapy they may choose to help them. On the other hand, many therapists find the whole area of research to be at odds with their practice. In this chapter we clarify what the research says and its implications for practice.

The chapter is developed thus:

1. **Does therapy work?** What evidence is there that therapy actually helps?
2. **Which therapy work best?** The reader is introduced to the most recent meta-studies which distil the differences across modalities.
3. **What works in therapy?** The evidence indicates that what are now called **common factors** are considered key skills in therapy. The common factors are deconstructed and explained in clear terms.
4. **Horses for courses?** Do some modalities work better from some clients and why?
5. **The therapeutic relationship**. Recent meta-studies clearly outline the alliance or relationship as being central to change.

6. **Specific factors in the relationship**. The reader is introduced to the key relationship factors that are proven to be effective in therapy. These key factors form the basis for practical therapeutic skills in later chapters.
7. **Issues of sex, age and race in therapy**. The reader is introduced to a summary of the research in these areas and the matching of therapist to client.
8. **The current context of research, new developments and areas for further research**. The state of research today and areas of further study are summarized.

Over the years, the different approaches have sought independently to prove their effectiveness. Often this has been in a move to maintain the superiority of their approach against another.

1. DOES THERAPY WORK?

From the early studies of the work of Rogers (1942), it is now proven beyond any reasonable doubt that therapy helps (Cooper, 2008; Lambert, 2013). Currently in the UK National Health Service (NHS), the CORE (Clinical Outcome in Routine Evaluation-Outcome Measure) shows that people report themselves as being less distressed after therapy than before (e.g. Stiles et al., 2006). Additionally, people who receive therapy report themselves as significantly improved compared with *control groups* of those who don't receive therapy (Lambert and Ogles, 2004). Other studies show that people who receive counselling fare better than those who receive GP care alone (Hansen et al., 2002).

Generally, meta-studies (Lambert and Ogles, 2004; Wampold, 2001) have shown that the level of improvement is considered highly *significant* – which in research language means that therapy is clearly proven to result in positive change for 75–90 per cent of people. This is a more successful outcome than for those having surgery or other medical procedures. Overall, Cooper (2008) found that around 80 per cent of people will do better after therapy than those who have not had therapy.

The effectiveness of therapy can be summarized thus:

- Improvements in mental health tend to be maintained for one or two years after therapy has ended, though the longer-term impact is less clear (Nicholson and Berman, 1983).
- Talking therapies are generally as effective as pharmacological treatments for psychological distress, and seem to have lower relapse and drop-out rates (Chilvers et al., 2001).
- Counselling and psychotherapy are relatively cost-effective forms of treatment – particularly for more psychologically distressed individuals – with an economic advantage above and beyond their contribution to psychological health and wellbeing (Gabbard et al., 1997).

- Approximately 5–10 per cent of clients deteriorate as a result of therapy (Lambert and Ogles, 2004).

(Adapted from Cooper, 2008)

We can be certain, therefore, that therapy is proven to be a worthwhile and effective treatment for people with psychological issues and mental health problems.

2. WHICH THERAPY WORKS BEST?

Debates over which therapy works best have to a large degree been minimized by the use of meta-analyses in the review of primary research (Lambert and Ogles, 2004). Early comparative or meta-analyses of many studies (Luborsky et al., 1975) found that *all* the different approaches to therapies were considered successful. What came to be called the **Dodo effect** (from Alice's *Adventures in Wonderland*) was realized in psychotherapy: '*All shall be winners and all shall have prizes*'. This is still the case when the relative differences in outcomes across different approaches are considered (Luborsky et al., 2002).

A major study by Stiles et al. (2006) found that different therapy treatments in the UK NHS had equivalently positive outcomes:

Over 1,300 people who received cognitive-behavioural therapy (CBT), person-centred therapy (PCT) and psychodynamic therapy (PDT) during a three-year period completed the Clinical Outcomes in Routine Evaluation-Outcome Measure (CORE-OM) at the beginning and end of their treatment. The researchers compared outcomes of six groups: three treated with CBT, PCT or PDT only, and three treated with one of these plus one additional approach (e.g. integrative, supportive, art therapy). They found all six groups averaged marked improvements. The treatment approach accounted for only tiny proportions of the variance in CORE-OM scores. They concluded that results for these three treatment approaches, as practised routinely across a range of NHS settings, were consistent with the previous studies that found that theoretically different approaches tend to have similar outcomes. This study further substantiated the view that the model of therapy in itself has no real difference on outcome.

Comparative studies exploring which therapy works best for which condition have been inconclusive in determining categorically any outright winners (e.g. Roth and Fonagy, 1996). Many researchers are now of the opinion that undertaking comparative studies of the different schools of therapy will not assist us in deciding what is best.

Many early research studies were undertaken by practitioners themselves or researchers seeking to prove effectiveness. Even today, studies are often carried out or funded by those who seek to prove that their preferred way is the best (Lambert, 2002). This investigator or **researcher allegiance** can therefore skew a study and reduce its objectivity.

Later in the chapter we review the debate as to what therapy works for whom. We can be assured that there is no overall evidence to say that one modality is significantly better than any other.

3. WHAT WORKS IN THERAPY?

When an RA was developed in Leeds in the UK in the 1990s, colleagues discussed developing a common way of understanding what we did, when it became clear that in many ways what actually happened in therapy was very similar for all of us. Very often it was language or conceptualization which differentiated. Current research suggests that even if practitioners believe they are following a model, there is clear evidence to suggest that therapists of the same modality vary widely in how they practice (Malik et al., 2003).

> *A number of blind men came up to an elephant and debated, 'What is the elephant like?' One of them touched its leg and said: 'It is like a pillar'. Another man touched its ears and said, 'The elephant is like a fan. Another touched its trunk and said 'It is like a water spout'. Yet another touched its tail and said 'It is like a rope'.*

This classic Hindu allegory shows us how we can all view the same thing very differently. All, from their own perspective, were correct in their understanding, but none could fully describe it. Similarly, there has been much research into what works in therapy.

Since it has been accepted de facto that therapy works and that virtually all of the major modalities have similar outcomes, researchers have been seeking to clarify what is it that works in therapy. Findings have strongly suggested that the different modalities have common components and that these common factors are central to successful outcome more than the specific techniques of a particular approach (Imel and Wampold, 2008).

Wampold determined that these factors affect the outcome of therapy:

1. General effects – those common factors that underlie all psychotherapies: 70 per cent.
2. Specific effects – that is, particular aspects linked to a specific model: 8 per cent.
3. Unexplained variability – linked to most likely client differences: 22 per cent.

These findings show that effects related to a model are indeed very small. He further states that there is little evidence for a model utilizing specific modality-based techniques or interventions. He proposes that the research indicates that there is clear evidence for a model linked to common factors.

What therefore are these common factors?

Lambert (1992) determined the four common factors as follows:

1. **Extratherapeutic change**: Those factors that are part of the client's personal life out of therapy (such as family, work and social support) that help recovery regardless of therapy.
2. **Hope/expectancy**: This can be called a placebo effect: improvement that results from the client's knowledge that she/he is being treated and from the belief that therapy will 'work'.
3. **Model or technique**: Those factors unique to particular therapies (homework tasks, desensitization *in vivo*, etc.).
4. **Therapeutic relationship**: This covers all variables that are found in therapy regardless of the therapist's theoretical orientation, such as empathy, warmth, acceptance, etc.

(after Paul and Haugh, 2008)

Asay and Lambert (1999) further identified the importance of these factors (see Figure 2.1).

While weightings of these factors vary according to different reviewers, the TR is consistently considered to be the most important factor which the therapist has some control over in therapy.

Orlinsky, Grawe and Parks (1994), in a **meta-analysis** of over 1,000 studies, noted the significance of the TR and identified key criteria, such as therapist credibility, skill, collaborativeness, empathic understanding, affirmation of the

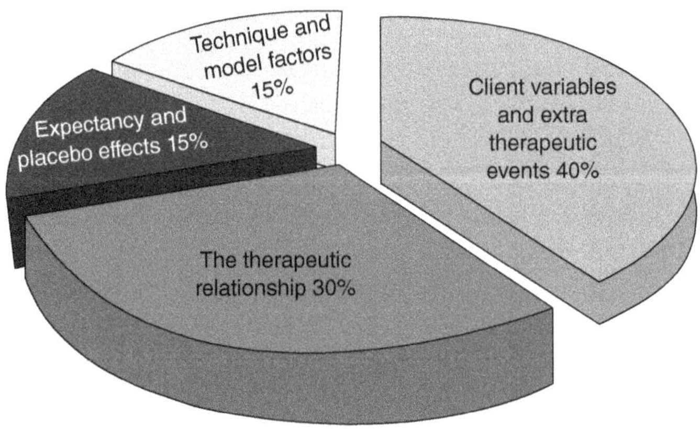

FIGURE 2.1 Lambert's pie: factors that affect the outcome of therapy (Asay and Lambert, 1999)

client, and attention to the client's affect (simply, emotional experiencing), as all being associated with positive outcomes. They further found that the most important determinants of outcome were:

- The quality of the patient's participation in the therapy – this was the most important determinant.
- The therapeutic bond, especially as determined by the client.
- The therapist's contribution, especially through 'empathic, affirmative, collaborative and self-congruent engagement' (p. 361) with the client.
- The skilful application of potent interventions.

They noted that these determinants 'can be considered *facts* established by 40+ years of research' (Orlinsky et al., 1994: 361–2).

REFLECTION POINT 2.1 COMMON FACTORS

- Are common factors simply a 'warm human relationship'?
- If so, does that in some way diminish these findings?

4. HORSES FOR COURSES? DO SOME MODALITIES WORK BETTER FOR SOME CLIENTS AND WHY?

The debate into which therapy works best for which client is a highly contentious one in the therapy community. *Overall*, the evidence is clear that, generally, all modalities are equally successful and none is significantly more so than any other. However, there has been a wealth of research to identify which approach may be best for which client group. Such research supports the need of commissioning bodies in determining the most effective, and cost-effective, treatment to put in place for any particular client.

There is a body of evidence that cognitive-behavioural therapies have been shown to be effective for a wide range of psychological issues, while there is less evidence for the other approaches (Cooper, 2008). This evidence is, however, widely contested by non-CBT practitioners and researchers:

- The CBT research, in the main, is been undertaken by researchers seeking to prove the effectiveness of researcher allegiance and research design. This brings into question the robustness of this research (Luborsky et al., 1999).
- People do not fit into neat 'disorders' and may not meet treatment criteria at all (Westen et al., 2004). The medicalization of distress may in effect factor out those with complex or non-standard psychological problems. The patient

uniformity myth suggests we are all the same or perhaps deviate from a norm rather than all being unique and different.

- Trials which have been used to determine effectiveness have been rigidly controlled. People with more than one presenting problem are often screened out as are those with severe problems. Little if any consideration is given for differences in clients, e.g. age, ethnicity, culture. Trials themselves may be so manualized that they bear little relevance to day-to-day therapeutic practice (Wampold, 2001).
- Meta-analyses which filter out all questionable variables suggest there is little difference in outcome between different approaches (Luborksy et al., 2002).

Furthermore, a number of independent major studies have clearly demonstrated the parity between modalities:

- King et al. (2013) evidenced equal success for non-directive counselling and CBT in the treatment of depression.
- Elkin et al. (1989) in the USA compared the effectiveness of CBT and interpersonal therapy in the treatment of depression and both were found to be equally successful.
- Stiles et al. (2006) (detailed above) in the UK evidenced comparative outcomes for cognitive-behavioural therapy, person-centred therapy and psychodynamic therapy.

CORE

The CORE (Clinical Outcomes in Routine Evaluation) was developed in the UK as a measure of outcome that is usable across the full range of therapeutic modalities. The CORE-Outcome Measure is a client self-report questionnaire designed to be administered before and after therapy and to evaluate therapeutic change.

Evans et al. (2000) highlighted analyses of over 2,000 responses showing good reliability and convergent validity of CORE against longer and less general measures. They showed large clinical/non-clinical differences and good sensitivity to change across different therapeutic modalities. CORE is therefore at the centre of the paradigm of 'practice-based evidence' (Margison et al., 2000). Its use has evidenced for many therapeutic services and for clients the efficacy of a wide range of modalities in psychotherapy (Evans et al., 2000).

There are further studies which suggest that different clients as opposed to different 'disorders' may benefit from different types of therapy. All clients are not the same. Researchers are considering that clients with certain characteristics may do better with one therapy than another. This 'aptitude–treatment' research may well help us understand further why one modality of therapy will work for one person and not for another. For example, there is evidence that clients with high cognitive functioning do better in cognitive therapy, whereas those with higher social functioning do better in interpersonal therapy (Sotsky et al., 1991).

Miller, Duncan and Hubbard (2004) found no evidence to suggest that an **eclectic** approach (see Chapter 3), that is, mixing theory and practice across models, is any more successful than school- or model-based approaches. They assert, however, that the focus should be in the practice of the therapist rather than the model:

> Significant improvements in client retention and outcome have been shown where therapists have feedback on the client's experience of the alliance and progress in treatment. Rather than evidence-based practice, therapists tailor their work through practice-based evidence. (Miller et al., 2004: 20)

5. THE THERAPEUTIC RELATIONSHIP

Most definitions of the therapeutic relationship (e.g. Bordin, 1979; Gaston, 1990) identify three key elements for successful outcome:

1. The collaborative nature of the relationship:

   That is, that therapist and client work mutually together.

2. The affective bond between client and therapist:

   There is an empathic understanding and trust *shared* by client and therapist

3. The client and therapist's ability to agree on treatment goals and tasks:

   Both parties have a *shared perspective* on the aim and activities in therapy.

Orlinksy et al. (2004) in their analysis of over 100 key studies note that no other area has attracted more attention by researchers investigating the link between the process of therapy and its outcome than what they call the 'therapeutic bond' (p. 345). They conclude that the TR is clearly related to positive outcome.

Horvath et al. (2011) differentiate between the **therapeutic alliance** and the therapeutic relationship. The TR is composed of several 'interlocking elements' (p. 56), called variably empathy, rapport, trust, etc., whereas the alliance is the conceptualization of what the relationship may achieve using these elements successfully. We look at the establishment of the working alliance in Chapter 6.

Martin et al. (2000) conducted a meta-analysis of 79 studies and concluded that the TR is consistently related to outcome, regardless of a range of possible variables, including the type of treatment. A further 62 studies, which were conducted in a wide range of modalities including cognitive-behavioural, psychodynamic, interpersonal and integrative approaches, were reviewed by Orlinsky et al. (2004). They noted a significant, consistent association between positive outcomes of therapy and the input of the therapist in sessions when rated by their clients. The relationship is directly related to the outcome in therapy: the better the relationship the better the outcome.

Professional bodies and others who have considered the body of research concur: 'The cumulative research convincingly shows that the therapy relationship is crucial to outcome' (Steering Committee of the American Psychological Association's Division 29 Task Force on Empirically Supported Therapy Relationships, 2002: 443. See Appendix).

6. SPECIFIC FACTORS IN THE RELATIONSHIP

The therapeutic conditions, as developed by Carl Rogers

Rogers' research led him to advocate that what came to be called the core conditions of **empathy**, **congruence** and **positive regard**, communicated to and received by the client, led to successful outcomes in therapy. Many practitioners become familiar with Rogers' (1957) six necessary and sufficient conditions. Rogers himself was an avid researcher. The extensive research which followed his original work indicates that the therapist variables of empathy, genuineness and positive regard may not be necessary and sufficient for *all* clients; however, a strong correlation has been found between levels of empathy and therapeutic outcomes and, similarly, positive regard and congruence also correlate with clients' reported levels of improvement (Sanders and Cooper, 2006).

There is now much less research focus on proving the efficacy of the original three conditions that arose out of Rogers' pioneering research. Virtually all modalities of therapy accept these as variably instrumental in the development of the TR.

Rogers was clear that these conditions need to be utilized in a theoretically coherent manner. Empathy, positive regard and congruence are explored in their practical application in Chapter 6.

Empathy

Empathy is one of the core competencies in the practice of therapy. In its simplest description, it can be the understanding of the client and their problem as they experience it. In its more complex description, it can be an understanding of all aspects of the client's experiencing without evaluation.

Bohart et al. (2002) found that levels of empathy make a significant contribution to the outcomes of therapy. Clients rated highly being understood by their therapist. Empathy is rated more highly than techniques. In fact, they further found a stronger correlation between empathy and outcome in CBT therapies than in experiential/humanistic therapies. For inexperienced therapists, empathy is more closely linked to outcomes, implying the importance of developing empathic communication for trainee and newly qualified therapists.

A meta-analysis by (Elliott et al., 2011) found strong evidence that empathy is linked to positive outcomes in therapy, regardless of therapist modality. They conclude with the following recommendations for practice:

1. Empathy is essential for all therapeutic practice regardless of therapist modality, treatment format or the severity of the client's problems.
2. The therapist's primary task is to understand the feelings of the client, not simply the words, and to not paraphrase back the content of what the client has said.
3. A range of empathic responses that carry forward the meaning of the client's communications are useful.
4. Therapists should attend to the unspoken as well as spoken, and the central themes as well as the peripheral themes.
5. Empathic responding needs to be individualized to the needs and perceptions of each client. One may value accurate immediate empathic responding, while another may wish there to be more distance in the relationship.
6. Therapists should not seek to predict the client's situation but offer empathy with humility.
7. Empathy should be offered in the context of positive regard and genuineness.

(after Elliott et al., 2011)

Positive regard

The second of the three competencies developed by Rogers, positive regard is variously described as 'non-possessive warmth', 'prizing', 'acceptance', 'unconditional positive regard', 'valuing' and 'affirmation' by writers.

Positive regard is considered to be significant to positive outcome in over half of studies (Orlinksy et al., 2004). Many studies report that a positive and warm relationship with therapists is highly valued by clients (Conte et al., 1995). **Ruptures** in the TR may be caused by the therapist's inability to consistently maintain helpful levels of positive regard (Farber and Doolin, 2011).

A meta-analysis by Farber and Doolin indicated that positive regard has a significant part to play in the outcomes of therapy. They offer the following recommendations for practice:

1. Positive regard is strongly recommended. It may 'set the scene' for other interventions or, in itself, lead to change.
2. There is no reason to refrain from communicating positive regard. It can do no harm. It can be considered 'kindness'.
3. Positive regard has a key role across different therapy modalities.
4. It may be particularly important to communicate positive regard where a 'non-minority therapist is working with a minority client'.
5. Positive regard must be communicated and it needs to be 'a caring, respectful, positive, attitude'.
6. Therapists vary in their ability to communicate positive regard and therapists need to monitor and adjust their conveying of it to the needs of each client.

(Farber and Doolin, 2011: 62–63)

In research into what is called **relational depth** (which we shall look at it in Chapter 7), Mearns and Cooper (2005) suggest that clients rate highly being cared for by their therapist.

Congruence

Variously described as 'genuineness', 'authenticity', 'realness' or 'presence', the third of Rogers' competencies is founded in the human presence of the therapist in relationship with their client. The therapist is open and honest in their communications.

Heavily researched by Rogers and his associates, congruence may be considered an intrinsic way of functioning for a therapist. It has proven difficult to directly link aspects of genuineness with outcome, due to methodological issues which have dogged many studies, but research indicates that while clients rate 'trustworthiness' (Burckell and Goldfried, 2006) as very important in therapy, overall only 38 per cent of clients directly link congruence with positive outcome (Orlinsky et al., 2004).

A meta-analysis by Kolden et al. (2011) concludes that there is strong evidence of the link between congruence and outcome, even though studies may have limitations. Orlinsky and Howard suggest that if study after study point in the same general direction, then 'we could not help believing that somewhere in all that variance there must be a reliable effect' (1978: 288–9).

These conditions may be considered to be central elements in the TR. Asay and Lambert (2001) found that therapists' facilitative skills directly linked to positive outcomes: **therapist facilitativeness** (as a generic term to describe therapist relational behaviours) is now accepted as a positive measure in terms of outcome.

What researchers now mean by the TR is more wide-ranging than the original client-centred research, which sought to prove a new approach to therapy based, in the main, around one modality: 'Therapeutic alliance is seen as a necessary, but not sufficient, condition for personality change' (Lambert and Ogles, 2004: 174).

6. SPECIFIC RELATIONSHIP FACTORS

In the modern era, research has moved on significantly from the early research which to some extent 'proved' the importance of Rogers' three conditions.

Orlinksy et al. (2004), in their meta-review of over 2,500 studies, distilled core relationship factors that have been directly linked with outcomes in therapy:

- The positive engagement in therapy by client and/or therapist
- Interactive coordination – the ability of both parties to work together on the therapeutic task
- Rapport or empathic communication
- Affective attitude, the communication of positive regard in the relationship
- Relational congruence, the development of a common understanding of what is happening in the relationship.

(after Paul and Haugh, 2008)

Positive engagement in therapy

This research examines the positive engagement by therapist and/or client in the therapeutic process. Where clients viewed their therapist as positively engaged and credible, therapy was found to have better outcomes. Other studies noted positive outcomes in relation to client engagement in therapy. There is little evidence of, or research into, joint or *mutual* engagement at this time (Paul and Haugh, 2008).

Interactive coordination

Interactive coordination is the joint collaboration by both parties in therapy. While not much research has been undertaken here, positive outcomes appear more likely where clients view therapists as more collaborative in the therapeutic process, as opposed to being more directive. Where there is considered to be a good TR, there is better goal and task agreement between client and therapist (Bordin, 1979).

Rapport

The term 'rapport' implies mutual empathic understanding and communication. There is now virtually universal acceptance of the place of therapist's empathic understanding in relationship to success in therapy (Bohart et al., 2002). Clients' ratings of therapist empathy are directly linked to outcome. However, there is little evidence to suggest that the therapist's self-reporting of empathy is linked to favourable outcomes. Therapists themselves can be considered a poor judge of this.

There is minimal research on rapport *between* client and therapist, but 17 studies (reviewed by Orlinsky et al., 2004) all show a consistent correlation with positive outcomes. Furthermore, most research is of the therapists' communication of empathy. Paul and Haugh (2008: 16) state: 'There has been almost no research on a client's empathic understanding in therapy, which is a real deficit in our understanding of the therapeutic relationship.' Orlinsky et al. (2004) note that if therapy is to be relational rather than therapist-led, research is needed in this area.

Affective attitude

This research examines the place of positive regard in therapy. Many studies link *therapist* positive regard to good outcome. A further 36 studies (reviewed by Orlinsky et al., 2004) link *client* positive regard to the therapist to positive outcome, while 26 studies link *reciprocal* positive regard to outcome. Clearly, therefore, positive regard is linked to successful outcomes. The evidence here further suggests gains where this is reciprocal.

Experiential congruence

This is where client and therapist have a common understanding of a shared experience in therapy. This area has been little studied. Research (Kivlighan and Arthur, 2000) indicates that where therapist and client move towards an experience of the '*same relational reality*' (Orlinsky et al., 2004: 354) there is a positive relation to outcome. Given the new interest in research in 'relational depth', where client and therapist report moments of meeting or changes to the quality of relationship, this area of study merits further research.

Phases of the relationship

While researchers mainly consider therapy to be a fluid process, consideration needs to be given to relationship formation in the early stages. Research indicates that positive changes early in therapy strengthen the relationship and lead to a positive outcome (Beutler et al., 2004). Other studies have clearly identified that the better the therapeutic bond or alliance is reported to be at its early stages, regardless of any positive gains, the better the outcome (e.g. Weerasekera et al., 2001). Early positive ratings of the relationship may be significant predictors of outcome (Bachelor and Horvath, 1999).

Developing an early positive relationship is more likely to lead to a positive outcome than one formed in later stages of therapy (Horvath and Symonds, 1991). Research further suggests that the establishment of a strong bond in the early stages of therapy allows for the safe exploration of negative feelings as therapy progresses. Safran et al. (2001) suggest that the collaborative working through of 'ruptures' in the TR in a non-defensive way leads to positive outcomes.

Evidence therefore suggests that forming a strong relationship from the beginning augurs well for positive outcomes in therapy.

7. ISSUES OF DIVERSITY, SEX, AGE AND RACE

All relationships are diverse and every therapeutic meeting is with another who is different. Whether professionals work as social workers, nurses, doctors, occupational therapists or other allied therapy professions, it is important to consider the impact of diversity, sex, age and race on the TR. However, as noted earlier, research tends to factor out differences in its variables. It looks, in the main, for the 'average'. This whole area therefore 'suffers from a paucity of research' (Paul and Haugh, 2008: 17).

Beutler et al. (2004), in their review of therapist variables, found only 10 studies after 1990. They found no link between therapist gender and outcome of therapy, including client drop-out rates. Similarly, age is not considered an area worth researching, and there are no significant studies up to 2003. One study (Beck, 1988) found that therapists who were over 10 years younger than their clients had the poorest outcomes.

There is a significant body of therapeutic literature which examines cultural, racial and ethnic compatibility. Beutler et al. (2004), however, could identify just 11 studies published between 1990 and 2000 that examined the ethnic/racial matching of therapist and client. There was evidence to suggest from this small sample that ethnic matching may be linked to outcomes, but the limitation in the number of studies and the research design of these studies cannot clearly identify the significant factors. (Variables such as drop-out rates in therapy, therapist-client mismatch and language all need further examination).

The American Psychological Association (2011 also see Appendix) notes the importance of adapting or tailoring the therapy relationship to specific patient characteristics, with particular reference to culture, religion and spirituality.

Issues relating to diversity are examined in detail in Chapter 11. Clearly, however, further research is much needed in this area.

8. THE CURRENT CONTEXT OF RESEARCH, NEW DEVELOPMENTS AND AREAS FOR FURTHER RESEARCH

One of the key issues in current research and its implications for practice is in the standardization of research studies, their findings, and implications for practice. In the UK, funding has favoured research grounded in **randomized control trials**: those approaches which can be clearly operationalized and favoured by those undertaking research seem to be more successful and are thus commissioned and funded (Mace and Moorey, 2001). This has implications too for the psychological therapies. In the UK, jobs as 'low impact' or 'high impact' therapists have been created based on manualized training.

While there is evidence that such approaches do well for a percentage of clients with simply defined problems, many people do not benefit from a number of sessions of problem-solving therapy.

REFLECTION POINT 2.2 RANDOMIZED CONTROL TRIALS

Randomized trials are now considered the 'gold standard' of research in the talking therapies. Many people question such research as being too generic or the wrong way to evaluate human suffering. Wessely (2001) suggests that while randomized control trials may be effective in determining the effects of a medicine, practitioners must have the right to retain clinical judgement in relation to the individual needs of each client.

- Should the clinical and professional opinion of the practitioner determine the best treatment?

The movement towards diagnosis in deciding what therapy works is clearly problematic. Many writers propose that people's life issues and the human condition should not be approached in this way. The classic schizophrenia study in the USA (Rosenhan, 1973), where researchers went to a range of medical settings describing the same symptoms and were diagnosed and treated in widely differing ways, is a clear example of this.

There is, furthermore, a move among practitioners to practice-based evidence: the ability of the practitioner to be self-reflexive in their practice and determine suitable therapy for the client rather than the 'one size fits all' approach in which there may ultimately be no winners or prizes. The way forward, as in medicine, may lie in the development of generalist therapists who may refer more complex or specialized cases to experts in these areas, such as eating disorders or addiction, for example. The focus may not be on a model of therapy but on the expertise and/or specialism of the therapist.

Recent research into relational depth (see Chapter 7) is promising, in helping understand how change may happen in therapy.

Neuroscience

Although research has been central in affirming the importance of the TR, there has actually been little 'hard' empirical evidence to demonstrate why the relationship seems so important. Recent knowledge of the brain and neuroscientific descriptions of the impact of the empathic relationship now enable us to understand what makes the therapeutic relationship curative and effective (Farmer, 2009). Research can now actively 'see' the emotions in the brain and how different aspects of the brain 'fire up' in response. Researchers can now directly evidence the effect of relationships, both good and bad, on the brain.

Neuroscience and attachment

The importance of love and attachments within primary relationships and their impact on children's mental and physical wellbeing is well documented (Gerhardt, 2004). Recent neuroscientific research findings confirm Bowlby and Ainsworth's attachment theories, as well as the importance of love and relationship throughout life. Joseph (1999) and Mikulincer and Shaver (2004) demonstrated that lack of love and a nurturing relationship in childhood affects the development of neurological pathways in the brain. Such studies have shown in the worst cases that children have died as a result of these circumstances.

Attachment research evidences how attachment patterns throughout life influence emotional and psychological wellbeing. Patterns formed in childhood also influence how individuals respond when faced with trauma or challenges later in life. Those with secure attachment styles often fare better in the face of psychologically distressing circumstances.

Neuroscience and empathy

There is now neuroscientific evidence to support the importance of empathy (Ivey et al., 2012). Empathic relationship-building involves activation of what are called **mirror neurons**. These neurons have important implications. When clients talk about their experiences, similar neurological changes occur in the therapist's brain. These neurological changes are activated through therapist's observing, listening and empathically responding to the client's experiences. The same process happens for the client as they listen and observe the therapist's responses and reactions to their content. The psychological and neurological processes operating in the therapist, which are communicated through empathic understanding of the client's problem/experience, trigger and activate new mirror neurons within the client.

Neuroscience and reparative relationships

Research has shown unequivocally that, through therapy, neurological changes are stimulated. The reparative aspect of relational encounter is not only influential in psychological change, but also causes *physiological* change. This enables an improvement in the client's sense of psychological wellbeing (Ivey et al., 2012).

This new research using neuroscientific methods is potentially ground-breaking for therapy. We can summarize thus:

1. The brain can change. **Neuroplasticity** means that the brain can create new neural pathways under the right conditions. The effects of the past are not irrevocably fixed. Effective therapy can change both the mind and brain of the client and therapist. In effect, the brain can rewire itself.
2. Therapy can lead to the building of new neurons. Effective therapy will help, as will positive life experiences and physical exercise.
3. When both client and therapist are *present* in therapy, neurological change will follow (see Chapter 5), as with individual meditation.
4. Positive emotional experiences have a similar effect on the brain. Focusing on positive thoughts and feelings overcomes negativity. If therapists focus on negative thoughts and feelings, it can create a circle of negativity in the brain. A focus on positive thoughts and feelings, transforms negative neural pathways.

(after Ivey et al., 2009)

A more detailed discussion of neuroscience is given in Chapters 4 and 5 where we explore developmental factors.

Neuroscientific research studies evidence the efficacy of the TR, to include empathy, presence and positive experiencing. It is important for therapists to link these findings to their practice.

TABLE 2.1 Implications for practice

The American Psychological Association Task Force (2011, see appendix) in their review of what works in psychotherapy, conclude:

- The therapy relationship makes substantial and consistent contributions to psychotherapy outcome independent of the specific type of treatment.
- The therapy relationship accounts for why clients improve (or fail to improve) at least as much as the particular treatment method.
- Practice and treatment guidelines should explicitly address therapist behaviours and qualities that promote a facilitative therapy relationship.
- Efforts to promulgate best practices or evidence-based practices (EBPs) without including the relationship are seriously incomplete and potentially misleading.
- Adapting or tailoring the therapy relationship to specific patient characteristics (in addition to diagnosis) enhances the effectiveness of treatment.
- The therapy relationship acts in concert with treatment methods, patient characteristics, and practitioner qualities in determining effectiveness; a comprehensive understanding of effective (and ineffective) psychotherapy will consider all of these determinants and their optimal combinations.

See Theory Clip 2.1 for Paul and Haugh's (2008) conclusion of their review of the research into the TR

T

THEORY CLIP 2.1 RESEARCH IN THE THERAPEUTIC RELATIONSHIP

- There is no evidence that any approach or manualized treatment is significantly better than any other. A small element of success is linked to model of therapy or treatment.
- There is evidence to suggest that a contextually-based approach to therapy will be more fruitful in future than a school- or model-based approach.
- The relationship is the most significant in-therapy factor for positive outcomes.
- Common factors have emerged across approaches that are intrinsic to success in therapy.
- It is accepted beyond doubt that the therapeutic conditions (variously described) originally developed by Rogers are central to success in all approaches.

(Continued)

(Continued)

Specific key factors that have proven effective in the TR are:

1. Positive engagement in therapy
2. Interactive coordination
3. Rapport
4. Positive regard
5. Relational/experiential congruence

- More consideration of these factors is needed, particularly the interactive or reciprocal elements which may guide us to further understanding of best practice.
- Evidence suggests that creating a good early TR augurs well for outcome, as does the ability to work through interpersonal issues.
- There is little evidence on the matching in age, sex and race and more research is needed in this area.

(adapted from Paul and Haugh, 2008: 18–19)

RESOURCE BOX 2

Cooper, M. (2008) *Essential Research Findings in Counselling and Psychotherapy*. London: Sage.
A clearly written book outlining the research and findings for therapists.

Cozolino, L. (2010) *The Neuroscience of Psychotherapy: Building and Rebuilding the Brain*. New York: W.W. Norton.
A useful text for learning more on neuroscience.

Norcross, J.C. (ed.) (2011) *Psychotherapy Relationships that Work: Evidence-Based Responsiveness*. New York: Oxford University Press.
A thorough in-depth review of the research with specialist chapters.

Paul, S. and Haugh, S. (2008) 'The relationship not the therapy? What the research tells us,' in Haugh, S. and Paul, S. (eds), *The Therapeutic Relationship: Perspectives and Themes*. Ross-on-Wye: PCCS Books. pp. 8–22.

Chapter succinctly summarizes the research into the TR.
Roth, A. and Fonagy, P. (2004) *What Works for Whom? A Critical Review of Psychotherapy Research*. New York: Guilford Press.

A resource on psychotherapy research.
Appendix (page 264): Recommendations of the American Psychological Association Task Force on Evidence-Based Therapy Relationships and Implications for practitioners.

CHAPTER SUMMARY

Research in the talking therapies now tell us:

- There is a wealth of research in counselling and psychotherapy which provides evidence for the efficacy of different modalities and it is proven beyond any doubt that therapy helps.
- The gold standard of research has been randomized control trials; however, they do not accurately represent what happens in everyday therapeutic practice.
- With regards to the question of which therapy works best, there is a body of evidence that cognitive-behavioural therapies have been shown to be effective for a range of psychological issues. While there is less research for the other approaches, this evidence is widely contested by non-CBT practitioners and researchers.
- Different studies have shown that different therapy treatments have equivalent outcomes.
- There is clear evidence for a model of therapy linked to the common factors of extratherapeutic change, hope/expectancy, model or technique, and the TR.
- Recent meta-studies clearly outline the therapeutic alliance or relationship as being central to change.
- Research which followed Rogers' work indicates that the therapist variables of empathy, genuineness and positive regard may not be necessary and sufficient for all clients.
- There is a strong correlation between levels of empathy, positive regard and congruence with client-reported therapeutic outcomes.
- Special relationship factors such as rapport and positive engagement in therapy between therapist and client are directly linked with outcomes.
- Client–counsellor matching with regards to diversity may be linked to outcomes; however, more research is needed in this area.
- Neuroscientific research shows that particular attachment styles result in maladjustment.
- Neuroscience shows that through the TR and provision of empathy and conditions which foster growth, positive therapy outcomes can be achieved.
- It is accepted beyond doubt that the TR is the most significant in-therapy factor for positive outcomes.

3

The relationship in different modalities

The aims of this chapter are for the reader to develop an understanding of:

- The foundations of practice in the different therapeutic modalities.
- The key figures, key concepts, the goals of therapy and the therapeutic relationship from the main modalities.
- The link between the traditional modalities and the development of relational key concepts.
- The importance of the therapeutic relationship in different modalities.
- A paradigm approach that has universal applicability.

This body of knowledge and practice informs us how we may choose to work effectively in practice. While the research clearly points to the centrality of the relationship in therapeutic change, the model of practice is the next most important consideration. There is no evidence to suggest that working with the TR alone, without a theoretical model to inform the practitioner, is any more effective. The use of eclecticism, a tool-kit approach to practice, drawing, in perhaps a haphazard way, from the different modalities may indeed be unhelpful to practice. Therefore, the modality and model of practice of the therapist is an important element in therapy.

In Chapter 1 what has come to be called the four forces of psychology was introduced:

1. Psychodynamic/psychoanalytic
2. Behaviourism
3. Existential-humanistic
4. Transpersonal

Out of these four forces have grown a number of different models of practice.

These forces of psychology can each be considered to have a philosophical overview of human nature. A philosophical worldview can be viewed as the way in which a person makes sense of life and the world in which they live. Out of this comes an understanding of the mechanics of the human psyche, or psychology, from which people develop ways of acting in the world. Much of this is not a conscious deliberation for most people. However, for therapists, it is important to consider:

1. A worldview, a philosophy of human nature and the world we live in
2. An understanding of the human psyche or psychology
3. An approach to how people change

As we saw in Chapter 1 (Figure 1.1) it is important to develop a philosophical understanding or worldview of the human condition. This can lead to a psychological understanding of how people live, operate and change. Finally, as therapists, we develop ways of working to help people change. Thus each therapist must consider their own philosophical perspective and psychological understanding of the psyche.

REFLECTION POINT 3.1 WHAT IS MY WORLDVIEW?

My philosophy is my worldview.

My psychology is how I make sense of the human mind.

My model of practice is how I work with others to help them change.

- What is your worldview?
- How does it link to your understanding of how the psyche works and your practice of therapy?

We now look at the four modalities in turn and their contribution to our understanding of the TR.

PSYCHOANALYTIC FOUNDATIONS

We start with the traditional psychoanalytic or **psychodynamic** approach. This school, which developed from Freudian psychoanalysis, was influenced by theories of interpersonal relationship (Sullivan), child development and early attachment

(Klein, Winnicott and Bowlby), and latterly relational theory (Kohut). The key concepts of this school can be summarized as:

- **Behaviour is determined by biological drives** and what may be considered unconscious motivations. Our motivation is to a large extent determined by our physiological needs and drives.
- **Personality develops as a result of the socialization of these instinctual drives**. Our social character is largely considered to be moulded by our interactions with others based on our motivation to satisfy and fulfil our inner needs.
- **The basis of personality structure is id, ego and super-ego**. This early psychological mode of the psyche was developed by Freud.

This psychodynamic **drive theory** sees human functioning as based upon the interaction of drives and forces within the person.

The human psyche is composed of an interaction of id, ego, super-ego. The ego, and to some degree the super-ego, is *conscious* or on the surface. The id is *unconscious*

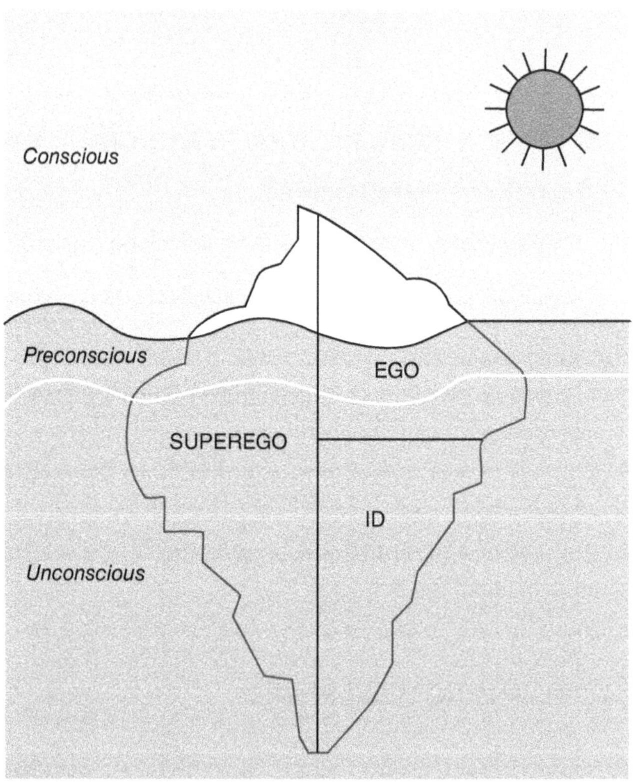

FIGURE 3.1 Freudian model of the psyche

and below the surface of our awareness according to this model. The **id** is the home of our instinctual drives. The **ego** is the sense of our conscious '*I*' which regulates our inner drives and our social self. And the **super-ego** is concerned with our place in society and how we behave in relation to the expectation of others (it can be considered to have a sort of parental quality). The id, ego and super-ego comprise the mind; they are not considered parts of the brain.

Psychological problems develop as a result of repressed childhood conflicts and the inadequate working through of developmental needs as the child grows. These repressed experiences are not worked through as the child grows into adulthood and are said to sit in the unconscious. Unresolved conflicts are brought to life in the TR and transferred on to the therapist. For example, a person wants love but actively rejects the therapist to avoid later pain if the therapist does not live up to their hopes.

Freud's psychology suggests we create a *template* based on our early primary relationships which mould how we behave in future relationships. If we have loving early relationships in which our needs are met, we expect adult relationships to follow similar courses. If our early relationships are unfulfilling in a variety of ways, we expect and in some way behave in our adult relationships in ways which lead to unfulfilment.

As well as this expectation of patterns that will repeat themselves, Freud suggested that we can drive ourselves to repeat the problematic primary relationship. This *repetition compulsion* causes people to act out the same problematic relationship dynamics in adult life, often again and again. For example, a person may seek out the same type of romantic relationship with the same problematic dynamics. It is as if the person tries to work out the pain or distress of the primary relationship in the adult relationship. However, for many people this is not resolved and the person behaves in the same unfulfilling ways to the same unfulfilling treatment. A dancer chooses the same type of partner again and again and is tripped up in the same ways. If only the person can see the patterns and understand why they follow them, then they will be better equipped to change.

Freud saw himself as the archaeologist of the human mind. His task was to look into the past with his patients and to recreate their unconscious drama by bringing to the surface and making sense of the many clues the patient presented. When these dynamics were brought to the surface, they could be 'worked through' so that they could be 'emotionally utilized' by the client. Insight alone is not enough. One of the many challenges of analytical therapy is to integrate into the current consciousness these dynamics we bring to awareness from our past experiences.

Goals of psychoanalytic/psychodynamic therapy

The aims of traditional psychoanalytic/psychodynamic therapy for the individual are threefold:

- To become conscious of their unconscious patterns, literally to make the unconscious conscious.
- To work through in the here-and-now of therapy, repressed conflicts that emerge in their relationship with the therapist. These are typically called transference behaviours.
- To gain insight and psychological awareness of the source of these restricting patterns and their emergence in everyday living.

The therapeutic relationship in psychoanalytic/ psychodynamic therapy

Traditionally, the focus of the TR is on the relationship of the client *to* the therapist. The client behaves towards the therapist based on past experiences of relating to others. The therapist therefore focuses on the client's transference towards them in this relationship.

The therapist behaves as a 'blank screen' with no personal or idiosyncratic behaviours to the clients so that this transference can develop. The client can more easily behave towards the therapist in ways borne of past experiences as there is little interpersonal relating.

The client behaves in a free-flowing manner, allowing whatever needs to emerge in themselves so that connections between internal conflicts can start to emerge. The therapist is the expert who interprets the meaning of a client's behaviour as related to past patterns and experiences so that the client can gain insight and awareness.

This classical Freudian approach has been developed over the years as a more RA to psychodynamic therapy has developed.

Object Relations theory

Freud's classical model was developed by, among others, Rank, Fairbairn, Anna Freud, Klein and Winnicott from the 1920s onwards. Evolving from Freud's view that we are pleasure-seeking beings, **Object Relations theory** is based on the principle that infants primarily seek relationship.

The development of Object Relations theory, with its challenge to classical psychoanalytic drive theory, opened the way for a new psychological theory by proposing that it is relationships with significant others that is at the heart of personality development, rather than instinctual, (libidinal) sexual or aggressive drives.

Object Relations theory proposes that people relate to people and situations in their adult lives as shaped by family experiences during early childhood. A person who experienced neglect in infancy from primary caregivers would expect similar behaviour from significant others in their adult life. These memories of people and events are processed into objects in the psyche that the person unconsciously carries with them into adulthood. These objects are then accessed by the subconscious to make sense of their social relationships and interactions. Much as a memory of an event is stored in the psyche, a similar event is approached and the mind accesses stored people to approach this new event. Where the individual has had difficult childhood relationships they project a similar outcome on to a new adult encounter. Therefore, as relationships are central to this approach, the client–therapist relationship is key to the success of therapy.

The Object Relations theory suggests that during the formation of primary relationships the infant relates to the caregiver as an object who responds to their needs. The infant will in fact organize positive or negative experiences from their caregiver separately in their psyche. Typically, the breast that provides milk is described as being the good breast. A breast that does not provide may be described as the bad breast. A mouth that kisses may be experienced as a loving mouth, whereas one that shouts may be seen as a bad mouth. The infant therefore has to process these different perceptions. Over a period of time the infant develops an internal representation of the caregiver and their good and bad parts.

These representations are subjective and may be inaccurate and yet over time grow in the psyche of the child to represent the caregiver. This can cause conflict in later life within a person, who has experienced good and bad parts of the same person and not been able to resolve them. Because these primary relationships are internalized in infancy, they continue to impact on a person's worldview, often unconsciously, into their adult life.

Object Relations theory therefore has two key concepts:

1. **Relations between people are the key to understanding human behaviour**. Our behaviour is learned in relation to others and our personality develops in relation to our primary experiences.
2. **We are driven by a need to relate, not by erotic feelings and drives**. We find fulfilment in relation to others.

The development of relational theory has been described as a shift from 'one-person to two-person psychologies' (Mitchell, 1988: 5). The classical Freudian approach views the infant as entering the world 'pre-wired', with a fixed human nature that develops in a life setting that either facilitates or distorts growth. (As we shall see, the classical humanistic approaches with human nature based upon self-actualization can be considered to be based on a similar supposition.) Two-person psychologies typically do not assume this fixed view of human nature, rather that the self is formed in relationship to a matrix of close personal interactions (described in Pelham, 2008).

In Britain from the 1930s onwards, the Object Relations School and Bowlby (attachment theory) radically transformed psychoanalysis (Greenberg and Mitchell, 1983) by introducing the importance of internal and external interactions with others. Fairbairn (1952) proposed that it is the desire for relationship, not sex or aggression drives, which is at the heart of being human. Fairbairn notes a client's comment that illustrates the difference between classical and relational psychoanalysis: 'You're always talking about me wanting this and that desire satisfied: but what I really want is a father' (Fairbairn, 1952: 137).

The therapeutic relationship in OR therapy

The OR therapist has a more active role in therapy than the passive, blank screen approach of the Freudian analyst. The OR therapist offers a supportive, reparative relationship to the client. They aim to allow the client to work through relational problems such as loss, powerlessness and issues with intimacy, in relationship with the therapist. **Interpretation** and challenge will be a part of the therapist's interventions within a boundaried, caring relationship.

The therapist will work through the client's unconscious pathological patterns, which are played out in therapy with the therapist. The aim is for the client to develop insight and awareness into these dysfunctional ways of behaving.

Interpersonal Psychology

In America, Harry Stack Sullivan (1953) developed a radically interpersonal psychoanalytic approach, which sought to rework the fixed concepts of Freudian psychology (such as innate drives: id, ego, super-ego) into concepts based upon relations between people.

Interpersonal theory sought to make sense of personality and psychological difficulties purely in relational terms. For Sullivan, personality is primarily created and sustained through interaction with others. The difficulties clients bring to therapy are not resolved primarily through bringing the causes etc. into conscious awareness, but through exploration in the here-and-now of the client's mode of relating.

The key concepts of interpersonal psychology are:

Personality is developed by social forces. It is not innate or determined in childhood.

Psychopathology is based on maladaptive interpersonal experiences.

Theorem of reciprocal emotion: we gain or suffer as our needs are met in relationships.

> **Parataxic distortions**: we base our perceptions of others on our own (distorted) inner experiences.
>
> Distortions are corrected by **consensual validation**: comparing our experience with the feedback of others through interpersonal therapy.

This disarmingly simple view of human nature was largely ignored at the time Sullivan developed this. However, to this day his propositions are simple and current.

Self Psychology

Self Psychology, developed by Heinz Kohut in the 1970s, sought to explore how the self developed in relation with others. The key concept is the *self object*, addressing how the infant's sense of self is developed and sustained through relations with others. Kohut describes how a rudimentary self emerges from our relatedness with others, becoming over a period time a cohesive self. The rudimentary self has both an *object*, which is the idealized parent image, and a *subject*, the grandiose, child, self. Gradually, the grandiose self becomes tamed and integrates with an intact integrated personality. The maturing self of the child allows it to begin to see the idealized object as a separate object, and aspects of the idealized parent image become **introjected** as the super-ego (Pelham, 2008).

Kohut (1984) used the word 'nutriment' to describe empathy as an important place in the healing process. He argued that therapy should be about the patient rather than analytic theory. To make therapy work, one needs to address the patient's self.

Kohut (1978) placed great emphasis on empathy in human development, referring to empathy as 'the recognition of the self in the other'. This led to the emergence of intersubjectivity theory (Stolorow et al., 1987), in which the TR is described as an intersubjective field co-created by both therapist and client.

Intersubjectivity theory

Intersubjectivity theory has as its basic premise that there is no such thing as a separate, independent mind. The mind develops as part of an 'intersubjective field' and that a therapeutic relationship is co-created by both client and therapist. Stolorow, Atwood and others highlight the interpersonal dimension and conceptualize the therapeutic relationship as an interactive process of 'reciprocal mutual influence' (Stolorow and Atwood, 1992: 18). They write: 'Clinical phenomena ... cannot be understood apart from the intersubjective contexts in which they take form. Patient and analyst together form an indissoluble psychological system' (Atwood and Storolow, 1984: 64). They use the term 'codetermination' (Stolorow and Atwood, 1992: 24) to describe this two-way process both in development and in therapy.

Developmental Psychology research

Studies have shown that subjectivity emerges in the intersubjective field of infant and significant others (e.g. Stern, 1985; Braselton and Cramer, 1991). The use of video-recording has demonstrated the delicate attunement between infant and adult and also the effects of misattunement. The subjectivity of the infant arises in an interpersonal field already populated with the hopes, fears, desires and fantasies of the caring adults.

The relational paradigm has been developed most explicitly in the Psychodynamic tradition. A key author is Mitchell, who explored and developed the ideas in a series of books in the 1980s and 1990s.

TABLE 3.1 Psychoanalytic/Psychodynamic summary

Key figures: Freud, Jung, Sullivan, Klein, Winnicott, Bowlby, Kohut

Key concepts:

Behaviour is determined by biological drives, unconscious motivations.

Personality develops as a result of the socialization of these instinctual drives.

The basis of the personality structure is the id, ego and super-ego.

Problems develop as a result of repressed childhood conflicts and inadequate resolution of a developmental stage.

Unresolved conflicts are brought into the therapeutic relationship and transferred on to the therapist, e.g. longing to be taken care of but the fear of being taken over.

Goals

To make the unconscious conscious

To work through repressed conflicts in transference

To gain insight, intellectual and emotional awareness

Therapeutic relationship in classical psychodynamic practice

The focus is the transference relationship

The therapist is a 'blank screen' so transference can develop

The client freely associates to uncover conflicts

The therapist is the expert who interprets the meaning of client's behaviour as related to the past

Therapeutic relationship in OR practice

The focus is on transferences and patterns that the client plays out in the relationship

The therapist offers a supportive, reparative relationship

The therapist uses expertise to interpret patterns of behaving based on past experiences

Reflections on the psychoanalytic foundations

This tradition has developed much of the *primary archaeology* of the human psyche. Freudian and post-Freudian therapists have determined, mainly from case studies, an understanding of how problems are formed, addressed and to some degree resolved.

The client's disturbance is their unique problem, in that they are perceived as having what can be seen to have a pathological psychic dysfunction. Social and cultural factors may not be addressed.

The client is often described as the 'patient', or in some cases the 'analysand', and they are analysed by the analyst who works from a body of theory and practice which locates the expertise with the practitioner. In some forms of practice the personality of the practitioner is put to one side and they operate as a 'blank screen'.

Table 3.2 introduces some of the key differences between a RA and a classical psychoanalytic approach.

TABLE 3.2 RA and classical psychoanalysis

Classical psychoanalysis
Psychoanalysis adopts a medical model: 'What's wrong with the client?' The goal is to cure neurotic symptoms.
The therapist interprets the client's material.
The focus is individualistic – the process of change takes place entirely in client's inner world.
The transference relationship is the medium of therapy.
Social factors are not important – the client is perceived as being in a pathological state.
RA
The focus is on 'What's wrong for the client?'
The therapist is interested in the meaning the client gives to their experience.
The therapist enters into a potential real human-to-human relationship.
Change happens in relationship – the therapist provides a more nourishing experience of self-with-other which is part of the therapeutic process.
The client's difficulties are not pathologized – they are seen as a creative adjustment to social and relational contexts.

BEHAVIOURAL/COGNITIVE-BEHAVIOURAL FOUNDATIONS

In the 1950s and 1960s, Behaviourism was a radical departure from psychoanalytic perspective. It took a scientific view of human nature, focusing on observable behaviour and not subjective experience. In its purest form, it did not consider inherited characteristics and rejected the notion of consciousness. Skinner, one of the founders of Behaviourism, believed 'neurotic' behaviour can be learned and unlearned. He developed Behaviour Therapy (BT).

In relation to the talking therapies, with the development of Cognitive Therapy (CT), it was found that when cognitive change (changing the way one thinks) was linked with behaviour (putting new ways of thinking into action) the combination of both methodologies was a more effective approach. Thus Cognitive Behavioural Therapy (CBT) was developed.

Behaviourism: Key concepts

The key concepts of Behaviourism can be summarized as:

- Behaviour is a product of learning.
- We learn through our actions and our behaviour is modified by what we have learned. Behaviour has consequences which are then filed away in relation to further actions.
- Behaviour can be encouraged by reward (positive reinforcement) or discouraged by being ignored or, in extremes, by punishment (lack of positive reinforcement).

Wolpe (1959) found that people can learn (or be conditioned) to become anxious in response to stimuli which would not normally give rise to anxiety. For example, a person who had a car crash in a tunnel becomes anxious when going through tunnels. He then found that anxiety can be extinguished if it is not reinforced. He developed 'reciprocal inhibition' – pairing an anxiety-provoking stimulus with an anxiety-reducing response weakens the association between the stimulus and the anxiety – so that, for example, relaxation is conditioned to the same stimulus, i.e. the tunnel. The person then experiences relaxation when driving through the previous anxiety-provoking stimulus, the tunnel (Wolpe, 1959).

Goals of Behavioural Therapy

1. Behavioural Therapy works on the elimination of problematic behaviours and learning of new, more productive behaviours.
2. Behaviour Therapy focuses on factors influencing behaviour and finding out what can be done about problematic behaviour.
3. It is concerned with the achievement of goals and targets.

Cognitive Therapy: Key concepts

> 'Men are disturbed not by things but by the views which they take of them'
> Epictetus (1st century CE)

Cognitive Therapy is often associated with Stoic philosophy. How a person interprets experience determines how they feel. For example, after a divorce you may feel happy if it means you are free, but depressed if it means you have failed in some way. Cognitive Therapy proposes that our interpretations of our subjective experiences are hypotheses or beliefs rather than facts, and as such they may be correct or incorrect to varying degrees.

Cognitive Therapy was developed by Beck, Ellis and others. They emphasized the central role of thoughts in mental processes. Ellis (1962) initially developed Rational Emotive Therapy (RET), later changed to Rational Emotive Behaviour Therapy (REBT). Beck (1976) identified distorted thinking about the self in people suffering from depression. Beck proposed that negative thinking originates in attitudes, or assumptions, which are laid down from childhood.

Goals of Cognitive Therapy

- Therapy aims to relieve symptoms and resolve problems.
- The approach helps clients acquire coping strategies.
- Therapy works to help clients modify underlying cognitive structures in order to avoid relapse.

Cognitive Behavioural Therapy: Key concepts

Cognitive Behavioural Therapy (CBT) developed as a more effective refinement of BT and CT. The underlying principles of CBT propose that problems have three components. These components are mood, cognition and behaviour (Thomas, 2008). Alongside the view that these three components should take the interventionist focus is another principle: that the client and therapist work together as a team to overcome identified problems.

CBT uses many of the techniques of Behaviour Therapy in a cognitive framework. Psychological disturbance arises from specific, habitual errors in thinking (called irrational thinking by Ellis). Unlike early Behaviour Therapy, introspection and the mind exist.

In a refinement of Stoic philosophy, Dryden, who contributed to the development of Rational Emotive Behaviour Therapy, suggested that it was more the type of thoughts than thoughts themselves that disturbed people: 'People are disturbed not by things, but by their rigid and extreme beliefs about things' (Dryden, 2008: 10).

T

THEORY CLIP 3.1 IRRATIONAL BELIEFS

Ellis developed the concept of irrational beliefs (Ellis, 1962, 1977):

- 'I must do well and win approval.' (Musturbations)
- 'Other people must treat me in exactly the way I want them to (otherwise they should be blamed and punished).'
- 'Life must give me everything I want and nothing I don't want.'

He proposed that irrational beliefs led to self-defeated thinking.

P

PRACTITIONER CLIP 3.1 WORKING WITH IRRATIONAL BELIEFS

I (Divine) once worked with a client who was a very successful banker. He came for therapy following a period of depression and anxiety after failing to succeed in an interview in which he could have been promoted to a higher post at work. In the same month his wife of four years had left him. He felt that his wife had left him because he had not been promoted and that his colleagues at work would now look down on him as a failure. Through therapy, it emerged that his core beliefs about himself included 'I must do well and cannot fail at anything otherwise no one will want me'. It also emerged that his parents only took him on holiday as a young boy when he had achieved top of the class when he was still in school.

Establishing, through the therapeutic relationship, these experiences and consequent irrational beliefs enabled us to start some cognitive behavioural work to help him change his thinking patterns (irrational beliefs) and self-defeating, withdrawing behaviours.

Goals of Cognitive Behavioural Therapy

Beck, the clinician who developed CTB in the late 1950s, proposed that the goal of therapy was to enable individuals to change perceptions of themselves and the world: to modify their thinking patterns (Beck, 1976). CBT therefore aims to replace maladaptive thoughts and beliefs with adaptive ones. Therapists aim to teach the client to modify underlying automatic thoughts and irrational beliefs so that there is relief of limiting symptoms.

Others goals can be to assist the client to achieve greater self-esteem to eliminate self-defeating outlooks on life, achieve better performance at work, or to gain more meaningful interpersonal relationships (Burns, 1989; Clarke and Fairburn, 2005; Thomas, 2008).

Therapeutic relationship (CBT and Behavioural)

Traditionally, CBT has been a formulation-based form of therapy which involves the use of tried and tested interventions by therapists. CBT has been critiqued for not taking into serious account the role of the TR. As a modality that uses case formulation and intervention, emphasis has often been on these aspects rather than the TR.

TABLE 3.3 Behavioural/cognitive-behavioural summary

Key figures:

Behavioural: Pavlov, Skinner, Watson, Wolpe.

Cognitive: Beck, Kelly (Personal Construct), Ellis (Rational Emotive)

In the 1950s and 1960s Behaviourism was a radical departure from the psychoanalytic perspective.

Scientific view of human nature – focuses on observable behaviour, not subjective experience.

Key concepts: Behavioural Therapy

Behaviour is a product of learning.

Behaviour can be encouraged by reward (positive reinforcement) or discouraged by punishment (lack of positive reinforcement).

Goals of therapy

Elimination of problematic behaviours and the learning of new, more productive behaviours.

Through behavioural techniques based on learning theory:

- Systematic desensitization
- Aversion therapy
- Relaxation therapy.

Key concepts: Cognitive Therapy

Interpretations of our subjective experiences are not facts.

Changing thinking changes feeling.

Goals of therapy

To relieve symptoms and resolve problems.

To help clients acquire coping strategies.

To help clients modify underlying cognitive structures in order to avoid relapse

(Continued)

TABLE 3.3 *(continued)*

Key concepts: Cognitive Behavioural
Uses many of the techniques of Behaviour Therapy in a cognitive framework.
Emphasizes thoughts, assumptions and beliefs.
Psychological disturbance arises from specific, habitual errors in thinking (irrational thinking).
Stoic philosophy – Epictetus: people are disturbed not by events themselves but by the view they take of them.
How a person interprets experience determines how they feel (e.g. after a divorce you may feel happy if it means you are free, but depressed if it means you are a failure).
Goals of therapy
To replace maladaptive thoughts and beliefs with adaptive ones.
To eliminate the client's self-defeating outlook on life.
To identify dysfunctional automatic thoughts and beliefs.
Therapeutic relationship (CBT and Behavioural)
The therapist is active and directive.
The therapist functions as a teacher to help clients learn more effective thinking/behaviours.
Clients must be active and experiment with new ways of thinking/behaviours.
A good working relationship is the groundwork – it is not highlighted or essential.
The therapist is active as a teacher.
Clients must actively participate in the process.
A good working relationship is the basis for implementing behavioural procedures.

There has, however, been increasing interest in the nature of the TR in Cognitive Behavioural Therapy (Gilbert and Leahy, 2007). Within CBT the TR reflects interpersonal schema, earlier attachment problems, emotional processing, failures in validation and compassion, and the origins of **resistance**. In order for the tools and interventions to be effective it is now accepted that it is important to have a good TR. There is also recognition that successfully resolving 'therapeutic ruptures' in the TR provides an often essential opportunity for using the relationship as a means to modify cognitive and emotional problems (Katzow and Safran, 2007).

The therapist is active and directive. They function as a teacher to help clients learn more effective thinking/behaviours. In many ways the approach is considered educational. Clients must be active and motivated to experiment with new ways of thinking and behaving.

A good collaborative working relationship is now considered to facilitate good outcomes: 'You will get further with a patient with a good therapeutic relationship & lousy techniques, than you will with good techniques & a lousy relationship' (Victor Meyer, cited in AuBuchon and Malatesta, 1998: 141).

Therapy is time-limited, problem-oriented and goal-oriented, with a clear rationale for emotional disturbance. Sessions are structured with an agenda. There is a strong emphasis on self-help and homework assignments. The work is mainly in the here-and-now, with a focus on practically trying out new ways of thinking and behaving.

Reflections on behavioural/cognitive-behavioural foundations

This tradition has done much to demonstrate how problems can be resolved by changes to thinking and behaviour. A more active approach to therapy can be successful. The practitioner is, in the main, an educator or teacher. Therapy is driven by goals.

Within CBT there remains a standard assumption that the TR is necessary to help promote client change, *but* is not sufficient to produce optimal change. According to CBT theory, this can only be achieved through effective behavioural techniques.

Table 3.4 introduces some of the key differences between a RA and a CBT approach.

TABLE 3.4 Differences between a RA and a CBT approach

CBT
CBT tools are used as a framework and a vehicle for the use of the therapist and client in a relationship.
The client is pathologized and the disorder effect on functionality is rated (i.e. as the obsessive compulsive/anxious client).
Some clients may be labelled as unsuitable/not fitting for CBT.
The therapist's 'expert' formulation is important and central to practice.
Focus is on changing faulty/irrational thinking and related behaviours.
RA
The focus is on 'What's wrong for the client?'
The therapist is interested in the meaning the client gives to their experience.
The therapist enters into a potential real human-to-human relationship and a collaborative approach rather than the therapist as expert formulation.
Change happens in relationship – the therapist provides a more nourishing experience of self-with-other which is part of the therapeutic process.
The client's difficulties are not pathologized (or faulty thinking, as in CBT) – they are seen as a creative adjustment to social and relational contexts.

There is *a third wave* of CBT which aims to help the client to accept their thoughts – Acceptance and Commitment Therapy and Mindfulness-based CBT. We look at these approaches in Chapter 12. Third wave CBT differs from traditional CBT in helping clients accept rather than attempt to get rid of thoughts when they emerge.

P

PRACTITIONER CLIP 3.2 RELATIONSHIP AND CBT

Amy presented with a diagnosis of Obsessive Compulsive Disorder (OCD). She also stated that she was feeling quite depressed and anxious. She had tried therapy before but said it had not worked because she 'could not cope with all the forms and the homework. The therapist was focused on teaching me what to do'.

In the assessment before using any tools or deciding what my formulation/understanding of her experience was, I (Divine) asked the client about her experience of OCD, depression and anxiety – how they affected her, what she felt were the root causes. This led to her talking about her relationship with her mother, who always criticized her and physically abused her if she felt she had not cleaned well enough.

As part of our relational encounter, I aimed at all times to work with her collaboratively. Through this offering, she reported feeling able to explore her experiences and behaviours. Although I did use some tools and she completed her thoughts record and diary as part of her homework, she gave useful feedback in evaluation. She reported being accepted as a person. The key ingredient to her engagement in therapy and consequent change was because the therapist did not rush to use cognitive tools.

This highlights the importance of the human-to-human, authentic relationship in successful therapeutic outcomes.

Drawing from the relational assumptions which we have noted in this book, therapists and clients can collaborate in understanding the importance of the skills and protocols used in CBT. These include case presentation by the client, conceptualization, validation, emotional philosophies, issues of resistance, schematic resistance, schematic mismatch, sunk-cost commitment, self-handicapping (after Leahy, 2008).

We propose that:

1. A relational approach to CBT needs to focus on a collaborative approach and on the therapist's use of self as the ultimate tool for facilitating change.
2. Conceptualizations and formulations are explored in therapy relating to client experiences and responses, not only to their environment but also to the client–therapist relationship.
3. Rather than pathologizing the client, their behaviours are seen as a creative adjustment to earlier patterns of relating in primary relationships.
4. The CBT tools need to be used collaboratively in order for the client to maximize changes to thoughts feelings and behaviours.

EXISTENTIAL-HUMANISTIC FOUNDATIONS

Humanistic psychology, also called **existential-humanistic** psychology, is interested in the subjective reality of the individual and the potential for self-determination. The approach builds from a tradition of phenomenology, whereby the focus lies in the experience and perception of a person (rather than in a notion of the unconscious or working only with behaviour). Maslow and Rogers brought to the fore the notion of self-actualization (Maslow) and the **actualizing tendency** (Rogers). These concepts were in sharp contrast to the psychoanalytical ideas that human beings were driven to adapt to unconscious conflicts and the behaviourist notion that human behaviour can be explained as conditioned responses or reflexes and the habits formed from those responses and reflexes. Bugental, Laing, Perls, Rogers and others contributed to the development of widely differing orientations within this tradition. Bugental and Laing, for example, were key figures in the development of existential therapy, a body of therapy that located the individual in the context of their life setting and emphasized living authentically within life's limitations. Perls and Rogers, on the other hand, placed the focus more clearly on the potential of the individual to actualize all their capacities in relationship to themselves and others.

Existentialism has its roots more profoundly in philosophy. Kierkegaard proposed that the personal meaning of life was central to existence and that subjective truth, was core to personal meaning as opposed to any objective truth, while Nietzsche proposed that each individual should live their own life to the full and embrace their fate.

Sartre proposed that the purpose of life was the search for **authenticity.** Like Nietzche, he believed in no external god; we all have to make of our lives what we can. Existence is the key – all life is alive but only man (sic) is conscious of it. His tripartite principles were *choice*, *freedom* and *responsibility*. We have the freedom to choose how we live in our personal world and it is our responsibility. The existentialists call is to wake up and live a fulfilling life.

> Ultimately, man [sic] should not ask what the meaning of life is, but rather he must recognize that it is *he* who is asked. In a word, each man is questioned by life; and he can only answer to life by answering for his own life, to life he can only respond by being responsible. (Frankl, 1963: 172–3)

Frankl described 'The Existential vacuum', a life without meaning is empty. The purpose of life is to find our meaning. He exemplified this with his notion of 'The Sunday Neurosis', that empty, dull feeling people get after the pleasure of the weekend, before returning to the futile working week. He further proposed that existential frustration of the will to meaning may be compensated by the will to pleasure, or the will to power. Sexual libido can, for example, become rampant in an existential vacuum.

For Yalom (1980), a person has four basic anxieties Death, Fear of Freedom, Existential Isolation, and Meaninglessness. The individual sets up defences against these basic anxieties. He saw engagement in life to be the only real medication against meaninglessness.

Laing was renowned for his radical beliefs. He developed the concept of Ontological Security. An individual who is ontologically secure will be able to deal with most obstacles in life, without the loss of a sense of reality, of his own or of others, and the world in general. If Primary Ontological Security is reached, life events have no threat on the individual. Laing (1960) rejected the disease model of mental illness. He saw extreme distress as the result of an individual attempting to contend with their frightening existential condition, which he saw as being caused by family dynamics and the behaviour of primary caregivers. What might be called psychotic behaviours were not a result of disease, but were defences to Ontological Security: a 'strategy that a person invents in order to live in an unlivable situation' (Laing and Esterson, 1964: 186).

Transactional Analysis

Transactional Analysis was developed by Berne (1961), who trained as a psychoanalyst but came to favour a transparent egalitarian relationship between therapist and client (Walford and Walford, 2008). He sought to demystify the therapeutic process, to empower the client and facilitate the TR. Like many humanistic therapists, he believed that human beings naturally move towards growth and health, given the right opportunities. Berne linked interpersonal relationships to three *ego-states* the *Parent*, *Adult* and *Child*. He called interpersonal interactions *transactions*, and the label '*games*' was given to the patterns of transactions which people found themselves repeating.

Barr (1987) described five relationship stages which impact the therapeutic process:

- The First Relationship – the original primary relationship and other significant relationships.
- The Intrapsychic Relationship – the internalization by the client, not simply of the whole primary relationship, into the developing sense of self. From this, the client develops an internalized sense of other people of relationship.
- The Transference Relationship – the client projects their experience of the intrapsychic relationship on to external relationships, including the TR.
- The Developmentally Needed Relationship – which the therapist works with in order to resolve developmental gaps.
- The Core Relationship – the potential *real* relationship the client in the here-and-now seeks with the therapist, as themselves in the here-and-now.

(from Walford and Walford, 2008: 83) (see comparison with Clarkson's model in Chapter 12)

Erskine (1997) described relationships as providing the experience from which the configuration of a sense of self and others is formed. He emphasized the need to connect with the early child within.

> In a relationship therapy the concept of contact is the theoretical basis from which clinical interventions are derived. … A major goal of therapy, then, is to use the therapist–client relationship – the ability to create full contact in the present – as a stepping-stone to healthier relationships with other people and a satisfying sense of self. Through respect, kindness and contactful listening we establish a personal presence and allow for an interpersonal relationship that provides affirmation of the client's integrity. This respectfulness may best be described as a consistent invitation to interpersonal contact between client and therapist, with simultaneous support for the client to contact his or her internal experiences and receive an external recognition for those experiences. (Erskine, 1997: 77–8)

Hargaden and Sills (2002) made a major contribution to the TR in Transactional Analysis, stating that the therapist and client need a shared understanding of their work together. They 'locate the transferential relationship at the heart of the therapeutic work' and propose 'the extent to which a therapist is informed of her own truths and has understood and integrated her unconscious self will inform the value of her interventions' (Hargaden and Sills, 2002: 115–16).

For a TA psychotherapist, therefore, working in the here-and-now in relationship with the client is fundamental:

> Through the therapist's full presence, the transformational potential of a relationship-orientated psychotherapy is possible. … More than just verbal communication, presence is a communion between client and therapist. (Erskine and Trautmann, 1996: 326)

Gestalt theory

The philosophical base of Gestalt draws primarily on existential phenomenology and the social psychological field theory of Lewin. We operate in relation to others. Optimally, we respond creatively in the moment to the other, encountering the other as a person in the here-and-now. The aim is to encounter another in an I–Thou encounter rather than in an I–it encounter (Buber, 1958; Hycner and Jacobs, 1995).

For Perls (Perls et al., 1951), the task of the Gestalt therapist was to invite the client into an active, experimental here-and-now partnership in which the client tried out new ways of relating. His approach was known to be particularly confrontational, using techniques to challenge clients in order to enhance their self-awareness.

Post Perls, the approach has become more supportive, empathic and collaborative. Therapy is focused in the therapeutic encounter and the space between therapist and client is the area in which healing takes place. Two key principles in Gestalt theory are (Latner, 2000):

1. The focus of therapy is in the 'now', the present experiential moment.
2. We only know ourselves through the web of our relational interconnections.

The therapist seeks to maintain their empathic, authentic presence while opening up to the relational space *between* therapist and client. 'If we take seriously the concept of the between, there is a reality that is greater than the sum total of the experience of the therapist and the client. Together they form a totality that provides a context for the individual experience of both' (Hycner, 1993: 134–5). The therapist commits to and trusts the 'process' of whatever comes to the fore at any moment in the encounter.

> Man [sic] and world are first and foremost in relation; it is only subsequently, at the reflective level of logic that we divide them into separate entities … meaning is neither in the mind alone, nor in the world alone, but in the intentional relation between the two. (Kearney, 1986: 13, 15)

As Gilligan (2008: 70) summarizes:

1. This situation of the therapy hour is new and unique and phenomenologically I cannot know it any better than my client.
2. Both I and my client are 'of the field'. I am part of my client's person–environment field as she is of mine. So as I create myself, I create her, and as she creates herself, she creates me.

For Gestalt therapy then, change comes about through relationship (Yontef, 2005), through transformation, which is possible only in relationship.

The key concepts of this modality can be summarized as:

- Individuals need to live their lives to the full, finding meaning and achieving their potential. Maslow initially suggested that self-actualization was an end point. However, Rogers and other are more concerned with the individual being fulfilled in the here-and-now on a daily basis.
- Personal and authentic encounter helps the client to transfer learning to other relationships. By having meaningful communication and contact with the therapist, the individual is enabled to have more complete encounters with people in other areas of their lives.
- Clients can find their own meaning. The subjective experiencing of the individual is fundamental. By finding meaning, one is enabled to live a fulfilling life.
- The focus is on developing awareness in the present of what one is experiencing. By bringing awareness into the here-and-now one is enabled to live more fully and be more in contact with all aspects on the self.

TABLE 3.5 Existential-humanistic summary

Key figures: Rogers, Mearns, Thorne (Person-centred), Perls (Gestalt), Berne (TA), Yalom, Laing, Esterson, Nietzsche, Sartre (Existential)

Key concepts

Personal and authentic encounters help the client to transfer learning to other relationships.

Focus on developing awareness in the present of what one is experiencing.

Expressing feelings.

Clients can find their own meaning.

Goals of therapy

To provide the relational conditions which support the client's growth and self-actualization.

To support the client's exploration so they can recognize blocks to growth, experience aspects of the self that were formerly denied or distorted.

Facilitate movement towards:

Greater trust in self.

Increased spontaneity.

Acceptance of responsibility for self and choices.

Therapeutic relationship

Real relationship with the therapist is of primary importance (not transference relationship).

Therapist communicates warmth, empathy, genuineness and respect to the client (core conditions).

Therapist is not an expert on the client's meaning.

Therapist has faith in the client's capacity for self-direction and their ability to resolve problems.

Goals of existential-humanistic therapies

The therapist aims to provide the space in which the relational conditions which support the client's growth and self-actualization can emerge and be communicated. The therapist aims to support the client's exploration so they can recognize blocks to their growth and more fully experience aspects of self which have been formerly denied or distorted. Therapy thus facilitates movement towards:

1. Greater trust in the self.
2. Increased spontaneity.
3. Acceptance of responsibility for the self and the choices which emerge.

Therapeutic relationship

What is considered the real relationship with the therapist is of primary importance (not the transference relationship or one based on interpretation or expertise).

The therapist communicates warmth, empathy, genuineness and respect to the client (what have been generically referred to as core conditions, after Rogers). The therapist is genuine in the relationship and communicates this and will, where considered helpful to the client, disclose their own perceptions, understandings, etc.

The therapist is not an expert on the client's internal meaning. They will work with the client's worldview.

The therapist has faith in the client's capacity for self-direction and their ability to resolve problems. Rogers called this the **organismic valuing process**. This is considered to be in relation to the actualizing tendency – the drive for every organism to grow and reach its potential.

Reflections on existential-humanistic foundations

These approaches focus on the client and their subjective experiencing as central. How my client sees the world is the reality I will work with. The therapist works to help the client become more fully functioning and perhaps self-actualizing in the humanistic tradition. In the existential tradition, the focus is more on working with the client to help them live an authentic and meaningful life. A human relationship has more emphasis in the classical practice of these approaches.

Table 3.6, as an example of an approach within the existential-humanistic modality, illustrates some of the differences between a classical person-centred practice and a RA.

TABLE 3.6 RA and classical person-centred therapy

Person-centred approach
The self of the client is viewed as pre-wired.
The focus is individualistic – and the goal is to become self-actualizing or fully-functioning.
The therapist's objective is to meet the client's needs – to provide the optimum environment for the client's growth.
The therapist does not get entangled in the growth process.
RA
In the RA there is no pre-wired 'self'.
The self is created in relationship and does not exist without those relationships.
The therapist is a facilitator and full participant in the relationship.
The relationship is a co-created process.

TRANSPERSONAL FOUNDATIONS

Key concepts

While Transpersonal therapy has not had a formative role in the development of relational therapies, the relationship between therapist and client is central to the therapy. Transpersonal psychology was created by Maslow and others due to the perceived limitations of humanistic psychology in dealing with personal and spiritual development and states of consciousness outside ordinary everyday experience (Shiers and Paul, 2008). Lajoie and Shapiro (1992: 91) note that transpersonal psychology 'is concerned with the study of humanity's highest potential, and with the recognition, understanding, and realization of unity, spiritual, and transcendent states of consciousness'.

Transpersonal psychotherapy is therefore concerned with a bigger picture of the human psyche and the need to have a height psychology *as well as* a depth psychology, as developed by Freud. A Transpersonal approach is interested in homonomy, union with the greater whole (Angyal, 1965). Areas of concern include individual development and balance, interconnectedness and selflessness, global identity. Lajoie and Shapiro suggest five key themes: states of consciousness, higher or ultimate potential, beyond the ego or personal self, transcendence, and the spiritual.

Therapists will work with the whole person. Key figures in this field include Jung and Assagioli and the Psychosynthesis model; Frankl and Logotherapy; Grof and spiritual emergencies; and the work of Wilber and a psychology of evolutionary development.

Goals of Transpersonal therapy

As a holistic approach to suffering, therapy may be concerned with the integration of physical, emotional, mental and spiritual aspects of the psyche. This will include the exploration and focus of the client's present state of being, their potential, and the development of inner resources and creativity. The aim of therapy may be explicitly spiritual to include spiritual development, integration of peak experiences, mystical and other metaphysical experiences. Therapy may also be involved in working with spiritual crisis, spiritual emergency and associated breakdown.

The relationship

For many transpersonal therapists the relationship is a key factor in the therapy. Vaughan (Walsh and Vaughan, 1993: 160) proposes three elements on therapy:

- The context is established by the beliefs and values of the therapist.
- The content consists of the client's experience.
- The process is the encounter between therapist and client through which healing occurs.

Wittine (in Walsh and Vaughan, 1993: 166) suggests that Transpersonal psychotherapy affirms:

1. The therapist's unfolding awareness of the Self, or deep centre of Being, and his or her spiritual perspective on life as central to the therapeutic process.
2. The transformative potential in the therapeutic relationship not only for the client but for the therapist as well.

Wilde McCormick (2000) proposes 'the vessel' of the therapist's awareness to describe the essence of the psychological dynamics between therapist and client in transpersonal therapy. The vital core of this vessel is

> that it will withstand the struggles and fragmentation of personality and difficult transferences will be able to bear the chill winds or suffocating cloaks of the past, and the fiery rages when the heat is on. This vessel holds the potential for fantasy – how I might have been, how it could be; for illumination, change, for healing, for transformation and the growth for love; for the ever present possibility of coming home to one's self and recognising it as such. (Wilde McCormick, 2000: 24)

The **I–Thou relationship**, as formulated by Buber (1958), is perhaps fully exemplified in Transpersonal therapy. For Buber, the Thou was in a sense a gateway to the divine or the ground of being. The potential unfolding between client and therapist, with both parties open to a transpersonal or possibly spiritual connection in which growth is possible, is key to the relationship in this approach. The therapist is seen as a facilitator of potential growth and not a teacher or guide.

TABLE 3.7 Transpersonal therapy summary

Key figures:
Assagioli, Grof, Jung, Maslow, Wilber.
Key concepts
Growth beyond the ego self.
Holistic development of mind, body and spirit.
A height and depth psychology.
The individual is part of a greater hole.
Goals of therapy
To grow spiritually as well as psychologically.
Evolutionary development.
To find meaning.
The therapeutic relationship
The therapist is a guide.
The therapist works in relationship to facilitate growth.
The co-created relationship may be transformational.
Techniques such as imagery, breath work and dream work may be used.

Reflections on Transpersonal therapy

Transpersonal therapy does put human development and suffering in a wider context than a one-person psychology. It locates the individual in relation to their environment with an implicit belief in a human spirit, be it energetic or connected to a religious belief system. Relationship is central to therapy, with a focus on the transformational elements in the meeting of client and therapist.

TABLE 3.8 RA and Transpersonal therapy

Transpersonal therapy

The focus is on holistic development as opposed to simple problem resolution.

Transpersonal psychology proposes that we grow on levels beyond the ego or individual psyche.

A therapist may use tools and techniques.

The therapist aims to facilitate growth and may be active in this.

RA

The focus is on the client and what they bring.

The therapist is interested in the meaning the client gives to their experiencing and works with the client to facilitate their needs.

Tools and techniques are not commonly used.

The therapist works with the client in the here-and-now of the relationship.

P

PRACTITIONER CLIP 3.3 TRANSPERSONAL PRACTICE

As a client, I (Steve) had a period of Transpersonal therapy. The focus was very much on all aspects of me, how they all connected and my integration and growth as a human being. The therapist used imagery to help bring to light aspects of the inner psyche and then worked with me with the concepts that evolved.

Let us now summarize the four forces of psychological therapy, and the role of the therapist and the relationship (Table 3.9).

TABLE 3.9 The four forces of therapy, the relationship and traditional position of therapist

	Methods	Position of therapist	Place of the relationship in therapy	Aim of therapy
Psychoanalysis	Interpretation of transference, countertransference and resistance	Expert 'Blank Screen' Works with transference and interpretation	Working with the relationship in the here-and-now to resolve past issues	To adjust To live more fully in the present reality based on the past

(Continued)

TABLE 3.9 *(Continued)*

	Methods	Position of therapist	Place of the relationship in therapy	Aim of therapy
Behaviourism and later Cognitive	Deciding goals Action plans New ways of behaving and thinking	Expert Educator Trainer	Focus on practical, goal-based working alliance	To change maladaptive thoughts, feelings and behaviours
Existential-humanistic	Human encounter In some cases particular techniques may be used	Facilitator or catalyst	Central Focus on working in the here-and-now	To live a full life Realization of potential To live an authentic life
Transpersonal Dialogue, Imagery,	Dialogue Imagery Creative visualization	Guide Facilitator Educator	To facilitate holistic change	To achieve spiritual growth To become integrated in mind, body and spirit

REFLECTION POINT 3.2 THE RELATIONSHIP IN EACH MODALITY

Research puts the TR at the heart of therapy whatever the modality followed.

- What do you consider is the focus of the relationship in each of the Psychoanalytic, Existential-humanistic, Cognitive/Behavioural and Transpersonal approaches?

MOVING TOWARDS A UNITARY PARADIGM

As we have noted, there has been a move over the last 20 years towards working in ways that:

- are proven effective
- allow the therapist to work in ways which are best for them
- draw from the rich vein of theory and practice that is evident across the traditions
- best serves the client
- are compatible with contemporary culture and its view of the individual – a shift towards a unitary paradigm

The four forces of psychology have come in their own ways to value the place of the relationship in therapy as a cornerstone to practice. Norcross (2005) estimated that there are more than 400 different types of therapy and today there are possibly more. Such a plethora of approaches can foster growth and creativity in the field and also offers clients choice. However, there is also the danger that the continual development of modalities can lead to an unproductive 'tribalism', in which the focus shifts to the 'this is the best approach' mentality. A **unitary paradigm**, however, is a holistic approach; it shifts towards the value of drawing on the skills and research evidence of other forms of therapy.

A unitary paradigm is not a move towards a therapeutic 'monoculture' in which one therapeutic modality dominates. Rather, it is a shift towards a stance that no one school has all the answers, and that different methods may be of help to different clients.

T

THEORY CLIP 3.2 PLURALISM, ECLECTICISM AND A RA

Pluralism

An emerging body of evidence suggests that some 'types' of client do better in one kind of therapy than another. For instance, clients with high levels of resistance and an internalizing coping style tend to do better in humanistic/non-directive therapies, while clients who are non-defensive and have a predominantly externalizing coping style tend to benefit from more technique-oriented approaches (Cooper, 2008).

Cooper and McLeod (2010) hypothesized a **pluralistic approach**. It is embedded in humanistic, person-centred and postmodern values but aims to be a way of practising, researching and thinking about therapy which also fully embraces the whole range of effective therapeutic methods and concepts. Different things are likely to help different people at different points in time and therefore there is no point arguing over which is the 'best' way of practising therapy. The pluralistic approach, then, clarifies the position that CBT can be helpful, and person-centred therapy can be helpful, and psychodynamic therapy can be helpful, rather than an 'either/or' approach. The decision on the focus and course of therapy may be a collaborative decision between therapist and client.

Undoubtedly, the pluralist approach is in line with a unitary paradigm and the centrality of decision making about the course and focus of therapy starts to highlight the importance of the TR.

Eclecticism

This term was used to describe a multi-modal approach to working effectively with clients. It draws from a range of different techniques to get the best result for the client. Typically, **eclecticism** has been criticized as an approach that can lack rigour or coherence.

(Continued)

(Continued)

RA

From a relational perspective we assert that the relationship is central and a collaborative way of working will ensure that a coherent approach to therapy that meets the needs of the client is maintained, rather than what can be, at worst, a pick-and-mix approach. The principles of our RA, as detailed in the next chapter, ensure that the growth and wellbeing of the client is the focus.

Many practitioners often find themselves working across models and developing their own model of practice, drawing from what makes sense for them and what is evidenced as effective from the different modalities.

REFLECTION POINT 3.3 ECLECTICISM AND COHERENCE

> Relational theory … is a domain of many diverse waters and much eclecticism even within defined streams of practice. (De Young, 2003: 39)

A RA, as presented here, is not considered an eclectic approach to the practice of therapy.

- What might be important considerations to ensure that a coherent model of practice is followed?

In the next chapter we outline a RA which draws from the wisdom and practice of the main approaches to theory and provides the foundations for a proven holistic and practical method of theory.

RESOURCE BOX 3

Charura, D. and Paul, S. (eds) (2014) *The Therapeutic Relationship Handbook: Theory and Practice*. Maidenhead: Open University Press.
Chapters explore the TR from all the major modalities.

Corey, G. (2013) *Theory and Practice of Counseling and Psychotherapy*. New York: Brooks Cole.
A clear, non-partisan outline of most of the major approaches to therapy.

DeYoung, P. (2003) *Relational Psychotherapy: A Primer*. New York: Brunner-Routledge.
Good background reading.

Dryden, W. and Branch, R. (eds) (2012) *The CBT Handbook*. London: Sage.
One of the most recent compilations of CBT practice and development.

Fadiman, J. and Frager, R. (2102) *Personality and Personal Growth* (7th edn). New York: Pearson.
Presents different theories on personality development and growth.

Haugh, S. and Paul, S. (eds) (2008) *The Therapeutic Relationship: Perspectives and Themes*. Ross-on-Wye: PCCS Books.
Clearly and succinctly lays the basis for the TR from the major modalities.

Lazarus, A.A. (2005) 'Multimodal therapy', in J.C. Norcross and M.R. Goldfried (eds), *Handbook of Psychotherapy Integration*. New York: Oxford University Press.
Introduces the reader to multimodal therapy and how it differs from traditional approaches.

CHAPTER SUMMARY

To help the reader to develop an understanding of the relationship from the different modalities, this chapter has presented the following:

- The four forces of therapy
  - Psychodynamic/psychoanalytic
  - Existential-humanistic
  - Behaviourism
  - Transpersonal
- The key figures and key concepts of psychodynamic/psychoanalytic, behaviourism, existential-humanistic and transpersonal approaches and their emerging models.
- The goals of therapy.
- The therapeutic relationship and its centrality to each of the forces of therapy.
- New developments (as appropriate).
- We also offered our reflections on each modality and how they interlink or differ from a RA.
- We set the foundations for a RA, drawing from these traditions of theory and practice.

4

A relational approach to therapy

In this chapter we outline the theory and practice of an approach to therapy from a relational paradigm. A RA is not based on one method of practice but is a paradigm or framework for the practice of therapy.

The aims of this chapter are for the reader to understand the RA, with a specific focus on the following:

- The key principles of this approach, underpinned by theory, research and practice.
- The context and underlying assumptions.
- The central ideas.
- The theory of personality and sense of self.
- How problems develop.
- The social context and its impact on the therapeutic relationship.
- The therapeutic relationship.
- The role of the therapist and therapist competencies essential to working therapeutically.
- The goals of therapy.

As we have seen, the TR is central to all approaches to therapy. Research has virtually proven its importance as an agent for change in therapy. New approaches have developed in all the different modalities focusing on the TR.

THE RELATIONAL PARADIGM

The relational paradigm has emerged in the past two decades, drawing upon the recognition of the importance of relationship in many different approaches to psychotherapy. The concept of 'relational' is now in common parlance across the

> range of therapies. It is an approach that invites exploration of the nature and dynamics of relationships and their importance in the development of the person, difficulties in living and the therapeutic process. (Pelham, 2008: 114)

We noted in Chapter 1 that a new therapeutic paradigm has emerged which takes the relationship as central to both theory and practice. Alongside this development have come models of practice that are called relational and also, more broadly, the concept of relationship has come to be regarded as central in therapy (for example, as we saw, it is one of the common factors in outcome research).

By paradigm, we mean a framework through which to work. In a paradigm there may be a number of different positions which fit within the framework and conceptualize themselves differently. We therefore maintain here *a* relational approach as opposed to *the* relational approach. There will be different formulations of working relationally. Some may be embedded in psychoanalytic theory and some in humanistic theory, and so on. We propose a RA that allows each and every practitioner to make sense of what they do coherently and consistently within their own formulation.

As we have seen, there are strong historical foundations to the development of effective TRs. The different approaches to therapy all maintain the importance of the TR. Cumulative research over many decades clearly identifies the relationship as a prerequisite therapeutic factor. Working with the relationship in therapy is considered essential, regardless of what model of therapy the person practises or what philosophical position or school the therapist considers themselves to follow.

In laying out an approach to the practice of therapy we are mindful, therefore, that some aspects of practice may fit more for some than others. We present here what are considered the main therapeutic factors without adhering to one ideology of practice.

T

THEORY CLIP 4.1 ORIGINS OF A RA

Context

The concept of 'relational' appeared in the 1980s in various forms of therapy. It has increasingly become an element of other forms of therapy as well as an organized methodological approach in itself.

From its psychoanalytical origins it draws from:

- Object Relations theory – we are motivated by a need to relate ('object' refers to the personal target of the need to relate)
- Self Psychology – our sense of self forms in the context of relationships.
- Intersubjectivity.

(Continued)

(Continued)

From its humanistic origins it draws from:

- Gestalt and social psychological theory. We are always part of something greater than both the human psyche and social contexts. The organism will always seek to improve itself.
- Person-centred psychology.

More recent developments can be recognized in:

- Cognitive Behavioural Psychology (Third Wave), in which the relationship and collaborative working are now established as central elements to therapy.
- Transpersonal approaches in which the therapist-in-relationship is a key agent for change and both parties are part of a greater whole.
- Transcultural approaches.
- Research into effective factors in therapy.
- Current research in neuroscience.

The key principles of the approach are expressed as:

> *Relations between people are the basis of social and individual life and relational concepts are used to understand human life in all its complexity.*

Relationships are of fundamental importance in:

- The development of personality and a sense of self.
- The difficulties clients bring to therapy (relations with the self and relations with other people).
- The therapeutic process (the therapy relationship is the heart of the process).

(Paul and Pelham, 2000: 110)

All models of therapy work through the relationship and make sense of it from different perspectives. For some it is the instrument for change, while for others it is the medium for forming a good working relationship. What matters is that the relationship is an essential factor in therapy.

Relational approaches draw from a basic given: *we are motivated by a need to relate*. From the moment of birth our phenomenological (subjective) worldview is grounded in and developed through our relationship with others. This can be illustrated in Object Relations theory, humanistic views of human development, Gestalt and cognitive psychologies.

Most importantly, our sense of self forms in the context of our relationships. In relational approaches we have seen that interactions between client and therapist are considered the vehicle for change.

The traditional psychodynamic and existential-humanistic approaches viewed the person as coming into the world pre-wired, with a predetermined instinctual nature. The person then encounters an environment that might encourage, facilitate, suppress, repress or distort this innate drive. In this approach there is one person meeting their environment.

In a RA there is still an innate drive but this drive is more focussed towards fulfilment *in relation* to others. Primary attachment experiences very much influence the development of internal security. Personality develops in a 'two-person' field: Who 'I' am is a co-creation of self and others. My identity is moulded through my experiences with others.

Central ideas

It is through relationships that we become and maintain who we are. Our sense of self is determined in relation to our life experiences in relation to others and the physical and socio-cultural environment in which we live.

All relationships take place in a social context. Every life interaction inhabits an environmental setting. We grow and live in a constellation of human engagements.

It is through the TR that change takes place. The relationship itself is the medium for change. This is examined and explained fully as we discuss the practice of therapy.

Principles

In the practice of therapy we consider these to be the main philosophical principles that underpin the relationship.

- **We are part of a growthful and evolving universe.** Every organism in our universe is part of a greater whole which is in a constant state of development. As human beings we are not separate from this process.
- **We are social beings. Without relationship we do not develop. Science show us this.** As human animals we need warm, caring relationships to grow. With such relations we are more likely to be happy and fulfilled. Without such relations we are likely to be unhappy, cope less well with stress, and form less productive relationships in adulthood.

- **We have a built-in propensity to grow to our full potential.** All organisms move to fulfil their potential given the right conditions. The organism will seek to fulfil itself, and will choose what may be called 'lesser ways' to meet its needs if thwarted in its movement by external circumstances.
- **We are born in and grow through relationships.** We learn in relationship to our primary caregivers in early life. Through our relations with friends, family and others in adulthood we learn and are fulfilled.
- **Our personal problems arise in and through relationship.** Life issues are, in the main, caused and/or maintained through our relationships with others. This is often as a result of early life experiences which lead us to perpetuate problems in relating in our adult lives.
- **Our ability to resolve practical problems is often facilitated when we can access our own internal resources.** We are all subject to the problems of day-to-day living and trauma. Those who are most likely to cope better are those who have had secure early relationships.

Basic assumptions for change in therapy.

Our problems are resolved in therapy through:

- **A relationship which offers the right conditions for healing and transformation.** Research and the wisdom of therapists of all persuasions show that a relationship with an empathic therapist is an essential ingredient in therapy.
- **A relationship which helps us work through issues from our past in relation to the therapist.** We believe that the working out, in the here-and-now, of relational difficulties arising from the past enables an individual to develop insight into the arising of these difficulties and explore new and growthful ways of relating.
- **A meeting with the therapist which enables growth and transformation.** A therapist can offer to their client the possibility of discovering or rediscovering their own internal natural tendencies to make positive life choices.

We believe the above conditions to be the cornerstone of good therapy. This necessitates in the therapist a number of factors:

- An explicit philosophy of life.
- A psychological understanding of the human psyche, of how problems develop and how they can be resolved.
- A discrete and coherent model of practice.
- The ability to form and sustain good relationships.
- To be living or working towards a fulfilling life outside the practice of therapy.
- Reflexive self-knowledge and awareness.

T

THEORY CLIP 4.2 KEY THEMES OF A RA

Central ideas

Key themes underpin a RA:

- It is through relationships that we become, know and maintain who we are.
- Relationships are important in:
  - Forming our personality/sense of self – early relationships are particularly important here.
  - The difficulties people bring to therapy.
- Relationships take place in a social context.
- It is through the TR that change takes place.

The importance of relationships

For the therapist, relationships are important for three reasons (Figure 1.2): It is through relationships that we become and regulate who we are; relationships take place in a social context; and it is through the TR that change takes place.

1. Relationships are important in understanding both what we call personality, the combination of characteristics, qualities and ways of relating that make up an individual's distinctive identity and sense of self, how we view and experience our self, including our attributes, behaviours and how we think and feel about ourself in our environment. Psychological therapists believe early relationships are particularly important.
2. In the main, the difficulties people bring to therapy are grounded in issues in relationships, both current and/or in the past, or the impact of traumatic experiences on relationship.

C

CLIENT CLIP 4.1 WORKING IN THE HERE-AND-NOW

Jim comes to therapy because he is not having much success with his work at university. In the course of counselling he reveals that he doesn't socialize with the people in his shared house. They are noisy and seem to be always partying. He says he keeps himself to himself and that is how he is, he prefers to be *alone*. Something in the tone of his voice suggests to the therapist that there is more to this. So the

(Continued)

(Continued)

therapist wonders if he is not perhaps alone but is in fact *lonely*. Jim hesitates, moves to deny this, and then rather quietly says: 'You might be right. I have never had any real friends. I have just accepted this is how I am.' This is a crux point in therapy and Jim then goes on to reveal the story of his childhood and domineering father.

In the example above, working in the present and the presenting symptoms, client and therapist are led to explore the causes based in the past.

The TR is the medium in which change takes place. The more present relational factors are, the more likelihood there is for therapeutic change.

> We are borne of relationship, nurtured in relationship, and educated in relationship. We represent every biological and social relationship of our forebears, as we interact and exist in a consensual domain called 'society'. (Cottone, 1988: 363)

Personality/sense of self

The human personality develops in relation to interactions with others. Primary caregivers are very important in the forming of this emergent personality. Life experiences and our reaction to them in relation to the love and support we receive from the important people around us are formative. Our sense of self, how good or not we feel about ourselves and the world we inhabit is determined in relation to these experiences.

We internalize early primary relationships as a template for future relationships. If we have a fulfilling relationship with our father, it is likely to set down a pattern for both future relationships with men and for our sense of self-worth. There is much evidence that points to the imprinting of these formative relationships in the developing child. We internalize early relational experiences as a template for future relationships. These become patterns of relating we play out in life, as illustrated in Client Clip 4.2.

C

CLIENT CLIP 4.2 PAST EXPERIENCES LEAD TO RELATIONAL PATTERNS

As young child John was constantly humiliated by his father. He has internalized a template of this *relational pattern*. Being shamed and shaming others: both are part of a dynamic he has introjected. He has the same attitude towards the self that the parent projected on to him, 'You're pathetic!'

In adult relationships John's internalized relational template leads him to expect others to ridicule and humiliate him (being shamed). He can also be like Dad and respond from the part of himself that humiliates others (shaming others). For example, he may respond by criticizing others or putting them down when he feels in danger of being criticized or put down himself.

Social context

All relationships take place in a social context. The home, the family and the environment all have an effect on the individual. The wider context impacts on this experiencing.

Prevailing socio-cultural attitudes and values all impact on relationships: for example, what it means to be a man/woman, to be white/black, to be gay/heterosexual, or to have a religious upbringing, physical ability or disability, a position in society, the agency or power and control you have in your life, and so on. (We look explicitly at social influences in Chapter 10. The example of Phil in Client Clip 4.3 shows how internal conflicts caused by the impact of family values can be played out in social contexts.

C

CLIENT CLIP 4.3 SOCIAL CONTEXT AND FAMILY VALUES

Phil is a white, male, heterosexual who works in a local government office. He carries with him a deep sense of inferiority because he feels he did not live up to the perfect image of the handsome, successful executive who had lots of money. He has internalized this from his father, who grew up in a different era. He has become aggressive and demeaning to one of his team, whom he believes to be gay.

Phil is conflicted due to his seeming failure not to live up to the expectations of his father. He is taking out his conflicts on a member of his team who he perceives as not being a true man, as he himself feels.

(Note: The film, *The Believer* (2001) illustrates similar themes.)

THE THERAPEUTIC RELATIONSHIP

The TR is co-created. Both parties are instrumental in it. It is created in context and in relation to the context. This is unlike a traditional classical approach where the therapist sets the scene for therapy or applies techniques to, or for, the client.

The relationship is fluid and changing and both client and therapist impact each other consciously and otherwise. In fact, therapist and client influence one another from moment to moment. The therapist helps the client to find meaning and understanding. This is a mutual co-constructed, intersubjective, process. The therapist is not the source of meaning, knowledge or answers, and does not attempt to overlay their meaning on the client's frame of reference. The therapist is not the expert.

All elements of the relationship are important to therapy. What we may call the *real relationship* and *transference relationship* are equally important. The here-and-now relationship between client and therapist and other dimensions to the relating are important, for example the transference relationship, where the client projects thoughts and feelings on to the therapist based on past experiences. The dimensions of the relationship as a whole are central to the joint work both parties engage in.

Role of the therapist

The role and functions of the therapist are key to the process of therapy. We propose the following principles for effective relational practice.

1. The therapist endeavours to enter into a real relationship with the client. They seek to be authentic and human, bringing with them human qualities.
2. The therapist is a participant in the therapy and therefore does not observe from an objective place, for example as the 'expert', the 'analyst', the 'doctor'.
3. The therapist knows that relational difficulties are likely to come to the fore in the room as the work develops. They are prepared to work with and through these with their client in a non-defensive way with the focused intention of helping their client.
4. The therapist knows that their own relational patterns will have an impact either in their own internal reaction to their client and/or their way of relating to their client. The therapist aims to be mindful of their own patterns and to ensure they do not negatively affect the therapy process. The therapist may to some degree 'bracket' thoughts and feelings that occur that may not be considered helpful.
5. The therapist helps clients to explore their difficulties and seeks to make sense of clients' past stories in terms of their present relationships, and vice versa.
6. The therapist is aware that clients' difficulties may be relational even if the story they are telling appears to have no other people in it.
7. The therapist trusts that the client will find their own resolution to their problems. The therapist further trusts that the client is doing the best they can in their present circumstances.

Goals of therapy

There are no specific goals of therapy as each case is unique and each client will bring their own problems and needs. The therapist will work with the client's perceived goals. However, there are general principles:

1. Therapy may help to bring to awareness the client's way of relating to their self and how this relates to current everyday problems.
2. Therapy may provide a safe, secure and supportive relationship in which the client has a positive, transformative experience with the therapist, as an 'other'.
3. Therapy may contribute to a more productive model or template of relating for the client.
4. Therapy may help a person become more integrated or congruent in relation to the different aspects or 'parts' of self.
5. Therapy may help a person be in touch with their own authenticity and make choices that are fulfilling and growthful.

WORKING WITH *THE* RELATIONSHIP

We now look at the relationship and explore ways of working with, and in a relationship. Kahn was one of those who proposed that the relationship *is* the therapy (1997). For him, there are two reasons why we need to study the relationship. First, relationship is the crux of therapy; through relationship therapy happens. Secondly, by raising our awareness of the relationship and its dynamics we have a powerful tool in our work with clients.

Kahn (1997) lays down five propositions for studying and working with the relationship:

1. Insight is not enough. We may see really clearly what we consider to be a central element to our client's life problems, and in the communicating of that to our client, nothing may change for the client. As Kahn says, 'Insight is necessary but not sufficient' (1997: 4).
2. Along with insight we need understanding of the relationship and what is happening in it. As Kahn says, virtually all schools of thought agree on this, even though they disagree on how to conceptualize the understanding and how the therapist should work with it.
3. The potency of the TR is that it is happening in the here-and-now. It is the live material that can be worked with.

4. An approach based on the relationship incorporates working with an understanding of relationship, historically the realm of the neutral analytical therapist, *and* working with acceptance and warmth, as per a humanistically-trained therapist. Therefore, the therapist may be considered doubly equipped in their work.
5. There has been a coming together of the analytical and humanistic approaches and now there is no need to choose between one and the other.

Kahn suggests that many analytically-trained therapists were torn between the need for theoretical reasons to maintain a blank-screen neutrality versus a need to create a therapeutic ambience of trust, warmth and acceptance.

Freud himself was much more personable in his early work with clients, maintaining that it was love that cured (see page 47). However, as he developed his practice he believed the patient's working out of the transference patterns to an objective therapist to be central to cure.

A relational therapist therefore works with relational patterns in a warm, accepting manner in the here-and-now of the relationship.

Existential-humanistic perspectives

The existential and humanistic schools believed the relationship to be central to change. There were distinct differences, though, in approach. Rogers and others, in the mainly American humanistic schools, believed in the *genuineness* of the therapist which was directed towards the client with positive regard and warmth.

Kahn notes Rogers' 'contribution to our understanding of the relationship between therapist and client was … monumental' (Kahn, 1997: 36), and 'If we exclude those of Freud, it is hard to name another set of books that has an impact on clinical practice equal to Rogers' (Kahn, 1997: 37).

Other humanistic therapists saw **authenticity** as more allied with an honest, open, 'no punches pulled' approach to human *encounter* (Kahn, 1997). The mainly European existential schools were concerned more with the authenticity of the therapist. By this they mean being as truly oneself as one can be in each moment and being with others in that way. The focus therefore was more on a truthful intimacy than the communication of warmth.

Existential writers (Heidegger, 1962) used the term '***Dasein***', literally meaning 'being there', to be truly present with another. Authenticity is one of a number of similar concepts, such as genuineness, congruence and being real in the TR. All these terms describe a process whereby the therapist does not try to hide their feelings behind a professional mask, but meets the client in a person-to-person relationship, with a willingness to share experience in the relationship.

The person-centred concept of *congruence* is an importance example of the humanistic perspective. A congruent response requires the therapist to be aware of their own inner experience and to communicate this to the client. The belief here is that the therapist's ability to be real will deepen the TR and the therapist's example will enable clients to take the risk of becoming more real, both to themselves and to the therapist. Rogers (1966: 185) states:

> Genuineness in therapy means that the therapist is his [sic] actual self during his encounter with his client. Without façade, he openly has the feelings and attitudes that are flowing in him at the moment. This involves self-awareness; that is, the therapist's feelings are available to him – to his awareness – and he is able to live them, to experience them in the relationship, and to communicate them if they persist. The therapist encounters his client directly, meeting him person to person. He is being himself, not denying himself.
>
> ...the therapist denies to himself none of the feelings he is experiencing and that he is willing to experience transparently any persistent feeling that exist in the relationship and to let these be known to the client. It means avoiding the temptation to present a façade, or assume a confessional-professional attitude.

Within the humanistic approach, the human quality of the TR is considered a core element in healing. The therapist seeks to meet the client in a person-to-person relationship. In Gestalt therapy, Parlett and Page (1990) propose such an open-ended enquiry can flourish only within a 'dialogic' relationship based upon the 'I–Thou' kind of person-to-person meeting and dialogue described by Buber (1958). They further state that this involves each party meeting the other as a person, not a role, and that Gestalt therapists let themselves be themselves and encourage those they work with to do the same.

Kohut (1971), who saw empathy as central to therapy, suggested that clients saw the cool neutral objectivity of some analysts as the most cruel rejection. Kohut (1982) and Gill (1982) were psychoanalysts who believed in working with what we may call unconscious processes and a warm TR. They and others (such as Kahn) suggest a middle way between the warm humanistic and cool analytical approaches.

Both Kohut and Gill saw *non-defensiveness* as vitally important for the practitioner. The therapist is willing to look at any response from their client in an open and reflective way, knowing that they don't need to be right or have all the answers. In the meeting of therapist and client, the healing or transformation happens not from the expertise of the therapist.

THERAPY AS A LOVING RELATIONSHIP

Consideration of music or the arts will illustrate the importance of love in human society. The basis of therapy as love has been noted by many theorists of differing orientations. Allport (1950: 80) wrote: 'Love is incomparably the greatest psychotherapeutic agent.' In considering an encompassing description of the therapeutic relationship, Burton (1967 102–3) wrote: 'After all research on psychotherapy is accounted for, psychotherapy still resolves itself into a relationship best subsumed by the word love.'

Rogers believed that what the Greeks called '***agape***', a selfless non-possessive approach to another love quite different from Eros or erotic love, is what is offered in therapy. Object Relations theorists Guntrip (1953) and Fairbairn (1954) used the word *agape* with regard to the therapy relationship: 'This kind of parental love … *agape* … is the kind of love the psycho-analyst and psychotherapist must give the patient because he did not get it from his parents in sufficient measure or in a satisfactory form' (Guntrip, 1953: 125). For Freud, the patient had to be treated and cured. For Rogers, the person had to be accepted and loved.

As we have seen, the TR is accepted as the most important factor in therapy that the therapist can impact on. The therapeutic functions include the conditions of empathy, warmth and acceptance. Patterson (1974: 89–90) believed that these conditions 'constitute love in the highest sense or *agape*'. If therapy provides some resolution of suffering for people who are missing love in their lives, then perhaps it is not implausible to suggest that some kind of love (*agape*) is *an indispensable ingredient* in the TR itself (Paul and Charura, 2012).

There have been developments within the psychoanalytic field and particularly an openness to explore both the TR, as a living dynamic, and the issue of love as curative. Ferenczi (1932: 169–70) wrote:

> …But if the patient notices that I feel a real compassion for her and that I am eagerly determined to search for the causes of her suffering, she then suddenly not only becomes capable of giving a dramatic account of the events but also can talk to me about them.

This view aligns itself with what Rogers and other broadly humanistic writers suggest. For Rogers, technique was not important; what was important was the successful communication of love – *agape*. Transpersonal and humanistic therapists may see the relationship created between client and therapist as facilitating love and growth.

Buber invited us to consider what it is to be human in relationship. He postulated the I–Thou quality of relating, rather than an I–it relationship in which the other is an object (Buber, 1958). In describing the quality of this love, Worsley (2008: 188) proposes:

> Love is near the heart of the I–Thou intimacy. Love is between the I and the Thou. Love is inherent in relating. I do not possess the one I love. In love all aspects of the other are open to acceptance. The good and the bad, the beautiful and the ugly, each may become engaged in accepting Loving.

In relational terms, this unconditionality in relationship is active, each moment acknowledging and communicating connection and working with the obstacles and difficulties as they emerge. This includes when therapist and client struggle to be in relationship and when it is difficult to be in contact. I–Thou relating is about being authentic and being with the other. 'If someone could give the suffering person a significant experience of the love so sorely missing, the confusion and pain would go away by itself' (Kahn, 1991: 36).

R

RESEARCH CLIP 4.1 NEUROSCIENCE AND LOVE

Research in neuroscience has recently continually evidenced the importance of love in human development and the importance of love in laying down the foundations for the healthy development of the brain many years after original neglect of abuse has impeded normal growth (Cozolino, 2010b; Joseph, 1999; Siegel, 2007).

> Loving in therapy cannot be reduced to particular words or therapeutic skills but rather is a relationship encounter with a quality of relating, dialogue, contact and process with each other moment by moment in a way that fully embraces our experiencing (Paul and Charura, 2012: 23).

THE INTERSUBJECTIVE CONTEXT

As such, there is no one reality of the client but both client and therapist have their own view of the world, their own subjective reality. Basically, there is not one reality (the client's) and an objective observer (the therapist) in the therapy room but

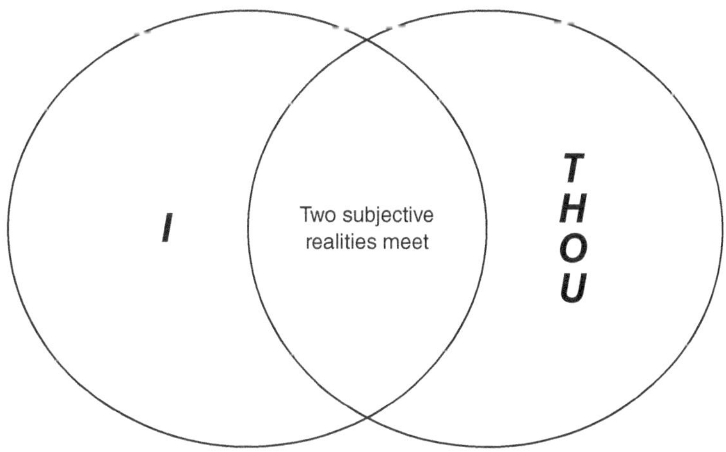

FIGURE 4.1 Intersubjectivity

two subjective realities. Stolorow and others call this **intersubjectivity** (Stolorow, 1994). There are two subjective participants in the therapy room, each of them trying to make sense of the client's issues.

As Kahn (1997: 70) explains it:

1. 'Therapists exert significant unconscious influence on the interaction, influence they can learn about only from the client.'
2. 'They must learn to be gently skeptikal [*sic*] about their own objectivity and their own view of the client's reality.'

There is no objective reality as such but a number of ways of making sense of experiences. The client tries in the best way they can to make sense of their past. In a sense, it is a *social construction* with accompanying strategies to help understand and work with its tensions. Hence, transference and inner resistances are the healthy striving of the psyche to resolve internal conflicts.

KOHUT AND SELF PSYCHOLOGY

Kohut (1984) was a classical psychoanalyst who developed his theory and practice around empathy. He believed mental health is the ability of an individual self to realize its own unique '*nuclear program in the course of its life span*' (a concept very similar to humanistic notions of self-actualization). He developed a theory that has become influential but differs significantly from classical analytic theory and practice. He called his approach **Self Psychology**. His approach is very similar in many ways to Object Relations, especially to Fairbairn and Winnicott, and to the Interpersonal approach of Sullivan. However, Kohut always denied being influenced by Object Relations theorists, and indeed sees Self Psychology as somehow different from all predecessors.

According to Kohut, the newborn is not born with a cohesive self, but the parents act and respond as if a self existed. The child's self arises out of this relationship – the interplay between the infant's innate potential and the responsiveness of the adult selves or **selfobjects** (very similar to Winnicott).

Classical theory implies intact structures of the personality: id, ego, super-ego. For Kohut, theory is based in the idea that the Self is a central structure of the personality, and it is formed over time in relation to impressions from parents or significant others by what he called **transmuting internalizations**. This is a process by which aspects of the selfobjects are absorbed into the child's self. Parents normally respond to the child by empathic attunement to the needs of the child. This empathic attunement will often fall short of the child's needs, but if the frustration is minimal (optimal) the child will take in an aspect of the selfobject in the form of a specific function (such as self-soothing). The child withdraws some of its magical (narcissistic) expectation from the selfobject and forms a particle of self-structure. The inner structure of the child then performs some function previously performed by the object. Due to needs being unfulfilled, this process may be defective and the person may develop secondary defensive or compensatory structures.

Kohut believed that the individual has three needs which must be fulfilled as the child grows for the self to develop fully:

1. The need to be '*mirrored*', which in essence requires the child to be accepted totally by the parent. This term is not be confused with the skill of mirroring in therapy. When a child has experienced significant mirroring over a period of time they are able to cope with times when they are not mirrored by adapting. Gradually, a self-structure develops with a healthy sense of self.
2. The need to idolize. The need to know that at least one parent is whole and powerful. If we have had and internalized a calm and powerful adult figure when we grow up, we develop the capacity to self-regulate our own feelings. Kohut further believed that the higher aspects of the personality are more readily developed in those who have internalized their idealized parent.
3. The need to be like others. The child needs to know that they are like a primary care figure. This helps with developing a sense of belonging in the world and that they fit in; that they are not odd.

For Kohut, if all these needs are adequately met, the growing child will develop in a healthy way. If they are not, and they often aren't, the child will develop what he called *compensatory structures* to enable them to cope.

> I began to entertain the thought that these people were not concerned with me as a separate person but that they were concerned with themselves; that they did not love or hate me, but that needed me as part of themselves, needed me as a set of functions which they had not acquired in early life; that what appeared to be their love and hate was in reality their need that I fulfil certain psychological functions for them and anger at me when I did not do so. (Kohut, 1991: 9)

A co-created relationship

It is clear that the TR is co-created and that both client and therapist are instrumental in it. The TR is created in context and in relation to the context. This is in contrast to traditional classical approaches where theory hypothesizes the direction of therapy through setting the scene and employing techniques. Within this approach the therapist and client impact on each other moment to moment.

The therapist helps the client find meaning and understanding and provides a safe, secure and supportive relationship. Therapy may contribute a template of relating for

(Continued)

(Continued)

the client which helps them become more integrated or congruent in relation to the different aspects or 'parts' of self. This relational encounter is transformational and fosters conditions which enable the client to be in touch with their own authenticity and make choices that are fulfilling and growthful. As each client case is unique, there are no specific goals of therapy. Each client will bring their own problems and experiences and the therapist will work with whatever the client perceives to be their goals.

P

PRACTITIONER CLIP 4.1 MIRRORING PAST RELATIONSHIPS IN THE PRESENT

Ken presented to me (Divine) following a period of three weeks' sick leave from work. He stated that he faced a lot of pressure at work and was off because of stress. He shared that what contributed to his stress was how he did not get on with his team and always felt he had to compete with two particular junior team members. He stated he also felt that although his managers never said it, he could tell they felt he was not good enough. His initial goals were therefore to manage the stress and to cope better. As therapy progressed, he stated that he wanted to drop out because there were other people 'out there' that needed it more than he did.

As we began to explore and work together, it emerged that this feeling of being in competition and not good enough was a feeling which emerged in his family since he was a child. Ken stated that his father always criticized him and that he could never do anything which was considered good.

Through therapy, Ken was able to see how his experiences at work and feelings of not being good enough mirrored his primary relationships with his father and sisters. They played out in the therapy room through him wanting to leave therapy when he stated he wanted to give others a chance. They may 'need it more than he did' – as if they were competing with him. He self-judged, as he had done in his family and at work. Therapy enabled him to see this and to self-accept in the 'here-and-now' of the reparative therapy relationship.

From our experience, even when clients share what they perceive to be their goals, once the therapy begins, past relational patterns, and the impact they have had on the client, often surface, as we have seen in Practitioner Clip 4.1 above. This then impacts on what the client perceived as their goal as new realizations emerge.

Thus the relational therapist's ability and competence to work with the clients' relational patterns in the here-and-now of the relationship enhances the potential of therapy.

RELATIONAL COMPETENCIES

While a RA is driven by philosophical principles and is not explicitly skill based, a professional practitioner needs to develop key competencies to be effective in their practice. We now present relational competencies for working effectively with all clients. These have been divided into four main domains: practical, personal, professional and contextual (Table 4.1).

TABLE 4.1 Relational competencies

Practical	Ability to foster and maintain and develop a good therapeutic relationship in the here-and-now.
	Ability to work with the client to establish and work with an agreed therapeutic aim.
	Ability to undertake relevant assessment (relevant history and identifying suitability for therapy).
	Ability to work collaboratively with the client, understanding their experiences and 'world view'.
	Ability to conclude the therapeutic relationship.
Personal	Ability to maintain authenticity in the therapeutic relationship.
	Ability to experience and communicate empathy and work with dynamics in the here-and-now
	Ability to respond non-defensively to client feedback.
	Ability to recognize and address own prejudices.
	Ability to work with difficult and complex processes.
	Ability to help clients reflect on and develop and articulate their emotions, experiences and personal meanings.
	Ability to be reflexively self-aware in relation to the client.
	Ability to facilitate the personal power and self-determination of the client.
Professional	Knowledge of, and ability to operate within, professional and ethical guidelines.
	Knowledge and understanding of a RA, mental health problems, and the ability to understand and employ the model in practice.
	Ability to undertake assessment using appropriate methodologies (assessment measures, tools, and so on).
	Ability to make use of supervision.
	Ability to recognize limitations in professional practice.
	Commitment to ongoing personal and professional development.
Contextual	Knowledge and understanding of how the particular context in which the therapist works impacts on the client–therapist relationship.
	Ability to reflect on how the therapist's own social and professional context impacts on their worldview.
	Ability to draw from the client how their social context is impacting on their experience.
	Ability to work collaboratively with the client in exploring potential barriers to change or challenges when considering the client's social context.
	Ability to record all elements of client's progress in relation to the professional context.

Source: adapted from Roth, Hill and Pilling, 2009

We developed these competencies building on the work of Roth et al. (2009) to maximize the effective practice of a relational therapist. In Chapters 6 and 7 we introduce the different competencies that are essential in establishing and developing the relationship. In Chapter 8, we build on the practical and personal competencies in facing challenges to the relationship and, in Chapter 11, in working with difference. A practical competency, for example, *an ability to conclude the therapeutic relationship*, is essential in managing the ending of a therapy contract. Other competencies, such as the therapist's *ability to be reflexively self-aware in relation to the client*, are explored more in the work in Chapter 10 on the therapist's self in relationship.

REFLECTION POINT 4.1 DEVELOPING YOUR CORE MODEL

A RA is described as operating within a paradigm which is not in itself a core model.

- What key elements can you draw from this chapter to inform your core model for the practice of therapy?

RESOURCE BOX 4

Cozolino, L. (2010) *The Neuroscience of Psychotherapy: Healing the Social Brain* (2nd edn). New York: W.W. Norton.
An overview of neuroscience, attachment and the TR.

Kahn, M. (1991) *Between Therapist and Client*. New York: W.H. Freeman.
A classic text which looks at psychoanalytical and humanistic elements in a relational paradigm.

Kohut, H. and Stepansky, P.E. (1984) *How Does Analysis Cure?* (Vol. 52). Edited by A. Goldberg. Chicago, IL: University of Chicago Press.
An important book looking at self-psychology and empathy.

Paul, S. and Charura, D. (2012) 'Accepting the therapeutic relationship as love', *The Psychotherapist*, 52: 22–3.
A simplified proposal for the place of love in therapy.

Roth, A., Hill, A. and Pilling, S. (2009) *The Competencies Required to Deliver Effective Humanistic Psychological Therapies*. London: University College of London.
Key competencies which have become central to therapists in evaluating their knowledge, practice and skills.

CHAPTER SUMMARY

A RA is not based on one method, but is rather a paradigm or framework for the practice of therapy. It has increasingly become an element of different models as well as an approach in itself.

Underlying assumptions

- A RA is based on self in relation to others and is thus a two-person psychology.
- Relational therapies posit that we have an inner drive, which is for connection, attachment with others.
- The personality develops in a 'two-person' field: who I am is a co-creation of me and others.

Central ideas

- It is through relationships that we become and maintain who we are.
- Relationships take place in a social context.
- It is through the therapeutic relationship that change takes place.

Personality/sense of self

- The personality forms in relation to primary experiences.
- Early relationships are particularly important.
- We internalize early relational experience as a template, or prototype, for future relationships.

Social context

- All relationships take place in a social context.
- Prevailing attitudes and values have an impact on relationships, for example, what it means to be a man/woman; to be white/black; to be gay/heterosexual; rich or poor, and so on.

Therapeutic relationship

- The therapeutic relationship is co-created.
- Therapist and client influence one another from moment to moment.
- Meaning is co-constructed between them.
- The here-and-now relationship and transference relationship are important.
- Therapy can be seen as a loving relationship.
- The relationship is the vehicle for therapy.

(Continued)

(Continued)

Role of therapist

- The therapist enters into an authentic, human relationship with the client.
- They do not observe from an objective place, e.g. the 'expert', the 'teacher', the 'doctor'.
- They know that interpersonal relational difficulties are likely to occur in therapy.
- They are prepared to work these through.
- They know that their own relational patterns will have an impact on the encounter.
- They help clients to explore their difficulties.
- They understand clients' stories in terms of what is going on in the day-to-day life of the client.
- They believe clients' difficulties are likely to be relational even if the story they are telling appears to have no people in it.
- They work from practical, personal and professional competencies.

Goals

Therapy aims to:

- Increase awareness of the client's way of relating to self and other (intellectual insight) and how this relates to current difficulties.
- Provide a safe and supportive relationship in which the client has a positive 'self with other' experience.
- Contributes to a new and more productive model of relating for the client.

5

Developmental factors in a relational approach

The aims of this chapter are for the reader to understand the formation of relational problems from a developmental perspective. This includes:

- Childhood attachment.
- Theories of human development.
- Neurobiology and neuroscience.
- How problems develop.
- Psychoanalytic and person-centred viewpoints.

In this chapter we introduce theories of human development and childhood attachment and their impact on interpersonal relationships. We review the evidence of neuroscientific research and the impact of developmental experiences on the brain. We also consider theories of personality development and psychological maladjustment based on the work of Carl Rogers and others. The material offered in this chapter offers a sound basis for the practice of therapy from a relational perspective.

DEVELOPMENTAL FACTORS

Many human problems have their origins in early experiences and in the ways of relating that an individual has learned to allow them to cope in everyday life. Understanding the roots of relational problems and childhood attachment is therefore central to a RA.

A RA draws from research on early childhood experience to help us understand patterns that an individual may act out in their day-to-day life. These may lead them to repeating cycles of behaviour that are problematic. Importantly, ways of relating based on these patterns may be re-enacted in the TR.

There are typically two elements in this:

1. Attachment: Basically, these are modes of relating based on childhood experiences. The individual is somehow stuck in their ability to relate freely as a result of parenting and primary caregiver experiences.
2. Transference relationships. The individual may behave towards the therapist in a way which reflects their inner, often unconscious, perceptions.

Bowlby's evolutionary theory of attachment (Bowlby, 1969) proposed that children come into the world biologically pre-wired to find attachment with others to enable them, and the species overall, to survive. Bowlby was influenced by ethological theory, particularly Lorenz's (1935) study of imprinting in ducks. Lorenz's research demonstrated that attachment is innate and a necessary function for survival.

Bowlby proposed that attachment behaviours are instinctive and will be activated by any conditions that seem to threaten the security of the child. Babies display certain innate behaviours, such as smiling and chuckling (he called these social releasers), which help ensure caregiving for their basic survival and consequent bonding with the primary caregiver. Where the mother responds with care and attention to this behaviour, positive bonding develops. Infants who develop a strong bond with the mother will have a statistically better chance of survival. Therefore, infants and mothers have evolved over millennia a biological need to stay in close contact. The basic attachment is not for food per se, but for care and attention to enable their survival.

Bowlby suggested that a child would form one primary attachment and that the attachment figure acted as a secure base for exploring the world. The attachment relationship becomes a blueprint for future social relationships, and rupture or disruption to it can have lasting consequences. His theory was later researched and developed by Ainsworth and others (1978).

Key elements of Bowlby's theory

The key elements of Bowlby's theory (adapted from McLeod, 2007) are:

1. A child has an innate need to bond with one main attachment figure (i.e. monotropy). This basic, primary relationship, for him, was with the mother. Deprivation of a good bond with the mother leads to problems later in life.

2. A child should receive the continuous care of this single most important attachment figure for approximately the first two years of life. Bowlby (1951) claimed that there is a critical period up to two years of age. If the attachment bond is disrupted during this critical time, the child will suffer long-term consequences. Bowlby used the term maternal deprivation to refer to the separation or loss of the mother as well as failure to develop an attachment.
3. The long-term consequences of maternal deprivation may include delinquency, reduced intelligence, aggression, affectionless psychopathy or the inability to show affection or concern for others. Individuals can act impulsively with no seeming regard for the consequences of their actions.
4. The child's attachment relationship with the primary caregiver leads to the development of the internal working model.

T

THEORY CLIP 5.1 INTERNAL WORKING MODEL

The **internal working model** is a cognitive conceptual framework for making sense of the world, the self and others. The model of the self reflects the messages communicated by primary caregiver(s) by word and action. This internal model governs how the child feels towards their parent, towards their self, how the child expects to be treated, and plans for their own behaviour towards others. The internal working model is:

- Based on early relationships (attachments).
- The source of transference patterns the individual operates in life.

According to Bowlby (1969), the primary caregiver acts as a prototype for future relationships via the internal working model. Adults' interactions with others are guided by memories from their internal model, which influence and help evaluate their contact with others (Bretherton and Munholland, 1999).

The main features of the internal working model can be considered to be:

1. A model of Others: 'How much can I trust other people?
2. A model of the Self: 'How do I feel about my self-worth?'
3. A model of the Self in Interaction with Others: 'What impact do I have on others, in this world?'

An infant who experiences frequent abuse may develop a negative internal working model that 'tells them' 'No one cares about me, I am unlovable, people who I hope will love me only hurt or reject me, it doesn't matter what I do or say, I am not good enough.'

If this 'model' of self, others and the world and how things work is not changed as the child grows, they may develop low self-esteem, be overly dependent or independent, sabotage jobs, friendships or relationships, and never get what they want in life. An infant who receives consistent, positive attention from their caregiver is most likely to develop a positive internal working model.

T

THEORY CLIP 5.2 ATTACHMENT BONDS

Bowlby created the term 'attachment' to describe the affective or emotional bond that develops between the infant and primary caregiver. He described attachment as a 'lasting psychological connectedness between human beings' (Bowlby, 1969: 194). Bowlby proposed that the earliest bonds formed by children with their caregivers have a profound impact that continues throughout life. According to Bowlby, attachment also serves as a drive to keep the infant close to the mother, thus improving the child's chances of survival. This attachment behaviour, therefore, is considered an innate evolutionary function to ensure the survival of the species. The type of attachment towards the caregiver develops in relation to the interaction between the two and this is also influenced by the caregiver's own attachment experiences as a child. Bowlby (1969, 1973, 1980) proposes that attachment bonds have four defining components:

- Safe haven: When the child feels threatened or fearful, they can turn to the caregiver for comfort and succour.
- Secure base: The caregiver provides a safe and dependable base from which the child can explore the world.
- Proximity maintenance: The child strives to stay near their caregiver and therefore keep safe.
- Separation distress: When separated from the caregiver, the child becomes worried and distressed.

Researchers have further noted that these early attachment relationships form during a time of significant neurological development of the brain (Siegel, 1999, 2003). So the early childhood years are considered very important in laying down psychological foundations for the future.

Ainsworth's 'Strange Situation' research into attachment

Ainsworth developed Bowlby's primary work. The first of a number of 'Strange Situation' studies demonstrated a clear link between attachment and behaviour. In a range of studies, researchers observed how young children responded to a situation in which they were left alone and then reunited with their mothers (Ainsworth et al., 1978). From these studies, Ainsworth described attachment styles: secure attachment, ambivalent-insecure attachment and avoidant-insecure attachment. Later, researchers Main and Solomon (1986) observed a fourth attachment style: disorganized-insecure attachment.

Many later studies have supported the link between childhood attachment, attachment styles developed from early childhood experiences and adult relationships and their outcomes.

Types of attachment

Secure attachment

A child who is considered securely attached exhibits distress when separated from their caregiver and is happy when their caregiver returns. Such children feel secure and able to depend on their caregivers. When the caregiver leaves, the child may demonstrate upset but appears confident that the caregiver will return.

When upset or fearful these children seek comfort from their caregiver. They know their caregiver will provide support, so they are confident to turn to them when in need.

Ambivalent attachment

Ambivalently attached children usually demonstrate a high level of distress when a caregiver leaves. Research suggests that ambivalent attachment results from inconsistent caregiving; sometimes the infant is responded to when in need, and at other times the infant is ignored. Additionally, the caregiver may tend to the physical needs of the child but ignore the child's need for love and interaction. These children cannot depend on their mother (or caregiver) to be there when in need.

Loving touch, play and interaction are considered very important for emotional development. Without this the infant does not 'feel felt' (Siegel, 1999). It can be difficult for these children to develop compassion and empathy.

With this type of caregiving, children learn that the world they inhabit is basically inconsistent – sometimes their needs are met, sometimes some of them are, and at other times they get nothing. Infants learn that others are neither dependable nor consistent. They may not learn or understand the world of emotions – their own or others' emotions.

Avoidant attachment

Children with an avoidant attachment tend to avoid caregivers. These children may in fact show no preference between a caregiver and a stranger. Research has suggested that this attachment style might be a result of abusive or neglectful caregivers. Children who are punished for relying on a caregiver will learn to avoid seeking help in the future. Avoidant attachment occurs when caregivers are unresponsive to the infant's needs – both physical and emotional. This neglect happens often in families where there is alcoholism and/or drug addiction, or in families who don't understand what their babies need. This happened in Romanian orphanages (Brown and Webb, 2005). The infants were kept in cots for the most of day and were taken out only to be fed or changed; they were shown little or no emotional interaction. Many became listless and passive in a world without love.

In this environment, infants learn that they have no impact on their world, or in relationship to others. The world is a stark, cold place in which no one really cares. These infants may become developmentally delayed. Human beings can actually die from lack of human contact.

Disorganized/disoriented attachment

A fourth category was added by Main and Soloman (1990). The child shows distress on separation but actively ignores and avoids the caregiver when they return. They may then freeze or fall to the floor, perhaps rocking or hitting themselves.

Evidence has suggested (Main and Hesse, 1990) that children with disorganized attachment may experience their caregivers as either frightening or frightened. A frightened caregiver is alarming to the world of a child, who uses triggers such as facial expressions from the caregiver to decide whether a situation is safe. A frightening caregiver demonstrates overt aggression to the child (physical or sexual) and creates a dilemma which Main has called 'fear without solution'. In other words, the caregiver is both the source of the child's alarm as well as the child's safe haven. The child is therefore caught in a no-win paradox, which could explain the 'freezing' behaviours observed in these children. Interactions with others are experienced as inconsistent and the child cannot internalize a coherent self-organizing model. A commonly used analogy is if the child uses the caregiver as their mirror to understand the self, the child looks into a mirror broken into a thousand pieces. The world is fragmented and uninterested and the child does not know how to deal with it.

REFLECTION POINT 5.1 ATTACHMENT AND THERAPY

Research on attachment helps us understand how early life experiences can affect relationships in later life.

- How might this inform the relational therapist working in the here-and-now with their client?

Problems with attachment

So what happens to children who do not form 'secure' attachments? There is much research (Gerhardt, 2004; Joseph, 1999) to suggest that failure to form secure attachments in childhood can have a detrimental effect on relationships later in life. There may be difficulty in forming or keeping close relationships and a sense of low self-worth, whereas those who are considered securely attached in childhood tend to have high self-esteem and strong, intimate and long-lasting relationships.

T

THEORY CLIP 5.3 IMPACT OF LACK OF LOVE AND ENVIRONMENTAL FACTORS ON DEVELOPMENT

We have seen in Chapter 2 the evidence from neuroscience which shows how lack of primary loving relationships in childhood impacts on brain development and functioning.

The effects of early attachment and environmental influences on neurons and social and emotional development are well documented (Cozolino, 2010a; Joseph, 1999). Deprived or abnormal rearing conditions induce severe disturbance in all aspects of social and emotional functioning, and affect the growth and survival of neurons, and many other parts of the brain. It also affects even physical growth, attachment patterns, play behaviour, and the oral and phallic stages of development. At birth, a part in the brain known as the limbic system is 'experience-expectant' and may develop abnormally, depending on the age at which they suffer deprivation. If there is a lack of primary loving relationships, insufficient stimulation within a child's environment and relationships, or the child is neglected, abused or traumatized, then this has a severe impact. The nuclei in the limbic system may atrophy (weaken), develop seizure-like activity, or maintain or form abnormal interconnections. This consequently results in social withdrawal, inabilities to interact appropriately, and an inability to form normal emotional attachments (Joseph, 1999).

Hazen and Shaver (1987) found varied beliefs about relationships among adults with differing attachment styles. Securely attached adults tend to believe that romantic love is enduring. Ambivalently attached adults report falling in love often. Those with avoidant attachment styles describe love as rare and temporary.

While we cannot say that infant attachment styles are identical to adult, romantic attachment styles, research has shown that early attachment styles *can* help predict patterns of behaviour and some psychological problems such as depression in adulthood. It is argued that depression is mostly associated with anxious ambivalent attachment style, as well as a preoccupation with, and fearful avoidance of, attachment relationships (Carnelley et al., 1994). Secure attachment is important and influential in supporting individuals through psychological distress, particularly where clients face major life stressors which may otherwise result in depression (Hammen et al., 1995).

NEUROSCIENTIFIC PERSPECTIVES AND THE RELATIONAL APPROACH

Traditionally, psychotherapeutic modalities offered explanations of how therapy facilitated change through therapeutic encounter. There was also an emphasis on *client-reported* outcomes. Although these are important, there was a missing link between the evidence base for therapeutic outcomes and objective empirical evidence.

In the last two decades the development of Computerized Tomography (CT) scans and **Magnetic Resonance Imaging** (MRI) brain imaging has enabled researchers to evidence important neuroscientific perspectives on the effects of therapy. Neuroscience has enabled therapists to show how therapeutic work is psychologically reparative.

The brain, neurological pathways and therapy: from childhood to adulthood

The brain is composed of billions of neurons that transmit electronic-chemical signals in the brain that affect the way that people think, feel, relate to others and behave. Abuse, neglect or trauma physiologically impacts on the development of the brain and the neuro-development process of children and young people. This often leads to physiological and behavioural problems manifesting in young people. Adult individuals who face traumatic or abusive experiences are also impacted on a neurological level.

We focus on three relational assumptions (see Chapter 3) to illuminate how neuroscientific research is important:

1. That we are social beings and without relationship we die.
2. Our problems arise in and through relationships.
3. Our problems are resolved in therapy through a relationship which offers the right conditions for healing and transformation.

We can now explore the human developmental process from a neuroscientific perspective and see how relationships impact on the individual. We can see the links between therapeutic change and physiological change in the brain. What previously has been evidenced through client behavioural/experience changes can only now be seen by MRI scans.

The importance of love and attachments within primary relationships and their impact on children's mental and physical wellbeing is well documented (Gerhardt, 2004; Joseph, 1999). Joseph (1999) highlighted the relationship between children's experiences and neurological development at different age stages. He based his arguments on earlier neurological studies which indicated that the human brain is almost fully functional at birth (Paus et al., 1999). However, the limbic forebrain (e.g. the hypothalamus and hippocampus) and neocortex (which mediates higher level cognitive, intellectual functions, human speech and language) develop and mature at a much slower pace and can take up to the first ten years of children's lives to fully mature. Joseph (1999) further argued that the limbic forebrain and neocortex depend on appropriate social interaction, emotional, perceptual stimulation and eye-to-eye contact to develop and fully mature (Charura et al., 2015; Joseph, 1999).

If this relational stimulation is not present within the child's environment, or if it is limited, neglectful or abusive, the developing neurons and dendrites will form abnormal connections, atrophy or even die. This may lead to cognitive difficulties, inability to socialize appropriately, or abnormal emotional and perceptual functioning. In worst case scenarios of abuse, lack of interaction or neglect, some studies have shown that the consequence may be death (Joseph, 1999).

Problems in relating can continue to be evident in early adulthood, manifesting as disruptive behaviour, inabilities to connect emotionally and personality complexities. It is through a relational therapeutic encounter in which the right conditions for transformation are provided that individuals can start to experience healing. The TR offers a safe environment in which individuals can start to explore the experiences which would have affected/impacted on them in their life.

R

RESEARCH CLIP 5.1 NEUROSCIENCE RESEARCH FINDINGS AND THERAPY

- Brody et al. (2001) studied the neurological and psychological impact of interpersonal therapy when working with clients experiencing depression. Their results showed that after 12 weeks of therapy there were significant neurological changes in the therapy group.
- Evans (2004) compiled cultural neuroscience research studies which unequivocally highlighted the adverse impact of poverty, exposure to increased levels of

(Continued)

(Continued)

stress, violence, separation and other turmoil on children's neural development. Stressful social factors, even in adulthood, contribute to the formation of unhealthy stress hormones such as cortisol, which can be permanently damaging to areas of the brain (Ivey et al., 2012).

- Fisher et al. (2005) demonstrated how love impacts physiologically on the brain. Her study confirmed how through loving relationships neural pathways can be transformed and relational patterns thus changed.

How does a relational encounter impact on neurological repair?

Neuroscience evidences the advantages of working relationally with clients. Therapists' responses to body language, ways of being and the expressed emotions are now evidenced to effect neurological repair (Hollan, 2012).

Researchers have indicated that emphatic and positive messages increase the production of **neurotransmitters** such as dopamine, which consequently increases the clients' sense of wellbeing. This is important because where an individual has experienced trauma, neglect or experiences which have inhibited development of healthy neurons and pathways, change is needed. Through therapy, neurological changes are stimulated. Ivey et al. (2012) demonstrated that a relational therapeutic encounter results in the generation of new neurones and neural networks that affect changes in the brain. This enables an improvement in the client's sense of psychological wellbeing.

Mirror neurons are central to how we give and respond to empathy. Mirror neurons are a network of neurons that become activated upon observation of the other. They are central to evaluation and adjustment of each other's behaviour moment by moment (Hollan, 2012; Kogler and Stueber, 2000).

When empathy is offered in the here-and-now of therapy, where the therapist endeavours to be present with their client, this targets the activation and integration of neural networks (Cozolino, 2010a, 2010b). Cozolino proposed that therapy is successful to the degree that therapists are able to create an experience that results in neuroplasticity. Empathy emerges from the human-to-human relationship between therapist and client. Moreover, from a neuroscientific perspective, what therapy actually does is to stimulate neuroplasticity. Through the TR, new neurons are stimulated, and existing neurons are enabled to grow and branch out and connect. Existing neural systems connect with each other in new and creative ways that support wellbeing (Cozolino, 2010b).

In summary:

1. The brain exists only in relationship to what goes on around it.
2. The therapeutic process is dependent on the client's natural biological propensity to generate new neurons. In other words, the therapeutic process is dependent on the brain's plasticity for it to be effective.
3. Relational therapy fosters conditions in which neurological alterations and optimal release of various neurotransmitters can occur.
4. Neurotransmitters are linked to cognitive, emotional, psychological and behavioural presentations. Empathic responses and a RA foster a safe and positive environment which enables neurological repair.
5. A RA enables neural development, neural network integration, coordination, repair and restoration. This relational approach is particularly crucial for the networks which specialize in emotions, cognitions, sensations and behaviour.

(adapted from Farmer, 2009 and Ivey et al., 2012)

REFLECTION POINT 5.2 NEUROSCIENCE AND THERAPIST QUALITIES

Recent neuroscientific research has transformed understanding of the impact of human relationships in the brain.

- In what ways might this research affect what qualities a therapist brings to the session?

Implications for practice

Research about early relationships can help us understand the relational patterns that our clients present to us in therapy. They can be particularly useful in understanding the ways in which our clients:

1. Have relational problems in everyday life.
2. Behave towards us as therapy progresses.

Of primary importance, however, is that our clients understand their own limiting thoughts feelings and actions which have led to the development of their internal working model. This helps raise awareness and helps the individual have more agency (personal power) in their day-to-day life by not repeating the same self-defeating patterns of behaviour.

Neuroscientific research, demonstrating the impact of attachment and love on relationships, enables us to understand how therapy has a transformational dimension on a physiological level. It enables us to see that even when clients have been 'damaged' in earlier primary relationships or present experiences, therapy can be reparative as new neuropathways and networks are formed. Cultural neuroscience highlights for practitioners the importance of understanding and taking into consideration clients' cultural experiences and social contexts. Overall, we can see the potential for positive impact that the therapist has in promoting psychological, neurological development and client transformation through a relational encounter.

We have now considered the research into childhood development, attachment and their impact on the development of the brain. We next consider psychological theories of personality development and maladjustment based on the research of Carl Rogers.

CARL ROGERS – THEORY OF PERSONALITY AND BEHAVIOUR

The theory and practice of person-centred therapy is based on Rogers' (1951) 19 propositions or principles about human development, the structure of the personality and the development and resolution of human distress. It is one of the most significant theories of human nature, and is now firmly grounded in research and practice. It provides a clear foundation for practitioners wishing to understand the principles of human development and, *furthermore*, the process of therapeutic change. The propositions are summarized here.

1. Every individual exists in a continually changing world of experience of which he (*sic*) is the centre.

See Figure 5.1.

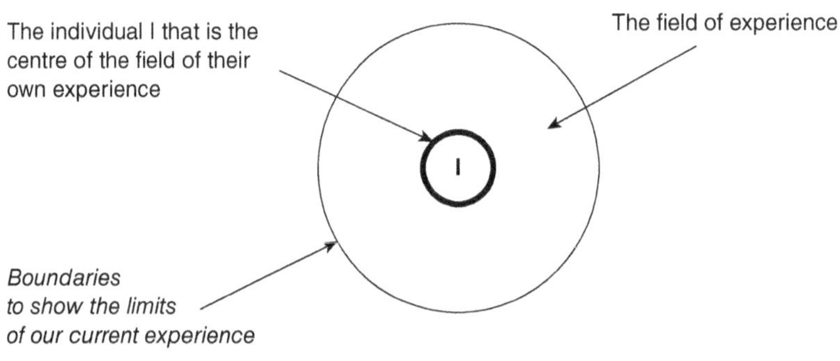

FIGURE 5.1 The field of experiencing

2. The organism reacts to the field as it is experienced and perceived. This perceptual world is for the individual 'reality'.

What the individual subjectively experiences or perceives is 'reality' for them.

3. The organism reacts as an organized whole to this phenomenal field.

Just like a jelly responds when touched, the individual responds to experience in a holistic way.

4. The organism has one basic tendency and striving – to actualize, maintain and enhance the experiencing organism.

A fundamental premise of humanistic psychology is based on the principle that the individual is affected by the same formative principle that covers our physical universe. We are all influenced by the 'actualizing tendency' to fulfil our potential and to grow and develop.

5. Behaviour is basically the goal-directed attempt of the organism to satisfy its needs as experienced, in the field as perceived.

An individual's behaviour is their movement towards meeting their needs as they experience them at any time.

6. Emotion accompanies and in general facilitates such goal-directed behaviour, the kind of emotion being related to the seeking versus consummatory aspects of the behaviour, and the intensity of emotion being related to the perceived significance of the behaviour for the maintenance and enhancement of the organism.

Any behaviour is linked to emotion. We move towards satisfying positive emotional drives. The significance of a behaviour and the intensity of emotion are linked to their importance to the individual in that moment in time.

7. The best vantage point for understanding behaviour is from the internal frame of reference of the individual himself (*sic*).

The unique, internal frame of reference or worldview of the individual is the best for understanding them, their thoughts, feelings and motivation.

8. A portion of the total perceptual field gradually becomes differentiated as the self.

As the infant develops, a part of their field of experiencing, responding to their name, their toys, their close caregivers and so on, becomes identified as their sense of self whereas other, non-significant experiences are not identified with in this way.

9. As a result of interaction with the environment, and particularly as a result of evaluative interaction with others, the structure of self is formed – an organized, fluid but consistent pattern of perceptions of characteristics and relationships of the 'I' or the 'me', together with values attached to these concepts.

The child comes to associate experiences and responses from others with their own developing personality and sense of self.

10. The values attached to experiences and the values which are part of the self-structure in some sense are values experienced directly by the organism, and in some instances are values introjected or taken over from others, but perceived in a distorted fashion, *as if* they had been experienced directly.

These values, which come to be associated as part of the self, may be based on their direct experiences or they may be values which have been internalized from other people, especially primary caregivers, and experienced as if the meaning of them was a reality.

11. As experiences occur in the life of the individual they are either: (a) symbolized, perceived, and organized into some relationship to the self, (b) ignored because there is no perceived relationship to the self-structure, (c) denied symbolization or given a distorted symbolization because the experience is inconsistent with the structure of self.

The individual has a range of experiences and they are filed away according to their meaning and value. Some are stored and integrated into the self-structure (e.g. a child learns how to ride her bike); some are ignored as having little meaning (e.g. the child sees another child who smiles at her but she does not know the child and thus carries on cycling); some are repressed because they are in conflict with the sense of self (e.g. the child's mother may call out to the child and tell her she is a bad child for getting her clothes dirty when she fell off the bike, but the child cannot accept she is bad).

12. Most of the ways of behaving which are adopted by the organism are those which are consistent with the concept of self.

The individual chooses ways of behaving which fit their self-image.

13. Behaviour may in some instance be brought about by organic experiences and needs which have not been symbolized. Such behaviour may be inconsistent with the concept of self, but in such instances the behaviour is not 'owned' by the individual.

A teenager may take drugs and steal from friends to fund the habit without in any sense taking responsibility for this behaviour. It is, in a sense, out of character.

14. Psychological maladjustment exists when the organism denies to awareness significant sensory and visceral experiences which constantly are not symbolized and organized into the gestalt of the self-structure. When this situation exists, there is a basic or potential psychological tension.

Distress occurs when the individual represses experiences which have not been correctly 'filed' in the psyche (as in proposition 11). These experiences have an energy of their own and this energy sits in the psyche and causes tension. One part of the psyche seeks to push away another part, causing incongruence or inner conflict.

15. Psychological adjustment exists when the concept of self is such that all sensory and visceral experiences of the organism are, or may be, assimilated on a symbolic level into a consistent relationship with the concept of self.

When the individual is open to all experiences and they can all be 'filed' without threat, then they are at ease or congruent in themselves.

16. Any experience which is inconsistent with the organization or structure of self may be perceived as a threat, and the more of these perceptions there are, the more rigidly the self-structure is organized to maintain itself.

The more the psyche is confronted with challenging experiences, the more it seeks to defend itself against them. The more rigid the defences become. The more tension the individual experiences.

17. Under certain conditions, involving primarily a complete absence of any threat to the self-structure, experiences which are inconsistent with it may be perceived, and examined, and the structure of self revised to assimilate and include such experiences.

When the individual is in a situation in which they feel safe and secure, they are able to look at the different conflicted aspects in the psyche, review them and allow them to be evaluated without threat and reduction of tension. With the right conditions this can happen in a therapeutic relationship.

18. When the individual perceives and accepts into one consistent and integrated system all his sensory and visceral experiences, then he is necessarily more understanding of others and is more accepting of others as separate individuals.

When a person begins to accept more aspects of their experiencing, they become more accepting of other people. They are less threatened by others and more at ease with themselves. They are then able to be open to others. This is one of the reasons why trainee therapists are encouraged to do work on themselves.

19. As the individual perceives and accepts into his self-structure more of his organic experiences, he finds that he is replacing his present value *system* – based so largely upon introjections which have been distortedly symbolized – with a continuing organismic valuing process.

When a person is more open to accepting experiences that threaten the psyche, they are able to discard the valuing system (described in proposition 10) and to live in manner in which their own internal values are in operation. They thus live more spontaneously and more fully.

As can be seen, Rogers' 19 propositions describe succinctly both human development and the acquisition and relief of psychological distress.

REFLECTION POINT 5.3 ROGERS' 19 PROPOSITIONS AND ATTACHMENT RESEARCH

Rogers' 19 propositions offer a coherent yet simple model to the development of problems as the growing person develops.

- In what ways does research on attachment concur or otherwise with this model?

Implications for practice

Rogers conceptualizes how the self develops and ways of behaving are internalized based on the conditions of others. This model also identifies that the individual can, when free from threat, reconceptualize their self and this becomes more integrated and functions more fully.

Rogers' theory of personality is further clarified by his description of infant development

The infant's experience is his perceived reality. No one can completely know his *internal* frame of reference.

- He (*sic*) is motivated by an innate *actualizing tendency* towards fulfilling his (organism's) potential.
- His behaviour is goal directed towards the actualization in his reality; he behaves as a unified organized whole (or *gestalt*).

The individual engages in an organismic valuing process. At this early stage all action is directly motivated towards immediate inner gratification and fulfilment. The person moves towards positively-valued experiences and away from negatively-valued experiences. A portion of experiencing becomes symbolized into an awareness of self and the development of self-awareness. This awareness thus becomes formed into a sense of self, or **self-concept**, in the infant's experiential field.

Positive regard

Individuals have a universal need for **positive-regard**, to feel good about themselves. The need for positive-regard is relational:

- It is based on experiences with others.
- It is wide-ranging.
- It is reciprocal and freely given back.
- It is dependent on the significance of the other – the more important the other, the more impact regard from them is valued.

There is a correlation between positive regard experienced by the individual from others and their own positive sense of self, which we can call positive *self-regard*. Rogers proposed that self-regard develops independently in relation to interaction with others.

Conditions of worth

As the child develops, he learns that some behaviours attract more positive regard than others. When the child actively chooses or avoids a self-experience because of the need for positive regard, they are said to have acquired a **condition of worth**. In order to feel good about themselves, they need to fulfil external conditions introjected by others. Their self-regard is dependent on them fulfilling conditions imposed by significant others.

Unconditional positive regard

If the infant only ever experienced **unconditional positive regard** from significant others, no conditions of worth would develop. Self-regard would be unconditional. The need for positive regard would be in harmony with the internal organismic valuing process. The individual would be psychologically adjusted. However, Rogers believed that this was never completely the case. He was of the view that all infants develop conditions of worth.

Locus of evaluation

As the individual learns to experience positive regard (to feel good about themselves) they have to meet conditions of worth – to get approval. Their experiencing self attaches more importance to the others' than to their own experience. Their **locus of evaluation** (LOE) becomes external rather than internal. Literally, the point from which they value themselves is outside themselves, from the perspective of others.

Living with an external locus of evaluation causes **incongruence**, which is an inner conflict between self-concept and experiencing. Because of the need for self-regard, the individual perceives their experiences selectively:

- Those in accord with the individual's conditions of worth are accepted.
- Those that don't are distorted or denied.

Consequently, numbers of experiences are not accurately organized/accepted into the self-structure.

C

CLIENT CLIP 5.1 THE IMPACT OF CONDITIONS OF WORTH

Peter was a banker working in central London. Every day he travelled into the city from a rural suburb on a tube train. He attended therapy with me (Steve) as he was starting to get anxiety attacks on his journey to work. In our sessions it became clear that he was experiencing internal conflict, or incongruence. He had a young family and there were high expectations that he would be a successful businessman. He had married at a young age and was carrying the responsibility of these expectations, which were shared by both his and, importantly, his wife's parents.

His life interests were in the environment and he really enjoyed being in the country. His career path was, literally, taking him far away from where he wanted to be. Peter started to dread going into work. He could not discuss this with his family or friends and this anxiety started to manifest as a fear of travelling underground in trains. Quite literally, he felt hemmed in and barely able to breathe.

In therapy he realized that he could no longer live in this way and that for his own health and wellbeing something needed to change. He discussed his aims with his family and found a job with an environmental charity outside London. While serving his notice, he had no anxiety symptoms when travelling on tube trains.

Peter was ultimately able to live a life which was more in harmony with his own aspirations, and a much better 'fit' for him. His family life improved as he was also able to spend more time with his growing children.

We can see here how Peter has 'introjected' conditions of worth from his family which conflicted with his own aspirations. This led to incongruence which eventually led to symptoms in his everyday life.

(Note: A purely cognitive-behavioural analysis may have led the therapist to focus on reducing symptoms. In this case, however, the work was explicitly relational.)

Psychological maladjustment

With the developing incongruence between experience and self-concept, behavioural incongruities also develop:

- Behaviours consistent with the self-concept are symbolized accurately.
- Behaviours which are not consistent with the self-concept but which dynamically actualize the experience of the organism are *denied* or are *distorted* in order to be congruent with the self-concept.

Threat and defence

An experience which continues to threaten the self-concept is subconsciously perceived as threatening. The threat has to be defended against because if the experience is accurately accepted it would be inconsistent with the self-concept. This would lead to the conditions of worth being undermined and the need for self-regard could no longer be met. The self-concept, which is a reference point for personal identity, and has grown to support the psyche, is itself thus endangered. Anxiety would ensue.

Defence is the selective perception or distortion or denial of the experience. This keeps the experience consistent with the individual's (false/incongruent) self-concept and maintains the integrity of the conditions of worth. The outcome is that the individual's perception of the world becomes limited and falsely defined.

The process of breakdown and disorganization

Breakdown may occur in some individuals where there is a significant incongruence and an event that acutely highlights this occurs. In this case:

- Defence cannot operate successfully.
- Anxiety is experienced.
- The experience is accurately perceived as it enters awareness and the split between the experience and self-structure causes a breakdown in the gestalt.

Disorganization results and experiences and behaviours occur which are no longer repressed. The tension between self-concept and experiences oscillates, causing disorientation.

Levels of disturbance

Rogers did not believe in diagnosis. However, a condition where a person was struggling with conditions of worth in order to function is more likely to be of a 'neurotic'-type nature. Conditions where there is a sustained breakdown of defences, to such an extent that the self-concept is seriously threatened, could in some cases be considered psychotic. The terminologies neurotic/psychotic were not used by Rogers.

Therapeutic implications

In order for the process of defence to be reversed:

- Conditions of worth must decrease.
- Positive self-regard must increase.

A process of reintegration is needed. The communication of unconditional positive regard from another will help:

- It must be empathic. As much as possible it needs to understand the frame of reference of the individual.
- As per Rogers' necessary and sufficient conditions, perception of unconditional positive regard will weaken/dissolve existing conditions of worth.
- The individual's own positive self-regard will increase and move towards becoming without conditions of worth and thus, ultimately, becomes unconditional.
- Perceived threat to the self-concept is reduced. Defences are reversed. Experiences previously considered threatening are accepted and accurately symbolized. The individual is less likely to encounter threatening experiences. Defences reduce in frequency.
- The concept of self and everyday experiences become more congruent. Self-regard is increased. Concurrently, positive regard for others increased.
- Psychological adjustment is regained. The innate organismic valuing process becomes more active. The individual becomes more **fully-functioning**.

Implications for practice

From a relational perspective, the primary experiences that a person has had will pre-mould to some degree how they form relationships. An understanding of research and understanding in this area informs the therapist of how a client may approach a TR.

We do not expect the therapist to seek to 'fit' the client to the theory. We expect the theory to assist the therapist in how a client may behave towards them and what the background to this may be based on. We note that each client is unique and different and must be related to as such.

Similarly, while there are many useful models of human personality, the model that Rogers developed is conceptually clear and not hidebound in theoretical underpinnings. It enables the ideas to be used with relative ease in a RA.

We can summarize the impact of developmental factors we have covered in this and earlier chapters and their impact on a RA thus:

1. The infant–caregiver relationship is of primary importance and plays a major part in moulding a person's intrapsychic structure, i.e. what they believe about themselves, others and the world.
2. A person's intrapsychic structure becomes formed into an internal working model which influences all subsequent relationships. This is based on:
   - The need to repeat what is familiar and works to some degree.
   - An attempt to work out any inner tensions resulting from their early experiences.
3. The self is socially constructed based on:
   - Early experiences with primary caregivers.
   - The social contexts of early experiences.
4. The repeated playing out of relational patterns in everyday life can be explored and understood in the here-and-now of therapy.
5. An accepting and caring relationship offered by the therapist can help resolve internal conflicts based on conditional relationships in early life.

REFLECTION POINT 5.4 MAKING SENSE OF THEORY AND WORKING IN THE HERE-AND-NOW

We have explored different theories of human development from psychoanalytical and existential-humanistic modalities

- How might such theoretical conceptualizations help and hinder the therapist's ability to be with the client in the here-and-now of therapy?

RESOURCE BOX 5

Bowlby, J. (1988) *A Secure Base*. New York: Basic Books.
Bowlby expounds his core theory.

Gerhardt, S. (2004) *Why Love Matters: How Affection Shapes a Baby's Brain*. London: Brunner Routledge.

(Continued)

(Continued)

A good book on infant development that explains why love is essential to brain development in the early years of life.

Mitchell, S. (2000) *Relationality: From Attachment to Intersubjectivity*. Hillsdale, NJ: The Analytic Press.

Provides interrelated ideas on, the relational links of human experience, explored from the work of Loewald, Fairbairn, Bowlby and Sullivan.

Nolan, P. (2012) *Therapist and Client: A Relational Approach to Psychotherapy*. Chichester: Wiley & Sons.

Clear description of theory and links well to practice.

Rogers, C.R. (1951) *Client-Centred Therapy: Its Current Practice, Implications and Theory*. London: Constable; Boston, MA: Houghton Mifflin.

Rogers outlines the foundations of his theory.

Sanders, P. (2006) *The Person-Centred Counselling Primer*. Ross-on-Wye: PCCS Books.

A clear introduction to person-centred theory and practice.

CHAPTER SUMMARY

To help the reader to understand developmental factors in a RA, in this chapter we have outlined and discussed the following:

- How theories of attachment influence our understanding of child development, the development of an individual's internal model and later relational patterns.
- Human development and the introjections of the values of others can cause us to develop in ways which are self-limiting and lead to psychological maladjustment.
- Abuse, neglect or trauma physiologically impact on the development of the brain and the neurodevelopment process.
- In relationship it is possible to reconceptualize both our sense of self and our ways of behaving, to live a more fulfilling life.
- Through the TR, new neurons are stimulated and existing neurons are enabled to grow and branch out and connect, thereby enabling us to conclude that the TR is transformational at personality and neurological levels.

Part II

Establishing and Maintaining the Relationship

This Part draws out the key concepts and skills, taking the reader through the process from Beginnings to Endings, and exploring the challenges along the way and the use of self in the relationship.

6

Establishing the relationship

The aims of this chapter are for the reader to develop an understanding of:

- Creating a safe space for therapy.
- Developing rapport.
- Beginning therapy and creating the basis of a good outcome.
- Agreeing therapy goals.
- Listening.
- The ethical framework and issues of power.
- I–Thou relatedness.

We look at challenges that may emerge during this beginning process. These include boundaries, defences and resistance. We also introduce competencies for developing and maintaining a successful therapeutic relationship.

RELATIONAL APPROACH

In order to understand how to develop and establish the TR, it is important to reconsider the principles and basic assumptions of the RA that we proposed in Chapter 4. As we have seen, there are historical foundations to the development of effective TRs in the different modalities of therapy. All maintain the importance of the relationship. Cumulative research over many decades clearly points to the relationship as an essential therapeutic factor. We consider that working with the relationship in therapy to be an intrinsic factor, regardless of what model of therapy the person

(Continued)

(Continued)

practises or philosophical position or school the therapist may consider themselves to be part of.

As the relational paradigm draws on other models when considering developing the relationship, each modality is considered as throwing light on a different dynamic on the relationship. This includes drawing from client-centred therapy perspectives of the facilitative and core conditions (Rogers, 1959), and the psychodynamic principles of transference, countertransference and defences. It is also important to consider differing dimensions to the relationship, such as relational depth and here-and-now working.

In approaching the practice of therapy we are mindful, therefore, that some aspects of practice may be more compatible with some therapists than others. We present here what are considered the main therapeutic factors without adhering to one ideology of practice.

Relational principles

As you will have seen in Chapter 4, in the practice of therapy we consider six main philosophical principles that underpin the relationship.

1. We are part of a growthful and evolving universe.
2. We are social beings; without relationship we do not develop.
3. We have a built-in propensity to grow to our full potential.
4. We are born in and grow through relationships.
5. Our personal problems arise in and through relationship.
6. Our ability to resolve practical problems is often facilitated when we can access our own internal resources.

Alongside these principles we also consider the basic assumptions for change in therapy and creating a safe space for therapy.

Basic assumptions for change in therapy

Our problems are resolved in therapy through:

1. A relationship which helps us work through issues from our past in relation to the therapist.
2. A meeting with the therapist which enables growth and transformation.

We believe the above principles and basic assumptions to be the cornerstone of good therapy. This requires the therapist to develop a number of factors:

- A clear philosophy on life and humanity.
- A psychological understanding of the human psyche, of how problems develop and how they can be resolved.
- A discrete and coherent model of practice.
- The ability to form and sustain good relationships.
- To be living or working towards a fulfilling life outside the practice of therapy.
- Reflexive self-knowledge and awareness.

Creating a safe space for therapy

The agency, physical environment, the contract agreed, the timing and length of sessions, how the therapist presents, and a variety of other factors all combine to help create a well boundaried and secure setting for therapy to take place.

C

CLIENT CLIP 6.1 ARRIVING IN THE THERAPY ROOM

> 'When I came to therapy I noticed the sign on the door of the clinic, every step of the journey up the stairs, how I was greeted in reception ... then when I came into the room I noticed the temperature, the smell, the chair that was for me, how my therapist dressed, their makeup and their scent, the view from the window, the quietness in the room. I could hear the music playing in reception. I could even hear the clock ticking.'

For the client, different variables impact on their senses as they approach therapy. All of which affect how they think and feel at the very outset of this process.

A number of writers point out the importance of creating a safe space for the therapy to happen. Winnicott's (1965) ideas, for example, were developed by what he saw as the nurturing emotional environment that a loving mother provides to her child. For Winnicott, a loving mother holds her baby, physically and emotionally, and is attuned and responds to the needs of the baby. He formulated the notion that the therapist develops a holding *environment* for their clients. Most therapists today agree that this 'holding environment' is a crucial component in therapy. Langs (1976) stressed the notion of maintaining the *frame*. Bion (1970) described this structure, in which the therapist holds the client in their process of self-exploration, as **containment**.

If we consider, as Perls (Perls et al., 1951) suggested, that the setting of psychotherapy is a *safe emergency*, then in essence it is a setting in place and time where

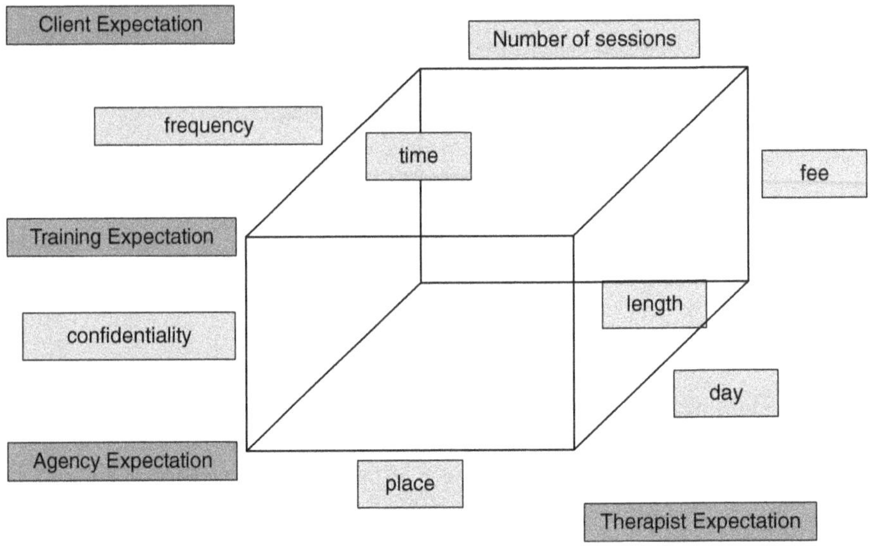

FIGURE 6.1 Factors impacting on the therapeutic frame

the individual can explore issues not easily or safely explored elsewhere. The importance of security and stability in the setting is therefore understood.

By maintaining the *frame*, the therapist is consistently present. They are clear about the tasks of therapy and maintain appropriate boundaries for and with the client. In itself, this safe space comes to be ever-present in the therapy process and a temporary receptacle for all that transpires. For a client in turmoil and/or with difficult relational patterns, knowing that their therapist consistently aims to provide a safe place for them to come to on a regular basis plays a large part in the unfolding of their therapeutic journey.

From Figure 6.1 it is clear that a number of external factors affect the creation of the space in which therapy is taking place.

THE THERAPEUTIC FRAME

The **therapeutic frame** is created through the initial contact made between therapist and clients. All the factors considered above help to create a potentially 'safe space' in which the client can securely explore the issues they bring. Pelham and Stacey (1999) state that at a working level this agreement can be seen as purely 'administrative', creating the necessary arrangements for the work. It can also be considered as an agreement which respects the autonomy of the client and provides a forum for them to work within clearly agreed boundaries. The client is informed of and can negotiate the arrangements and can take an informed judgement as to whether or not to enter therapy.

It is important to establish a clear and boundaried therapeutic frame for the safe space in which therapeutic work can happen. Client and therapist bring their hopes, fears, desires and conflicts to the meeting, based on their own personal histories. The frame can become the forum and at times the battleground for these feelings (Pelham and Stacey, 1999). It is important, therefore, to clearly manage the frame. It may become the structure towards which past experiences and hopes and fears around power, authority, security, containment, desire, anxiety, and so on are activated.

From this perspective, it is important to have a contract, which once agreed can be changed by mutual agreement. For example, changes in time or frequency could be made to meet the needs of either party. This contracting process takes place at a rational conscious level and is the first step in establishing the **working alliance** (please see below and Chapter 12) (Clarkson, 2003). Both parties bring their unconscious hopes, fears, desires and conflicts, which stem from their own cultural/personal history, to the encounter. The therapeutic frame will come to be the living vehicle for expression of these feelings.

The setting

The physical setting itself will have a great bearing on how client and therapist settle into working together. In any physical environment the immediate sensory impact of the therapy room will be instrumental in first impressions. The wellbeing, comfort and security of the client are paramount. While we do not dwell on the detail here, the therapist needs to give attention to seating arrangements, room layout, images, books and other items that will impact on the client. In order that it can become a safe therapeutic space for the client, a certain amount of neutrality in décor is recommended.

The therapist

Similarly, how we dress as therapists will have an impact on most clients. Our aim is not to impress or unduly influence, but to help our clients feel at ease. It is common for beginning therapists to give considerable attention to how they present. We are perhaps more visible to our client than we realize. Every nuance of our behaviour, habits, tics and observable propensities are available to our client, who is preparing to have with us one of the most intimate life relationships. As Kottler (1986) notes, the therapist is working in a glass box and as such is eminently visible.

While neutrality in dress and behaviour may be considered important, we are not advocating that the therapist becomes a 'blank screen'. The therapist needs to be present in the therapy because being present is a very important ingredient. It is better to be more fully yourself while at the same time being there for your client.

How therapists present themselves can also convey their norms and values to the client. Clients often link how they see the therapist presenting or what they are wearing to a bigger cultural, social and political context. An example of this may be a therapist using speech in a way that the client finds difficult to relate to. Thus, language also becomes an important factor in the therapeutic frame.

Language

The therapist may use language that some clients, particularly those from ethnic or minority groups, may find unfamiliar or difficult. Language has a cultural context (see Chapter 11) and therefore the role of language, its construction and interpretation in therapy is vital. Therapists need to consider this when working with a diverse range of clients. Proctor (2002) considers language to be associated with issues of power and oppression in therapy. The use of jargon and specialized language can be a catalyst in the formation of impressions of a therapist's superiority of knowledge and expertise. We believe it is important for therapists to be aware of inadvertent discriminatory practice in the way they speak, email or communicate with clients.

Timing

It is very important in establishing the therapeutic frame for sessions to be clearly time boundaried. Length and frequency of sessions needs to be clearly agreed at the start. Commonly, therapists offer a 50 minute 'hour' in order for the session to be ended in good time and, if necessary, for future bookings and perhaps payment to be sorted. When client and therapist are clear, the 'safe space' is agreed and the work can progress within this. It is common for new therapists to have problems ending sessions on occasion. This can be due to a number of factors, for example, late arrival, difficulty in advising clients of the time, session content and what we may call 'door handle' moments, where the client divulges something profound at the very end of the session. Wherever possible, clear time boundaries are recommended to help maintain the therapeutic space and to ensure that the client is comfortable that the work will end as agreed. However, when a client is clearly distressed, the therapist will need to attend to the ending of the session sensitively.

In the contracting meeting, the therapist will explain timings and ending of sessions with their client. A clock or clocks that are visible to both client and therapist will help both parties manage the time. The therapist may choose to advise the client that the end of a session is approaching. It is the therapist's responsibility to monitor timing. It is important to establish a pattern of meetings with which you are comfortable. Gutheil and Gabbard (1993) point out the potential dangers of making unusual times and places for meetings.

From the moment we meet a client we are starting the process of forming a relationship. The first impressions both client and therapist have of each other will be important in the development of a working relationship. The physical setting itself, the therapist's dress, behaviour and ability to manage time, will have a great bearing on how client and therapist settle into working together. We have seen how the TR is central to change in therapy. We have further seen how the relationship itself is considered the main change element in a RA.

BEGINNING THERAPY, DEVELOPING RAPPORT AND CREATING THE BASIS OF A GOOD OUTCOME

The relationship is the most significant in-therapy factor for positive outcomes. It is accepted beyond doubt that the therapeutic conditions (variously described) originally developed by Rogers are central to success in all approaches. In Chapter 2 it was noted that the TR can be said to have three elements:

1. The collaborative nature of the relationship.
2. The bond between therapist and client.
3. The client and therapist's ability to agree on the task of therapy.

(see also Paul and Haugh, 2008: 9–23)

Establishing the TR is therefore the most important early task in therapy.

RESEARCH CLIP 6.1 KEY FACTORS IN ESTABLISHING A GOOD THERAPY RELATIONSHIP

- The relationship is the most significant in-therapy factor for positive outcomes.
- It is accepted beyond doubt that the therapeutic conditions (variously described) originally developed by Rogers are central to success in all approaches.

(Continued)

(Continued)

- Specific key factors that have been proven to be effective in the TR are:

  1. Positive engagement in therapy
  2. Interactive coordination
  3. Rapport
  4. Positive regard
  5. Relational congruence

Creating a good early TR augurs well for outcome.
(Paul and Haugh, 2008: 19)

Many practitioners talk about developing a *working alliance*: 'The part of the client–psychotherapist relationship that enables the client and therapist to work together even when the patient or client experiences strong desires to the contrary' (Clarkson, 1995: 11).

The working alliance can be considered as the agreement that forms the container for the TR. In essence, it is:

1. A working agreement.
2. Mutually agreed.
3. With goals that have been mutually agreed between therapist and client.
4. It is an adult–adult relationship, freely entered into by both parties.

This working alliance can be said to be comprised of three interrelated components (Bordin, 1994):

1. Emotional bonds
2. Goals
3. Tasks

Goals and tasks

Goals will typically be agreed first as they are more tangible. Client and therapist will then agree how they will work towards these outcomes. Agreement on goals at the beginning stages of therapy is proven to have a positive indication to relationship formation and eventual positive outcomes. The working alliance therefore contains an agreement about what the work comprises: the focus of the work – what the client wants to achieve (goals) – and how the client will get there – the role and responsibilities of the therapist and client (tasks).

At this first meeting, in order for the therapist to work with the client, they need to develop a clear understanding of the client's situation as they present it and to communicate this to the client.

REFLECTION POINT 6.1 GOAL-RELATED COMPETENCIES

In Chapter 4 you have seen the relational competencies that are needed to work effectively with all clients.

- What professional competency do you think is necessary in working with the client in developing a good therapeutic relationship?
- What professional competency do you think is necessary in eliciting what the client wants?

Goals and tasks in the first session

It may not always be the case to clarify the goals and/or task of therapy. It may be that with a more disturbed client or one coming to explore lifelong relational patterns that the task of therapy will emerge as rapport is developed. Furthermore, the goals and tasks may be very simple in their initial expression, and the complexities will only become apparent over time. Key questions are:

- Why are we here?
- What do we hope to achieve?
- What is our therapeutic contract?
- How will we work together?
- How do we get there?

Bonds

Bonds are likely to be felt in terms of liking, trusting and respect for each other and a sense of common commitment and a shared understanding. An effective TR is one in which the client feels understood and attended to, and experiences mutual trust and respect (Horvarth and Greenberg, 1994).

The therapeutic alliance involves:

- An attitude of commitment to engage with the client's presenting problem.
- The therapist's skill in supporting and maintaining this attitude of engagement.
- An understanding of what is involved in the work of therapy for both client and therapist.
- A framework for considering the working alliance.

So the first session will most likely be spent agreeing a contract for the work that is to be done.

The contract

What is a contract in therapy? The contract is the agreement between therapist and client to establish the structure for the work that is to follow. Depending on the setting, it may be called a *contract* or perhaps an *agreement*, for example. It typically deals with two distinct areas:

1 The business

This part of the contract is very important for providing the foundations for the development of the therapeutic frame and the safe space for therapy to happen.

2 Therapy

This is the mutually agreed understanding of the client's reasons for coming to counselling and of what they can expect to happen in sessions.

Why do we need a contract?

- The client has a right to know what to expect from the therapist so they can make an informed choice about whether to enter into counselling.
- A clear contract helps to avoid misunderstandings and disappointments later on. This is vital, particularly where the therapeutic work may become complex, challenging and/or dense. The contract then becomes a reference point to which both parties can return to for clarity.

It is important, therefore, when contracting to consider and clarify all the factors that will impact on the counselling that is to follow.

What may be included in the business contract?

Depending on the agency or practice, setting the content of a contract will differ. Most agencies will have their own standardized contracts. Practitioners in private practice settings need to take care in the composition of a safe and meaningful contract.

A contract may include the following:

- Time and frequency of sessions
- Duration – number of sessions available and reviews
- Fees

- Contact between sessions
- Missed sessions
- Cancellations, illness and holidays
- Confidentiality and its limits
- Reviewing
- Ending arrangements
- Record keeping, taping and use of personal information
- Aims of therapy
- Type of therapy
- Dealing with emergencies
- Dealing with complaints

So far we have identified the key factors in establishing a good therapy relationship. When contracting, it is important that therapists recognize their own limitations, be cognizant of issues of diversity and treat clients with respect and dignity. Such recognition of limitations helps reduce potential problems, such as complaints or ruptures which may arise in the therapeutic relationship.

REFLECTION POINT 6.2 THERAPIST LIMITATIONS

In Chapter 4 you have seen relational competencies for working effectively with all clients.

What professional competencies do you think are necessary to demonstrate that you recognize your limitations? Points to consider in reflecting on the competencies include:

- What you need to do in order to establish whether you can offer therapy to the client or not, and
- What may need to be done in order to formulate a clear working contract that the client understands.

Working within an ethical framework

Working within an ethical framework provides both therapists and clients with a structure for what is morally right or wrong. Another dimension of the ethical framework is about protecting clients by ensuring that therapists deliver professional, competent therapy in a way that is consistent with the occupational role of a therapist. This is based on the assumption that the therapist can be relied upon with regard to their personal and professional knowledge, skills and abilities, as well as their wider values and attitudes (Barger-Charleson and Van Rijin, 2011).

It is also important to note that therapists need to abide by an ethical framework and relevant codes and guidelines for professional practice. An ethical framework is important because clients access therapy at vulnerable points in their lives and hence should be safeguarded against any unethical practice (Ivey et al., 2012). Where complaints are made against therapists, where practice is questionable, or where difficult events may be occurring both inside and outside the therapy room, an ethical framework enables sound decisions to be explored. The key ethical principles are presented in Table 6.1.

TABLE 6.1 Ethical principles

- Fidelity (keeping faith with clients: Can I do what I said to the client I would do? Be clear about your own boundaries)
- Autonomy (empowering clients and allowing them to make informed choices)
- Beneficence (actively benefiting clients, duty of care: Am I qualified, appropriately trained and competent for this particular client work?)
- Non-maleficence (avoiding harm to clients: What harm can I cause directly or indirectly to clients? A clear contract clarifies expectations and reduces misunderstandings)
- Justice (treating clients fairly: Can I give all clients equal treatment, time and energy, also taking into account difference and diversity?)
- Self-respect (applying all the above to self)

(*Sources*: BACP, 2010; Barger-Charleson and Van Rijin, 2011; Sills, 2006)

EARLY STAGE OF THE THERAPEUTIC RELATIONSHIP

A main part of early work with a client will normally be in facilitating the client's telling of their story. Key qualities on the part of the therapist which will come to the fore here are:

- Empathy
- Positive regard/warmth
- Genuineness

Widely accepted as core to any TR with any therapist of any modality, these qualities were originally developed after extensive research by Carl Rogers in 'The necessary and sufficient conditions of therapeutic personality change' (1957). Rogers formulated the following conditions:

1. Two persons are in psychological contact.
2. The first person, whom we shall term the client, is in a state of incongruence, being vulnerable or anxious.
3. The second person, whom we shall term the therapist, is congruent or integrated in the relationship.
4. The therapist experiences unconditional positive regard for the client.
5. The therapist experiences an empathic understanding of the client's internal frame of reference and endeavours to *communicate* this experience to the client.
6. The communication to the client of the therapist's empathic understanding and unconditional positive regard is to a minimal degree achieved.

For constructive personality change to occur, it is necessary that these conditions exist and continue over a period of time. Let us now examine these conditions.

1 Two persons are in Psychological contact

For Rogers, both client and therapist needed to have a basic level of contact, a '*minimal relationship*'. He saw this as either on or off. Today, writers are suggesting that the quality or level of contact will contribute to the outcome (Mearns, 1997). We believe that the quality of contact will ebb and flow over the duration of therapy.

Attendance by the therapist to developing rapport will enable a deepening of contact between client and therapist. Some clients may not be in a position to make psychological contact due to psychosis, organic disease, dissociative states, and so on. It may be that pre-therapy (Prouty, 1990) may be needed. Pre-therapy is a continued re-presentation of elements of shared reality in order to co-create a common ground in which to work.

2 The first, whom we shall term the client is in a state of incongruence, being vulnerable or anxious

Incongruence means a discrepancy between the actual experience of the individual and their self-picture or self-concept. This discrepancy, when experienced in day-to-day living, may cause a tension state to occur which is experienced perhaps as anxiety or depression. This anxiety is often seen in therapy as the individual becomes aware of some element of their experiencing which is in contradiction to their self-concept. The client therefore approaches therapy in some state they recognize as unsatisfactory.

3 The second person, whom we shall term the therapist, is congruent or integrated in the relationship

This means that, within this relationship, the therapist is an integrated person without internal conflicts. They are freely and deeply themselves in relation to their client. They are not presenting a façade, either knowingly or unknowingly. In this way they are able to be integrated in their relation to their client in the relationship. They are therefore in a position to facilitate client change without withdrawing due to fear or threat. Some writers will define congruence as genuineness, and others as authenticity, although this may have a different meaning which we look at in Theory Clip 6.4.

4 The therapist experiences unconditional positive regard for the client

Here the therapist experiences a prizing or valuing of all aspects, good and bad, of the client's experiencing – there are no conditions in this acceptance. The therapist cares for the client in a non-possessive way or to satisfy their own needs. It means a caring for the client as a unique individual, with permission to have and explore their own feelings and experiences. Researchers may call unconditional positive regard, warmth, valuing or prizing, although there are slight differences in meaning.

5 The therapist experiences an empathic understanding of the client's internal frame of reference and endeavours to *communicate* this experience to the client

The therapist experiences an accurate understanding of the client's awareness of their own experiencing. The therapist senses the client's world as if it were their own, but without ever losing the 'as if' quality. The therapist is separate from the client but experiences their sense of the client's world as if they were the client without being encumbered by their own reaction to this.

> When the client's world is this clear to the therapist, and he moves about in it freely, then he can both communicate his understanding of what is clearly known to the client and can also voice meanings in the client's experience of which the client is scarcely aware. (Rogers, 1957: 284)

6 The communication to the client of the therapist's empathic understanding and unconditional positive regard is to a minimal degree achieved

This final condition requires that the client perceives, to some degree, the unconditional positive regard (UPR) and empathy which the therapist experiences for them. Unless this is achieved to some minimal level, then therapeutic change cannot take place.

> The very basis of the practice of these conditions in the therapeutic relationship is the practice of empathy, warmth/positive regard and genuineness. They can be considered as attitudes grounded in a philosophical paradigm. In some cases they can be superficially communicated by certain skills. For the therapist, however, we believe they are attitudes to develop in oneself. Any 'techniques' are embedded in the therapeutic attitudes: that is, they are grounded in the inner experiences of the therapist in response to the client's frame of reference.

Let us now look at them in more detail.

Empathy

> It means entering the private perceptual world of the other and becoming thoroughly at home in it. It involves being sensitive, moment by moment, to the changing felt meanings which flow in this other person, to the fear or rage or tenderness or confusion or whatever he or she is experiencing. It means temporarily living in the other's life, moving about in it delicately without making judgments. (Rogers, 1980: 142)

Empathy in client-centred theory is a concept that is integrated with the conditions of congruence and UPR. It was developed by Rogers within a context of non-directivity and is predicated on the foundation block of the actualizing tendency, the belief that with the right conditions the organism will choose what is most growthful. Any 'techniques' are embedded in the therapeutic attitudes: that is, grounded in the inner experiences of the therapist in response to the client's frame of reference. For Rogers, empathy is not necessarily the same as 'communication' of empathy or 'empathic responses'.

T

THEORY CLIP 6.1 A CLIENT'S PERSPECTIVE OF EMPATHY IN PRACTICE

A client reported:

> Every now and again, with me in a tangle of thought and feeling, screwed up in a web of mutually divergent lines of movement, with impulses from different parts of me, and me feeling the feeling of it being all too much and such like – then whomp, just like a sunbeam thrusting its way through cloudbanks and tangles of foliage to spread a circle of light on a tangle of forest paths, came some comment from you. [It was] clarity, even disentanglement, an additional twist to the picture, a putting in place. Then the consequence – the sense of moving on, the relaxation. These were sunbeams. (Rogers, 1957: 142)

This client's description evidences the power of empathy in helping the client to clarify and disentangle what they may be struggling with or unclear about.

Truax and Carkhuff (1967), who did significant research into the use of empathy in counselling sessions, summarize the key qualities of an empathic therapist as that they:

- Behave in ways which indicate they take the relationship seriously.
- Are aware of what the client is feeling in the here-and-now.
- Are able to communicate their understanding of these feelings appropriately.
- Communicate in a way which reflects the mood and content of the client, with sensitivity to the client's feelings.
- Communicate in a way which serves to clarify and expand the client's awareness of their feelings and experiences, including those of which the client may only be partly aware.
- Are able to stay in tune with their client's shifting emotional state with an ability to correct and realign their responding accordingly.
- Are sensitive to any mistakes they make and able to respond and change their responding non-defensively.

(Kahn, 1997: 44–5)

Developing empathy

Many people believe that the practice of empathy is at the heart of healing relationships. From both psychoanalytic and humanistic modalities, practitioners recognize the importance of developing a deep understanding of the client and their worldview. Psychodynamic writers talk of empathic *attunement* (Stern, 1985), *resonance* (Weiss, 1950) and *communicative matching* (Masterson, 1985). Kohut writes extensively on its importance (1984). In the humanistic tradition, Rogers based his model of therapy around *empathic understanding*.

T

THEORY CLIP 6.2 KOHUT AND EMPATHY

Kohut (1984) pioneered the term 'empathy' as a technical, therapeutic concept plus an important component of the healing process. Empathy is more than 'feeling for the client'. Empathy is the 'scientific tool' of psychotherapy. The therapist has only one tool; that tool is their self. 'Empathy is the means by which a psychological observer gathers information about the inner world of the human experience.'

Empathy is active listening through:

- Hearing the client's story
- Communicating understanding of that story and its impact on the client's life.

Being understood by the therapist gives the client an affirming experience vital for establishing other meaningful relationships.

For Kohut, the main task of therapy was to provide a corrective emotional experience, and empathy was central to this. Empathy is not simply mirroring to the client with total acceptance and positive regard; it is helping the client understand their feelings in relation to their childhood experiences and their basic needs not being met.

Although, as an analyst, Kohut believed in the power of the unconscious and the importance of working with transference, he stressed the importance of being human in the relationship:

> I have come to feel freer, and, without guilt and misgivings, to show (my clients) my deep involvement and concern via the warmth of my voice, the words that I choose, and other similarly subtle means. (Kohut, 1984: 221)

Kahn (1997) proposes key advantages of feeling free to empathize with our clients. In our empathic responding we offer them:

1. A sense of being listened to by someone who is truly willing to try to understand them.
2. A sense of having been deeply understood.
3. A sense of being accepted when they are experiencing conflict and/or expressing negative thoughts and feelings.
4. An opportunity to explore and understand the deep roots of their problems and a real chance to make sense of them.
5. An opportunity to build new self-structures to compensate for past deficits.

A look at the Gloria film with Carl Rogers (Shostrom, 1965), although dated, will demonstrate the intentionality of the therapist to respond empathically and their willingness to alter their responding as their understanding is modified by their client's responses.

T

THEORY CLIP 6.3 WHY EMPATHY WORKS

Kahn (1997) explains that when the therapist communicates empathic understanding to their client, the client realizes that their therapist is seeking to understand their world and is thus encouraged to understand it themselves. This encourages the client to be empathic with their self and to seek to understand their self in a non-judgemental way as their therapist is doing. The willingness of the therapist to understand without prejudice the world of the client increases their self-esteem and their willingness to understand themselves more fully.

As a client, if I can understand the different aspects in myself without judgement and with a sense of neutral appraising, as my therapist endeavours to do, then I am more able to look at and find new ways of accepting these previously conflicting aspects.

Alexander was a psychoanalyst who saw therapy as providing a corrective emotional experience (Alexander et al., 1946). In therapy the client gets the care and understanding for their pain that they didn't get when it was needed. While, at the time, many analysts disagreed with this, we can agree today that the empathy of the therapist does allow the client to work through inner pain and suffering in a secure caring environment.

In developing the therapeutic relationship, we believe it is important to be responsive to all aspects of the client's presentation. We need to be aware of and be responsive to nuances of our client's body language, emotions and often conflicting and disparate communicating. We need to be empathic to the whole person and to each and every aspect of their experiencing. In the beginning stage of therapy the communication of empathic understanding is central in the establishment of the relationship. Some practitioners state that it is the sole essential attitude. As the relationship forms through the process of therapy, it is the responsibility of the therapist to continue to offer a secure therapeutic space to the client.

Congruence

Congruence can be defined as rapport within oneself, or consistency between thought, behaviour and values.

A person's *ideal self* may not be consistent with what actually happens in their day-to-day life and the life and experiencing of the person. A difference therefore exists between their ideal self and actual experiencing. This is called incongruence. Where a person's ideal self and actual experiencing are consistent or similar, it can be said that a state of inner congruence exists. The closer our *self-image* and ideal-self are to one another, the more congruent we are and the more integrated we are in ourselves.

> The therapist should be within the confines of this relationship a congruent, genuine, integrated person. It means that within the relationship he is freely and deeply himself, with his actual experience accurately represented by his awareness of himself. It is the opposite of presenting a façade either knowingly or unknowingly. (Rogers, 1957: 98)

In effect, in the practice of therapy there is consistency within the person in the sense that: (i) their underlying experience, (ii) conscious perceptions, and (iii) outward behaviour are all harmoniously matched to some degree.

> The more I accept myself and am able to be present in a comfortable way with everything that bubbles up in me, without fear and defence, the more I can be receptive to everything that lives in my client. (Lietaer, 1984: 44)

Genuineness can be said to have two sides – an inner and an outer. The inner refers to the degree to which the therapist has conscious access to all aspects of his flow of experiencing – congruence. The outer can be said to refer to the explicit communication by the therapist of his conscious perceptions and feelings. This may also be called Transparency (Rogers, 1959).

The more integrated in themselves a therapist can be in the practice of therapy, the more they are able to work with their client in the exploration of their own incongruence. The more *genuine* and present they are, then the more they are able to be with their client.

T

THEORY CLIP 6.4 AUTHENTICITY, GENUINENESS, CONGRUENCE, TRANSPARENCY

There are a number of terms used by writers to describe aspects of the person of the therapist in the therapy encounter:

Authenticity was a term developed by existentialists to describe the degree to which one is true to one's own individuality, personality and character, regardless of external conditions or pressures. It relates to living and behaving authentically in day-to-day life. *If I am fully myself I am being authentic.*

(Continued)

(Continued)

Genuineness was used initially by Rogers to describe the willingness to relate to clients without hiding behind a façade, to be real in the relationship with one's client.

Congruence is a development of the term 'genuineness' and is concerned with how integrated the therapist is in relation to parts of themselves and in their relationship with their client.

Transparency describes the openness of the therapist and the willingness to share of their being, their authentic self with others. This is different from self-disclosure, which is the sharing of concrete information about oneself to another.

Positive regard

> Unconditional positive regard is the label given to the fundamental attitude of the … counsellor towards her client. The counsellor who holds this attitude deeply values the humanity of her client and is not deflected in that valuing by any particular client behaviours. The attitude manifests itself in the counsellor's consistent acceptance of and enduring warmth towards her client. (Mearns and Thorne, 1988: 59)

The communication without judgement of positive regard to all aspects of the client's experiencing allows them, without a sense of judgement, to explore different aspects of themselves with impartiality. Psychological distress is founded on a sense of self-judgement, where one part of the experiencing self values negatively, or distorts, or denies another. The positive regard of the therapist enables the client to move towards positive self regard and a dissolving of inner incongruence.

> It involves as much feeling of acceptance for the client's expression of 'negative' ... feelings as for his expression of 'good' … feelings, as much acceptance of ways in which he is inconsistent as of ways in which he is consistent. … It means a caring for the client as a separate person, with permission to have his own feelings, his own experiences. (Rogers, 1957: 99)

Many writers suggest that these conditions are in fact integrated aspects of a more profound attitude. The attitude and behaviour of the therapist models to the client a more integrated self-acceptance. Bozarth (1998) proposes that all the conditions are so intertwined as to be theoretically inseparable. He postulates that there is one core condition, the *actualizing tendency*, in which the others are integral elements.

The development of the TR is central in offering these therapeutic conditions or attitudes:

- I, the therapist, am comfortable with myself in the here-and-now in this relationship. (I am experiencing internal congruence and Unconditional Positive Self-regard).
- I am not threatened by you, therefore am able to engage openly with you.
- I experience acceptance towards all aspects of you, (Unconditional Positive Regard), and can freely communicate that to you (Transparency).
- I communicate my unconditional regard (UPR) to you by (empathic) understanding and acceptance and this enables your own natural healing process (actualizing tendency) to be promoted.
- The very nature of my presence is demonstrated through my attempt to understand you (empathy), my wholehearted acceptance of you (UPR) and my natural movement to engage with you fully (Congruence, Authenticity).

COMPETENCIES

The competencies in Table 6.2 underpin the practice of relationship formation.

TABLE 6.2 Competencies specifically relating to establishing the relationship (adapted from Roth et al., 2009)

Practical
Ability to foster and maintain and develop a good relational TR in the here-and-now.
Ability to work with the client's material to establish and work with an agreed therapeutic aim.
Personal
Ability to respond non-defensively to client feedback.
Ability to work with difficult and complex processes.
Ability to facilitate the personal power and self-determination of the client.
Professional
Knowledge of, and ability to operate within, professional and ethical guidelines.
Ability to recognize limitations in professional practice.

RESOURCE BOX 6

Haugh, S. and Merry, T. (eds) (2001) *Rogers Therapeutic Conditions. Volume 2: Empathy*. Ross-on-Wye: PCCS Books.
A practical guide to empathy.

Rogers, C.R. (1957) 'The necessary and sufficient conditions of therapeutic personality change', *Journal of Consulting Psychology*, 21(2): 95–103.

(Continued)

(Continued)

This article offers a detailed hypothesis on the conditions for therapeutic personality change.

FURTHER PERSON-CENTRED READING

Bozarth, J. and Wilkins, P. (eds) (2001) *Rogers Therapeutic Conditions. Volume 3: Unconditional Positive Regard*. Ross-on-Wye: PCCS Books.
Sanders, P. (2006) *The Person-Centred Counselling Primer*. Ross-on-Wye: PCCS Books.
Tolan, J. (2012) *Skills in Person-Centred Counselling & Psychotherapy*. London: Sage.
Wyatt, G. and Sanders, P. (eds) (2002) *Rogers Therapeutic Conditions. Volume 4: Contact and Perception*. Ross-on-Wye: PCCS Books.

BOOKS ABOUT THE THERAPEUTIC FRAME

Gray, A. (1994) *An Introduction to the Therapeutic Frame*. London: Routledge.
Luca, M. (2004) *The Therapeutic Frame in the Clinical Context*. Hove: Brunner-Routledge.

ETHICAL CONSIDERATIONS

Sills, C. (2006) *Contracts in Counselling and Psychotherapy*. London: Sage.

A PRACTICAL GUIDE TO ESTABLISHING THERAPY

Green, J. (2010) *Creating the Therapeutic Relationship in Counselling and Psychotherapy*. Exeter: Learning Matters.
A straightforward readable book especially useful for beginning therapists.

ON THE WORKING ALLIANCE

Clarkson, P. (2003) *The Therapeutic Relationship*. London: Whurr.
Tolan, J. (2012) *Skills in Person-Centred Counselling and Psychotherapy*. London: Sage.

WEBSITES

www.allanturner.co.uk/
This website is a resource with references to person-centred books and articles.

CHAPTER SUMMARY

To help the reader to understand elements in establishing the relationship, in this chapter the following were discussed:

- The TR as a key factor regardless of what model of therapy the therapist may work in.
- The main philosophical principles that underpin the relationship and its effective use.

- Basic assumptions of therapy and a relationship which offers the right conditions for healing and transformation by enabling clients to work through issues from the past in the here-and-now of therapy.
- The importance of creating a safe space for therapy, including consideration of the physical environment, the contract and timing, and the length of sessions.
- The therapeutic frame, which is formed in contracting between the therapist and client.
- How therapy develops from the early stages, including the importance of maintaining rapport, developing empathy, collaborative working and mutual understanding.
- How empathy, congruence and unconditional positive regard are integrated.

7

Developing the relationship

The aims of this chapter are for the reader to develop an understanding of:

- Maintaining rapport and strengthening the relationship.
- The middle phase of therapy and reviewing.
- Issues of power and authority.
- Difficult and complex processes.
- Working in the here-and-now, relational depth and I–Thou relatedness.
- Configurations of self.
- Stages in the therapy processes.
- Transference, countertransference and defences.
- Relational patterns.

We also highlight competencies for developing and maintaining a successful therapeutic relationship.

We have noted that developing the TR is the keystone to a good outcome for our clients. In the beginning stage of therapy the development of empathy between the therapist and client is a prerequisite. As the work evolves, it continues to be important that the therapist demonstrates basic relational conditions. The therapist needs to continue to seek to understand the multifaceted experiencing of the client. This communication of continued empathic understanding will give the client permission to follow their own unfolding story.

MAINTAINING RAPPORT AND STRENGTHENING THE RELATIONSHIP

As therapy develops, the client may encounter and seek to divulge difficult feelings and memories which they may be ambivalent about sharing. It is therefore important to maintain a non-judgemental attitude to all aspects of the client's experiencing. It is important to maintain a positive approach to the client in relation to all the material they share. The authenticity or genuineness of the therapist becomes more important to the client as they express difficult material. The therapist models themselves as being at ease and open to the client and responds to them with humanity.

THEORY CLIP 7.1 MAINTAINING RAPPORT AND STRENGTHENING THE RELATIONSHIP

To maintain rapport and strengthen the relationship in therapy it is important to:

1. Continue to maintain rapport by developing the use of empathy, positive regard and genuineness in the relationship.
2. Use empathy non-selectively in relation to all aspects of the client's experiencing.
3. Endeavour to work collaboratively with mutual understanding in relation to the client's problem.
4. Review aims and process of therapy as needed, relating to the contract, as appropriate.
5. Maintain a non-defensive way of working in relation to the client.
6. Work with the dynamics and pace of therapy as they emerge.
7. Work in the here-and-now with the client.

In a RA this is not a manualized or skill-based model of practice. Therapists develop their own personal style based on the key principles of successful relational practice. Review of practice in supervision, through feedback from clients and in relation to their own personal development will help maintain an effective TR.

A simple model of the psyche, called the Johari window, created by Joseph Luft and Harrington Ingham in 1955 in the United States, is used to help people better understand their relationship with self and others.

Before therapy

	KNOWN TO ME	UNKNOWN TO ME
KNOWN TO OTHERS	Public Arena Open	Blind Spot
UNKNOWN TO OTHERS	Hidden Avoided Private	Unknown Unconscious

As therapy develops

	KNOWN TO ME	UNKNOWN TO ME
KNOWN TO OTHERS	Public Arena Open	Blind Spot
UNKNOWN TO OTHERS	Hidden Avoided Private	Unknown Unconscious

FIGURE 7.1 Johari window– developing awareness of self and others

Public Arena: This quadrant represents traits of the subject that both client and therapist have open access to.

Hidden or **Private**: This quadrant represents information about the client which they keep to themselves. It is up to the client if they wish to disclose this information or not.

Blind Spot: This quadrant represents information that the client is not aware of, but the therapist is. The therapist can give feedback to the client about their behaviour which will be helpful to the client in developing their understanding.

Unknown/Unconscious: This quadrant represents the client's behaviours or traits that neither party is aware of. This may be hidden material from the past or equally inner potential.

When a TR develops, the client is more trusting of the therapist and thus divulges more hidden/private material. The therapist is able to effectively give feedback to the client about their 'blind spots'. This process enables the client to be more fully aware of and comfortable with their self and thus their public arena expands in relation to the therapist. This process allows new understandings to emerge from the previously unknown/unconscious quadrant.

We saw in the previous chapters the importance of the working alliance: 'the quality and strength of the collaborative relationship between client and therapist in therapy' (Horvath and Bedi, 2002: 41). There has also been clear evidence to support establishing shared goals between therapist and client (Tryon and Winograd, 2002). Where both parties are working together and are able to develop a common understanding of the issues and dynamics, the outcome is likely to be better. The therapist is therefore not the expert in the process and expertise needs to be shared. A transparent and humble approach will help.

MIDDLE PHASE OF THERAPY AND REVIEWING

During the middle phase of therapy, it can be very helpful to review from time to time how therapy is progressing in relation to initial hopes and aims. Both parties can review and this process will help develop mutuality and collaboration. It can be very useful where client and/or therapist feels stuck, patterns are repeating, or there is conflict or confusion.

It is important to review the process of therapy as much as the original aims. When both parties review what has been happening from their own perspective it can raise awareness of the dynamics that are taking place and help bring insight into the situation. Sometimes it is useful to suggest an ad hoc review, particularly when therapy is experienced as blocked. Therapists working in statutory or agency settings may be required to do a more formal or standardized review. The material arising from such an evaluation can also be usefully explored by client and therapist.

Working non-defensively

REFLECTION POINT 7.1 RELATIONAL COMPETENCY FOR WORKING NON-DEFENSIVELY

- What professional competency do you think is necessary for working non-defensively with clients?

THEORY CLIP 7.2 THE IMPORTANCE OF NON-DEFENSIVENESS

For Kohut (1984), non-defensiveness in the practice of therapy is indispensable. Defensiveness against external threat to the psyche is likely what has characterized our client's previous important relationships and that this is may be why those relationships have not been healing. Non-defensiveness is therefore one of the main gifts we, as therapists, have to offer our client.

This is especially apparent when a client is sharing their feelings about us. At such times defensiveness and empathy are mutually exclusive. To respond with interpretation and process analysis to the client will not help. As Kohut puts it:

> If we can empathize with clients, we can open ourselves to discovering just how they see us. Of course their view may not coincide with the way we see ourselves, but we're not there to empathize with ourselves, we're there to empathize with our clients. And empathizing with our clients when they're seeing us in a bad light is very hard – and very therapeutic. (Kohut, 1984: 122)

It is far better to acknowledge the clumsiness and errors in our responding than to take it as personal affront.

As noted so far, in the middle phase of therapy both therapist and client may have an opportunity to review their progress together. Theory Clip 7.2 outlines the importance of non-defensiveness. In line with this, working non-defensively is a competency in itself. It shows the therapist's ability to review their practice as well as to work ethically with power within the therapeutic frame.

Power and authority

We now explore the importance of working effectively with power and authority. However, before we do, we encourage you to reflect on the competence which relates to this.

> **REFLECTION POINT 7.2 WORKING WITH POWER AND AUTHORITY**
>
> - What professional competency needs to be in place for the therapist to work effectively with the power in therapy?

The frame and the therapist, in their position as the guardian of the frame, are likely to be the targets against which dynamics of power and authority are played out. As we have seen earlier in this chapter, the creation of the frame ensures a secure and safe place for internal dynamics and unresolved conflicts to be explored. On the one hand, the 'secure base' is created with love and care and, on the other hand, that very security allows for oppositional feelings to be explored. As a client may be experiencing complex inner material, the frame becomes the receptacle for both positive and negative elements of the client's experiencing, often at the same time.

The client may see in the structure of the frame an authority that reminds them of previous difficult experiences and primary relationships. This can evoke very powerful feelings for the client which may then spill out.

Maintaining a power balance in relational therapy is therefore important. While in the beginning of therapy the client may defer to the therapist, as therapy progresses the intention is that the client feels in control of their process and can take responsibility for their experiencing. The therapist needs to be mindful of this and to work towards ensuring:

1. That the client is aware of their own relationship with power.
2. How the therapist works with this power and authority in the TR.

Often clients become powerless because of their life experiences, or family or social environments, which may be oppressive and disempowering.

We draw on an expression used by Buber (1950): '*realphantasie*'. This indicates the process in which the other's reality is touched in the therapeutic process. To relate to a person in this way goes beyond valuing them as a client in the here-and-now, but it is to try to enter their essence and to imagine them as the person they are and can become with all their possibilities (Schmid, 2001). This view of the client assumes, therefore, that where clients come to therapy disempowered, through a relational encounter in which they are viewed with all their potential, they become more and more aware of their power as the therapy progresses. This way of relating is affirmative, facilitates growth, empowerment and nourishes the development of the client.

P

PRACTITIONER CLIP 7.1 WORKING TO EMPOWER A CLIENT

I (Divine) worked with a client, Mo, who was an asylum seeker after fleeing his home country, Iran, where he stated he was a political activist, following being tortured in prison. Mo described this process as breaking his spirit and he presented with low confidence, feeling worthless and had what he described as moments of uncontrollable raging anger. As an asylum seeker he struggled to engage in the therapeutic process because he stated it was not a way of dealing with problems in his country. Mo often stated that I knew best and as I was the professional I should help him.

I shifted this balance in power by exploring the collaborative nature of a RA and naming my limitations to accomplish any of the agreed therapeutic goals without his commitment to the therapeutic process. As therapy progressed and we explored his life in then the present moment, he became more in control of his process and started to take more responsibility for his experiencing.

Relationships based on class, gender, sexuality, race, culture, disability and so on are saturated with issues of power (Pelham and Stacey, 1999). A generic offering of 'unconditional positive regard' by the therapist may neutralize such cultural power dynamics. If they are rendered unconscious, they are likely to manifest in non-rational ways. It is therefore particularly important to be mindful of these factors.

We have seen how in the middle phase of therapy it is important for the therapist and client to review their work. We have looked at the competencies that are essential in working non-defensively and effectively with power and authority with clients in this middle phase of therapy. Not only are issues of working non-defensively and empowering the client important, but so too is 'containment' of whatever the client brings to therapy.

Containment

As the sessions progress, the client will often bring with them beliefs that certain aspects of themselves are bad or unacceptable. They may have an unconscious hope that someone may be able to hold or contain (and thus make acceptable and manageable) these aspects of the self. As Casement (1985: 132–3) puts it:

> There are times when people cannot cope with their own feelings without some assistance. … Basically, the help being searched for is always for a person to be available to help with those difficult feelings. Often, however, the response from the people around is to treat those feelings as if they were abnormal or dangerous. Medication can subdue them. Referral elsewhere … seldom changes anything for the patient, who inwardly still feels victim to powerful feeling. … These deflective or suppressive measures can add to the sense that there is an intensity of feeling which nobody could manage. … We are using the notion of containment here as a general term for the management of another person's difficult feelings, which are otherwise uncontained. … It is usually a personal form of containment that is being looked for. In more human terms, what is needed is a form of holding, such as a mother gives to her distressed child. … It can be crucial for a patient to be thus held in order to recover, or to discover maybe for the first time, a capacity for managing life's difficulties without continued avoidance or suppression.

Working with difficult and complex processes

REFLECTION POINT 7.3 DIFFICULT AND COMPLEX PROCESSES

- What professional competency do you think is necessary in working with difficult and complex processes?

We present here two Client Clips on different difficult and complex processes.

CLIENT CLIP 7.1 THERAPIST CONTAINMENT OF CLIENT RAGE

Amy was a student at a special school for children with emotional and behavioural difficulties. One day she had what she later described as 'a major freak out' in her classroom and was brought to me (Steve) by a teacher. She became filled with rage and we had to restrain her. The inner rage she was experiencing caused her to hit out, scream and threaten us both with violence. We held her and talked to her calmly. After several minutes she started to sob uncontrollably. She was then able to sit with me, drink tea, and talk about how unhappy she was and how difficult it was for her to handle the extreme feelings she felt. Within half an hour she had returned to her class.

It is imperative, therefore, for the therapist to seek to 'hold' the frame. In this forum, both acceptable and unacceptable parts of self can emerge. This holding of the frame can be a message for the client that it is safe to explore complex feelings with them and that the therapist is willing to work with all that they present.

C

CLIENT CLIP 7.2 CONTAINING PROJECTION

Wendy came to therapy to explore her feelings about her father. For several sessions therapy was a polite and respectful meeting in which past experiences were explored. She then became withdrawn for two sessions and appeared to be struggling with herself. I (Steve) shared with her my sense of what was happening. In a matter of seconds she filled up with rage, accusing me of intruding into her privacy. The anger was palpable and I strove to keep calm and stay with her. After a few minutes she started to cry and revealed her memories of being locked up in a cupboard by her dad for being naughty. In the subsequent session she thanked me for staying with her.

If the therapist is unwilling to hold the frame and finds themselves wanting to give advice, placate, give extra time and so on, this may give a message to the client that they are not able or willing to keep the boundary of the frame or that the client's problems are not containable, are just too bad.

It is important to maintain the boundary and the security of the safe space as the client may be struggling with thoughts and feelings that have not been acceptable elsewhere. If it is not perceived as safe, they may repress these aspects of themselves. Inexperienced therapists may find themselves struggling to end on time, seeking to solve the client's problems, and so on. Working in the here-and-now to contain whatever the client brings to each session is therefore important.

Working in the here-and-now

As we have said earlier, working with material arising from past experiences or patterns in the here-and-now can be instrumental in developing awareness, insight and a new understanding. The therapist therefore endeavours to be present in the here-and-now of the therapy relationship.

REFLECTION POINT 7.4 WORKING IN THE HERE-AND-NOW

- What professional competency do you think is necessary in working with the client in the here-and-now?

A number of theorists have written about a way of working, within which both parties experience a sense of connectedness in the moment. This connectedness is becoming recognized as having an important place in the therapy process.

Buber (1988), a philosopher whose writing crosses therapeutic modalities, suggests that growth does not take place in relation to ourselves but in relation to another. We are only fully ourselves in relation *with* another. For Buber, this involves an encounter with the being of the other. I no longer see you as I–it; that is, I am the therapist and you with whom I am contracting are the *it*, the client. As we get to know each other and I make myself available to meet you more deeply, an *I–Thou* relationship is possible, in which both parties meet as subject-subject, not subject to object. Friedman (1995) proposes that in the meeting itself healing happens, we are fulfilled through our meeting with others. Techniques or skills per se do not heal, but what does is in the encounter between therapist and client. The person of the other is in their dynamic centre and I cannot perceive that when I am seeing the other as separate from me. In encounter, therefore, the other can become present for me and I for them.

Mearns and Cooper (2005: xii) propose a meeting at 'relational depth': 'A state of profound contact and engagement between two people in which each person is fully real with the Other, and able to understand and value the Other's experiences at a high level.'

Relational depth describes feelings of connectedness and relating that, for many therapists, are at the core of their practice (Friedman, 1985; Mearns and Cooper, 2005; Stern, 2004). They may be moments of encounter or refer to a particular *quality* of relationship. Cooper (2005) summarizes these processes from the perspectives of the different therapeutic orientations:

> In the psychodynamic modality, Stern (2004; Stern et al., 1998) described 'moments of meeting,' in which a 'mutual interpenetration of minds' occurs. Ehrenberg identified the 'intimate edge': 'the point of maximum and acknowledged contact at any given moment in a relationship without fusion'. (2005: 3)

Jordan, a feminist psychotherapist, proposes a 'mutual intersubjectivity' in which

> one is both affecting the other and being affected by the other; one extends oneself out to the other and is also receptive to the impact of the other. There is openness to influence, emotional availability and a constant changing pattern of responding to and affecting the others' state There is both receptivity and active initiative towards the other. (Jordan, 1991: 82)

Existential and humanistic therapists, such as Friedman (1985), Laing (1971) and Hycner (1993), have also described moments of 'I–Thou' meeting and 'dialogue' in the therapeutic encounter, drawing upon the work of the existential philosopher Buber (1958).

This relational depth consists of a 'blending together of high degrees of the three core conditions of empathy, unconditional positive regard and congruence' (Mearns 2003: 8), in concert with 'conditions' of 'contact' and 'perception', that is, the client perceives the counsellor's empathic understanding and unconditional positive regard to a minimal degree (Rogers, 1957). Mearns further links relational depth with Rogers' (1986) notion of 'presence': moments in which the therapist's 'inner spirit' seems to connect with the inner spirit of their client in a moment of seeming oneness. This meeting resonates the I–Thou relating as described by Buber. Whereas the meeting of both parties creates an energetic presence, the therapist endeavours to be present in their relating to their client.

From an existential perspective:

> 'staying with' and 'attuning oneself to' the client's current way of being – no matter how debilitating, restrictive, limiting, and irrational it may appear to be to the therapist (if not all others in the client's world, client included) that the existential psychotherapist, simply via this client-attuned presence, begins to challenge profoundly the client's expectations regarding how others are, how others expect the client to be, and how the client expects others to be with him or her. (Spinelli, 2008: 54)

Or, as we saw earlier, from the perspective of Transactional Analysis:

> Through the therapist's full presence, the transformational potential of a relationship-orientated psychotherapy is possible. … More than just verbal communication, presence is a communion between client and therapist. (Erskine and Trautmann, 1996: 326)

From an energetic perspective, the offering of self in the here-and-now creates a space for a meeting. 'Presence' is perhaps a conceptual term for the ground in which client and therapist meet and therapy takes place.

> We have seen how clients may present with thoughts and feelings that have not been acceptable elsewhere. It is important for therapists to be competent in working with difficult and complex processes. Working in the here-and-now to contain whatever the client brings to each session is therefore important. In fully meeting the client, the therapists may engage in an *I–Thou* encounter with the client which can be transformational. Through the different phases of therapy, from the beginning to the middle phase, right through to the ending, different configurations of a client may emerge and this helps the relationship to continue developing.

Configurations of self

Sometimes people experience themselves as having, and behaving in and with, different 'parts' or elements to their self. Each part, or 'configuration' (Mearns and Thorne, 2000), has developed with its unique feelings, thoughts and behaviours, which may be quite different from other parts. For Mearns, a 'configuration' is a construct made up of a pattern of feelings, thoughts and behavioural responses which represents to the person one aspect of their self.

Sometimes these **configurations of self** may be growthful and other times they may be limiting or restricting. They may arise because of internal conflicts at different stages of life, due to not being able to meet one's needs. In some cases the differentiation between the different parts may be so severe that is causes suffering.

P

PRACTITIONER CLIP 7.2 WORKING WITH CONFIGURATIONS OF SELF

I (Steve) worked with a client, Alan, who experienced an internal dialogue between three parts of himself:

'Part of me wants to work hard and have a decent relationship, another just has this impulse to drive my van off the road and run someone over. I wrestle constantly with this in myself. Another part of me just wants to sort this out and really has brought me to therapy.'

Alan struggled with parts of himself, a configuration which for him caused incongruence and great discomfort. In therapy, these different parts were highlighted and he started to dialogue with and between the parts.

In some cases the client might talk of being 'in two minds' in relation to decision making: 'Half of me wants to take the job, whereas the other half of me wants to travel.' Mearns and Thorne (2000) advise on working with these parts:

- *Listen* for the different parts, but don't *invent* them.
- Parts may emerge in the process of therapy; it is not the task of therapy to seek them out.
- Avoid 'zero-sum' responding.
- Seek to respond empathically and non-selectively to all the different aspects of the client that present. Avoid making a global comment as each element of the client's experiencing contributes towards an integrated understanding of their self.
- Empathic mediation: help the parts to hear each other.
- The therapist responds to each part and facilitates an internal dialogue between them to help move towards integration.

- Practice multi-directional partiality: prize *all* the parts.
- Give equal value to each part; they are each part of the client's Self which they are struggling with.
- Therapist's use of their configurational Self.
- Be aware of your own internal processes and how they impact on your experiencing.

As we have seen, each therapy session contributes towards the development of therapy though the therapeutic relationship. Containing whatever the client brings and working with their configurations of Self, giving value to each part, enables therapy to progress. At the same time, each session is part of a process of therapy.

THE PROCESS OF THERAPY

In his research into therapy, Rogers proposed there were seven stages of change. The stages themselves he considered to be notional. They describe a journey from stuck, fixed rigidity to a spontaneous free-flowing state that, he noted, individuals who were functioning fully demonstrated. Clients' experiences tend to be grouped around a particular stage or stages. There is no expectation that a client will enter or exit at any stage or complete all stages of therapy.

Step 1	Step 2	Step 3	Step 4	Step 5	Step 6	Step 7
Rigid, fixed position not seeking therapy. The problem is external	Process of change					Living fully in the here-and-now. No longer needing therapeutic help

FIGURE 7.2 Rogers' seven stages of change in therapy

Stage One: In the first stage, the client is defensive and resistant to change.

There is an unwillingness to reveal anything about the client's self except about externals. Feelings and meanings are externalized. Rigid personal views are expressed. Close communications invoke anxiety. Problems of a personal nature are generally denied. There is a blocking of internal communication/reflexions in the psyche.

Stage Two: In this stage the client becomes slightly less rigid and will talk about external events or people.

When the person can begin to experience themselves as *fully received* by the therapist there is a slight easing and flowing of constructs and symbolization. The client can begin to express non-personal material. Problems are still perceived as external to the self and no personal responsibility is taken for problems – others are blamed. Feelings are not owned in the here-and-now and there is some linkage into past events. Personal constructs or worldviews are viewed as facts and clients tend to assign stereotypical meaning to events. Little insight into personal contradictions is evident.

Stage Three: The client talks about themselves as an object and avoids discussion of present events.

There is a further loosening of the rigid self-structure and freer talking about self – often in the third person as an object of others. The client may talk more about feelings, but usually past feelings, and there may be very little acceptance of feelings which may be seen mainly as bad or unacceptable. However, there is a move towards awareness of feelings.

Stage Four: The client begins to talk about feelings and relates more to the therapist.

There is some exploration of deeper *past* feelings. Present feelings are talked about objectively and often negatively. There may be fear and mistrust of emerging feelings. Some acceptance of feelings may be evident but it is not consciously expressed. The client begins to recognize self-concept as a construct and questions this validity. There may be attempts to clarify mixed feelings and thoughts. The client will recognize incongruity between their experiencing and their self-concept. Some awareness of personal responsibilities for problems may emerge at this stage. There will be some movement towards a closer relationship with the therapist, but this may be with expressed anxiety.

Stage Five: The client expresses here-and-now feelings and increasingly accepts more responsibility for their actions.

The client is able to express feelings in the present. Feelings bubble up into awareness, although the client is still experiencing threat and anxiety. There may be awareness of getting close to something important and surprise and fright at the feelings which 'bubble up'.

There is increasing acceptance of emerging feelings as part of the self and a willingness to accept these feelings. Experiencing is much more in the here-and-now rather than the there-and-then. There is a loosening and discovering of rigid constructs and movement towards re-evaluation and understanding of feelings and personal meanings. The client begins to face up to personal contradictions and incongruities. There is increasing acceptance of responsibility and dialogue between parts of the self.

Stage Six: After the insight of the last phase the client enters a crucial and perhaps dramatic phase in which increasing self-congruence is evident. This may signal the ending of therapy.

Stuck feelings are experienced in the here-and-now. Feelings 'flow' and are fully felt. A present feeling is experienced with immediacy and richness. There is a quality of living subjectively *in* the experience not feeling *about it.* The self is experienced as a feeling not an object. Experiencing is realized as a process not a fixed state. There may be physiological changes. The body is more relaxed, stress symptoms abate, and so on. Incongruities are realized and let go of as the inner blocks dissolve. Limiting self-concepts and constructs dissolve and the client is cut loose from his previous framework. Experiencing becomes full – the client experiences positive self-regard which may be associated with positive regard for others. The client no longer has a 'problem'.

> Once an experience is fully in awareness, fully accepted, then it can be coped with effectively, like any other clear reality. (Rogers, 1961: 148)

Stage Seven: The client is fully-*functioning*, and able to live spontaneously and happily.

Feelings are experienced fully and richly. There is an acceptance and trust of the changing, emerging self. Experiencing moves from structure-bound, rigid thinking to a subjective experiencing in the here-and-now. Personal constructs/concepts are freely reformulated. Internal communication is clear. The individual takes full responsibility for their thoughts, feelings and actions.

Rogers' model of notional stages of therapy can be helpful to us, aiding our understanding of where a client may be in their therapeutic journey in relation to the therapist. It demonstrates how a client may develop their relationship in therapy and how this relationship can change over time. A client may well have left therapy before the final stage.

DEFENCES, TRANSFERENCE AND PROJECTION DYNAMICS IN THE RELATIONSHIP

As the relational paradigm draws on a range of models, it is helpful to consider psychodynamic dimensions of defences, projection transference, countertransference and resistance. We acknowledge that these principles may be present through the different stages of every therapeutic relationship.

Defences

According to Freud, defences are mechanisms the ego uses to protect against the potentially destructive impulses from the id. In a sense, they are normal processes the psyche uses to maintain equilibrium. From a humanistic perspective, defences are what the psyche creates to protect the self-concept from threat. From a cognitive-behavioural perspective, defences are thinking strategies or actions the individual will employ to avoid facing memories, thoughts, or feelings that they are unwilling or unable to accept or consider.

Writers have gone on to detail different manifestations of defences and given them the overall term 'defence mechanisms'. These include, for example, denial, distortion, repression, sublimation, projection, etc., from a traditional psychodynamic perspective. Humanistic therapists will accept these notions, although traditionally they may have worked with them quite differently. Cognitive behavioural therapists will consider problems with thinking and behaving to be defence mechanisms. Obsessional thoughts, ritualizing and phobias may all be examples.

From a relational perspective, it is important to understand that a person will have defences to protect themselves from threat. These defences may form into habits or patterns. The individual may further develop ways of thinking, feeling and behaving to maintain themselves. These, however, will be unique to each individual. Each person will develop their own defences and defensive strategies to survive. A relational therapist will therefore work with each person's defensive behaviours in the here-and-now in relationship with the client and not relate back to a set of theoretical responses based on fixed notions of defence mechanisms.

Transference

Transference is a term often used by therapists to describe feelings, thoughts or memories that a client has from their past that they project on to another person. This is done out of conscious awareness and can be quite innocuous or have more complex dynamics.

For example, when I (Steve) was a teacher working in an inner London primary school, a girl who I was working with asked 'What do I do now daddy?' and as she said it, she immediately realized her error. She saw me as a father figure and in that moment she behaved towards me as to her father.

A more complex transference dynamic may be where an individual directs painful or repressed thoughts and feelings on to another without knowing. A worker may hate their boss quite passionately, for example, out of proportion to their boss's behaviour. This may simply be because even the position of the boss brings up in the worker their own issues with authority which they then project on to their boss.

Countertransference

Countertransference is the process by which an individual is stimulated by the behaviour of their client and responds personally. The therapist experiences feelings, thoughts and behaviours in response to the client's material, without reference to processing the content and its meaning. This can often be spontaneous and powerful. For example, a particular client may talk to their therapist about issues to do with their father. This may stimulate in the therapist issues around their own father or around being a father. The therapist then responds from their own personal perspective as opposed to seeking to understand and make sense of the client's thoughts and feelings.

Such responses can be unhelpful and it is for this purpose that personal awareness-raising is recommended in the form of personal development work and/or personal therapy for the therapist so that they can be as clear as they can be of areas of personal inner unresolved dynamics which can spill into the relationship with the client. Supervision for therapists is also central to working with and understanding such processes.

There are parallels between the history of transference and countertransference in psychoanalysis: each was first seen as a hindrance in therapy and then it was realized that they could be the 'royal road' to successful therapeutic work.

T

THEORY CLIP 7.3 CLARKSON'S TRANSFERENTIAL/COUNTERTRANSFERENTIAL RELATIONSHIP

1. Proactive transference: what the client brings to the relationship/the client's projections of past experiences onto the therapist.
2. Proactive countertransference: what the therapist brings to the relationship/the therapist's transference towards the client.
3. Reactive transference (or countertransference): what the client reacts to because of what the therapist brings in the relationship.
4. Reactive countertransference: what the therapist reacts to in the client.

(Clarkson, 2003)

(Note: The concept of countertransference is different from congruence, in which one is acting with a sense of integrated conscious awareness. With countertransference the therapist's response is from their personal reaction to the client.)

Projection

Projection is the act of locating one's own thoughts and feelings on to another person. Quite simply, the individual projects their ideas on to the other without seeing them for what they are and with little regard for the other. A young person may idealize a TV personality and thus see them in this way without having any personal relationship on which to base this fantasy.

Projective identification

Projective identification is a form of countertransference in which the client projects on to the therapist unconsciously a part of their self they are at odds with to some degree, for example rage or fear. The therapist picks up this projection and since there is no obvious reason for them to feel it from their client, they may believe in some way that the feeling or thought originates in them. The therapist identifies with it and seeks to manage this rather than working with it as another element of their client's material (Casement, 1985; Gray, 1994). This is further explored in Chapter 8.

Many psychodynamic therapists see the above concepts as central to understanding and working with clients in therapy. For other therapists, these are important dynamics to understand and may be present in therapy. However, they may not be central to therapy.

From a relational perspective, the concepts above are considered to be part of the dynamic that the client brings to therapy:

- The developing person organizes their experiences to make sense of the world and their relations with others. This helps form the self-concept out of which they relate to people.
- This way of relating is brought into the therapeutic relationship and acted out in relationship with the therapist.

In the relationship with the therapist, experiences, insights and new understandings lead to the transformation of established/limiting relational patterns.

Working with resistance

Some therapists, typically with a psychoanalytical orientation, will talk about the client's resistance. Resistance, as initially conceptualized by Freud, referred to the blocking of memories from conscious awareness. This was a key concept since it involved bringing these repressed memories in to the individual's consciousness. For relational therapists, resistance can be seen as a healthy defence to threat. For Aron (1996), for example, it may be seen as a legitimate self-protection against some aspect of the therapist's behaviour which is threatening to them. The therapist's role, therefore, is to help the client make sense of what is causing them to act in this way in relation to the therapist at this time.

C

CLIENT CLIP 7.3 RESISTANCE AND RELATIONAL PATTERNS

Jim (Client Clip 4.1) had been referred to student counselling because he had problems making friends. He talked about his inability to form friendships with fellow students as they were from other areas of the UK and were unlike him in many ways. After a number of sessions, in dialogue he revealed something of his feelings about his situation, which up to that point he had been very rational about. His therapist asked him how he felt about things and he replied 'I feel quite alone'. His therapist had an empathic sense of something deeper, not yet acknowledged and asked 'By alone, do you mean lonely?' Jim froze, his face hardened up. He then seemed to slump and said, 'Yes, I think so, you are right, I am lonely.'

This was a transformational moment in therapy. It had not been safe for him to allow himself to feel how he was in the here-and-now of therapy. In fact, he had resisted going there for a number of sessions, placing the blame for his situation on external factors. He was then able to use therapy to explore his relational patterns and their roots.

Elements of Rogers' process model of stages of therapy can be illustrated here. For a period of time Jim saw his problems as external to him and could not allow himself to feel what was troubling him. As he felt safer in the relationship he was able to allow himself to feel what needed to be made conscious, in the here-and-now of therapy.

Gill (1982) saw it as a very important task for the therapist to work with the client's transference and their perceived *resistance* to the therapist's attempts to throw light on the client's problems. An important task, therefore, is to help the client *decode* the transference, the projections they may put on the therapist. It is also to help the client make sense of the feelings they may experience in therapy in the here-and-now. Therapy is a two-way, interpersonal process. The therapist is not a blank screen. The client will therefore be influenced by:

1. What they themselves bring to the session – their hopes, needs and expectations.
2. What is happening in the here-and-now of the therapeutic meeting, how the therapist and client both respond to each other.

For Gill, the social context cannot be ignored; therapy does not take place in a vacuum:

> The therapist may deny that he is reacting to the patient, but it is impossible for him to avoid such reaction. … The therapist who does not recognize the inevitably social nature of the therapeutic situation is in the grip of the companion illusion of himself as a blank screen. … It is the illusion that the patient is naïve. (Gill, 1982: 543)

Gill suggests three ways of making sense of a perceived client's resistance to their therapist: here-and-now interpretation; contemporary life interpretation; and genetic interpretation.

Here-and-now interpretation

This is when the client expresses a strong feeling in relation to something that is transpiring in therapy. The cause of the client's feelings is in the here-and-now. For example, the therapist's train is delayed and they arrive late. The client has been waiting out in the cold and feels rejected. There is no immediate cause for the strength of reaction the client feels.

Contemporary life interpretation

Here, there may be some connection between the feelings the client experiences in therapy with a range of current life events. The client expresses anger to the therapist and parallels may be found in the day-to-day experiences of the client. Perhaps a number of life events are causing the client to feel frustration and this is spilled out on to the therapist.

Genetic interpretation

For Gill, the meaning is not to do with DNA but the 'genesis' or original cause. The client feels perhaps that their therapist is failing them in some way and this comes out in therapy. The therapist remembers that they expressed early on in their work together that their parents never met their need. This is the type of interpretation typically used by classical analysts.

(Note: For many practitioners, for example those with a person-centred orientation, the emphasis will be more on empathic responding and the making of connections in sharing with the client an understanding of their situation rather than on making an interpretation.)

Gill suggests there are two types of transference interpretation. The first is the dynamic with the therapist and what the client projects on to the therapist. Here the therapist helps the client to make sense of their thoughts and feelings towards the therapist. The second is where the therapist helps the client to see the link between their early attitudes and perspectives and how they relate to the therapist currently.

Relational perspectives on resistance

For a relational therapist, no interpretation is right – it is an attempt to understand and help the client to work through what is happening in the here-and-now. The only one who will know if it is 'right', if it fits, is the client. Interpretation will always, therefore, be exploratory in nature and shared tentatively.

T

THEORY CLIP 7.4 RELATIONAL PERSPECTIVES ON RESISTANCE

1. Resistance is a natural defence against threat. It is quite normal for a person to protect themselves in this way.
2. A client's defence may be explored by the therapist empathically as they seek to understand the meaning for the client.
3. Resistance may be a way in to important material for the client. If the therapist goes into it headlong, the door may be barred and therapist and client will be in an impasse.
4. As Gill notes, we all give off signals, many of which we may only be partially aware of. The impact of the therapist on the client's experiencing cannot be underestimated.
5. People resist change, partly because of the security provided by what is familiar to them, and also provided by the success of their script – a way of thinking and behaving that has worked in the past to help manage their inner conflicts.
6. Resistance is in a sense the meaning the client has made of the past in the here-and-now. An understanding of the client's past can help the therapist work with the client in the here-and-now.

Working with relational patterns and other dynamics

Many people bring to therapy patterns of behaving which are causing them distress or frustration in their lives. As the work develops, these patterns may then emerge in therapy and become part of the dynamic in the therapeutic process. Part of the work of the therapist, which helps to strengthen the relationship, may be to help the person become aware of these patterns, develop insight into them and find new ways of relating.

For other people, based on their early childhood experiences, they may have identified attachment patterns (see Chapter 5) which they then recreate as the therapy relationship continues. The task of the therapist may be to bring this attachment behaviour to the client's attention so they can work on it and help find new ways of being in relationship. In the past, there would have been significant focus in some modalities of therapy to interpret such pattern of behaviour. In this way the therapist was the expert and the client was the 'patient'. In relational therapies, the focus is now on finding a common understanding and making sense of the dynamics in the here-and-now. Relational therapists therefore need to be mindful of working from a position of expertise. While the theory of the core conditions, stages of therapy, transference, countertransference, and resistance etc. is helpful in understanding the human psyche, each person is unique and different, with their own heritage.

TABLE 7.1 Summary of specific competencies necessary in developing the TR (adapted from Roth et al., 2009)

Practical
Ability to foster, maintain and develop a good relational therapeutic relationship in the here-and-now.
Ability to work with the client's material to establish and work with an agreed therapeutic aim.
Ability to work with the client's relational patterns.
Personal
Ability to respond non-defensively to client feedback.
Ability to work with difficult and complex processes.
Ability to facilitate the personal power and self-determination of the client.
Professional
Knowledge of, and ability to operate within, professional and ethical guidelines.
Ability to recognize limitations in professional practice.

RESOURCE BOX 7

ROGERS' STAGES IN THERAPY

Merry, T. (1998) *Learning and Being in Person-Centred Counselling*. London: Sage.
Sanders, P. (2006) *The Person-Centred Counselling Primer*. Ross-on-Wye: PCCS Books.
Both books offer a clear explanation of this continuum.

RELATIONAL DEPTH AND CONFIGURATIONS OF SELF

Mearns, D. (2005) *Working at Relational Depth in Counselling and Psychotherapy*. London: Sage.
Mearns, D. and Thorne, B. (2000) 'The nature of "configurations" with self', in D. Mearns and B. Thorne, *Person-Centered Therapy Today: New Frontiers in Theory and Practice*. London: Sage. pp. 101–19.
Two texts which detail the theory.

WORKING WITH TRANSFERENCE AND RESISTANCE

DeYoung, P. (2003) Relational Psychotherapy: A Primer. New York: Brunner-Routledge.
An overview of working with such phenomena.
Kahn, M. (1991) *Between Therapist and Client*. New York: W.H. Freeman.
An easily readable book which works with humanistic and psychodynamic perspectives.

CHAPTER SUMMARY

To help the reader to understand elements in developing the relationship, the following were discussed in this chapter:

- The process of therapy with reference to Roger's seven stages from stuck, fixed rigidity to a spontaneous free-flowing state in which an individual is hypothesized to be functioning fully.
- How the relationship is strengthened through working non-defensively, being empathic to the person and to the totality of their experiencing.
- The importance of Buber's concept of the I–Thou relationship as a process of authentic encounter, dialogue and presence in the therapeutic relationship.

(Continued)

(Continued)

- Working in the here-and-now, maintaining a power balance and empowering the client through the course of the therapeutic relationship.
- Concepts such as transference – a term often used to describe feelings, thoughts or memories that a client has from their past that they project on to another person – and countertransference – a process by which an individual is stimulated by the behaviour of their client and responds personally.
- The implications for practice of developing the relationship and how this relationship can change over time.

8

Challenges to the relationship: When things get tricky

This aims of this chapter are for the reader to understand and develop ways of working with challenges to the therapeutic relationship from the following perspectives:

- Transference and countertransference.
- Attachment.
- Working with resistance and stuckness.
- Shame and guilt.
- Ruptures and threats to the frame.

Professional codes of conduct and ethical principles are also explored.

For many practitioners, when the TR gets challenged in some way, worry, anxiety or even a sense of threat sets in. With the development of a sound working alliance and the similar building of a good therapeutic rapport, the relationship becomes strong. It is to be considered part of the work that a therapist can expect to be challenged at some point, the client will feel stuck, and a range of thoughts and feelings may emerge from the client in therapy that a therapist will have to respond to. In this chapter we consider different perspectives on the dynamics that emerge in the relationship and how to deal with them when things 'get tricky'.

We look at perspectives from different modalities. For example, psychoanalytic therapists traditionally saw the challenge to the TR, or even to the therapist, as very much part of the therapeutic process.

It is therefore quite normal and to be expected that at some point in therapy something will emerge that may be difficult. The importance of regular supervision and a level of self-awareness and personal development will equip the therapist to be able to work freely through these difficult issues without feeling personally threatened in relation to the client.

CHALLENGES TO WORKING WITH TRANSFERENCE AND COUNTERTRANSFERENCE

The terms transference and countertransference had their roots in psychoanalytic theory. We invite the reader to explore and make sense of the issues discussed here from their own perspective. First, let us look at some examples.

P

PRACTITIONER CLIP 8.1 THE CHALLENGE OF TRANSFERENCE

Phil and I (Steve) had been working together for over a year. At times I would want to broach something in the pattern of his behaving in the sessions and he would clearly not want to go there. Then, during one session I mentioned this pattern to him again. He got aggressive, angry and shouted at me: 'If I had 100 therapists you would be the worst ever.' The session ended soon after. I phoned up my supervisor after the session to discuss my response to this. I was pretty shocked by the strength of his outburst. In the week that followed I often reflected on the session and rehearsed how I would go into the next session. The following week Phil turned up and immediately apologized for his 'out of order' behaviour the previous week … and 'yes' I was 'right'. The work we did together that week was deeper and more meaningful than previously.

The relationship was strengthened by what had happened. The fact that, in the therapy room, it had been safe for Phil to express his feelings and that I had not responded defensively, had allowed the in-therapy expression of some very powerful emotions. The feelings expressed were his; I was in some sense the object, but not the source of his anger. It had been contained safely in the therapeutic setting. This enabled it to be worked on later.

P

PRACTITIONER CLIP 8.2 THE CLIENT WHO LIKED ME TOO MUCH

A client Monica once came to see me (Steve) in a clinic I worked at in London some years back. Her issues were mainly due to relationships at work and her desire to improve her career prospects. The work was, to my mind, very slow paced and she would explore in detail issues relating to the day-to-day events of her work relations. Monica very much enjoyed coming. After a period of time I began to feel that what she got out of the session was being with me rather than the work issues she presented with. I took this to supervision and we worked with how I could best help her. The feelings she displayed when with me (what some might call positive transference) led me to feeling less than positive towards her. At the same time it was not possible for me to share my own perceptions of her situation as she presented in a very literal way.

In time, I would say I experienced revulsion in myself to her (some might call this countertransference or others might call it projective identification). I continued to offer the therapeutic conditions to her and worked with my own negative feelings to her in supervision. At one point, the receptionist would tell me that M's eyes would light up when I entered the waiting room. After 18 months, Monica got a new job and moved away.

What is the learning in this? A simplistic analysis might be that I was reacting (countertransference) to her projection of feelings on to me (transference). In supervision I reflected on that perhaps what I was experiencing was the unconscious projection of a part of herself that she did not feel good about (what is called projective identification). Through supervision I was able to separate out my feelings and what was her behaviour. This helped me maintain a positive therapeutic relationship with her, which she clearly found helpful.

In both Practitioner Clips 8.1 and 8.2, in a sense, the therapist was able to *bracket* his own inner responses, work on them in supervision and offer the best possible relationship to his client.

P

PRACTITIONER CLIP 8.3 WORKING WITH THERAPIST COUNTERTRANSFERENCE

Nikki came to see me (Steve) early in my professional career. She was in the process of going through a female to male gender reassignment. As the work progressed, it became clear to me that I was having trouble myself with the session content and the nature of the procedures she was undertaking. This could be termed my countertransferential feelings. Nikki was excited about the progress she was making.

In supervision we explored my feelings and if I could effectively work with her. We decided that it was more helpful for me to stay working with her, bracket my own feelings, and work on them in supervision. She continued to work with me over several months and completed a successful gender reassignment.

At that stage in my professional development, I struggled to work with some issues which I later addressed. The competency *ability to recognize and address own prejudices* is highlighted here.

In this situation, my own (countertransference) responses were processed outside the therapy room and I was able to continue to provide a safe TR for her to explore her movement from female to male.

Working with transference

When working with transference, there are a number of ways of responding (after Clarkson (2003):

- Interpretation: The therapist can share their understanding of the client's process and invite the client to reflect on this.
- Interruption: The therapist can seek to break through the client's behaviour and draw them back to the work in progress.
- Confrontation: The therapist can challenge the client's behaviour.
- Empathy: The therapist can empathically respond to the client.
- Dialogue: The therapist can share their sense of what is going on relationally at that moment and invite the client to explore with them.

REFLECTION POINT 8.1 COMPETENCIES AND CLIENT'S EMOTION

In Chapter 4 we discussed the relational competencies needed for working effectively with all clients.

- What professional competency do you think needs to be demonstrated when working with transference with a client to help articulate what may be going on in the here-and-now?

In the Client Clip below, there are a number of ways in which the therapist can respond.

CLIENT CLIP 8.1 WAYS OF WORKING WITH TRANSFERENCE

Jan is exploring issues to do with her father's domination over her as a child. She has arrived late for the session and when the therapist asks about this, she has become angry and exclaimed that the therapist is always putting her down.

There are a number possible ways the therapist may respond:

- Interpretation

  For example: 'I note that whenever I ask how you are doing you get angry with me and blame me for these angry feeling, yet when you are working through issues with me you behave quite differently. I am wondering what you make of this?'

- Interruption

  For example: 'I am not seeking to put you down J. I am just wondering what is happening with you as you were so late today.'

- Confrontation

  For example: 'You are really angry with me J. and I would like to ask you to explore what this is about. This has come up before.'

- Empathy

  For example: 'You are feeling that I am putting you down again and again.'

- Dialogue

  For example: 'I am feeling quite a lot of strength in what you are saying there J. and it doesn't quite match where I am coming from and what I thought I was meaning. Shall we have a look at what is going on between us?'

When working relationally, therefore, there are a number of ways of working with clients' material to help them reflect on their thoughts and feelings and the patterns that motivate these difficulties. The challenge is to work non-defensively and collaboratively.

ATTACHMENT

Some people play out in the relationship with their therapist their own difficult relational patterns.

Mearns (1994) talked about 'the dance of psychotherapy': the too-ing and fro-ing that happens between client and therapist over the course of their work together, in each session, and over a number of sessions. The client may open up at some point and come closer and then withdraw. The therapist responds to that and at the same time holds in their awareness the pattern that is being played out. At some stage, the therapist may share with the client their perception of the dance, the process, which is unfolding.

In traditional psychoanalysis, the therapist would comment on the resistance of the client, in essence to the therapist. In relational therapy, the therapist reflects their perception of the pattern. Of course the therapist is a living part of this pattern and is not separate to it. Relational therapy, as indicated elsewhere, proposes that there is an innate drive for connection, attachment with others. Based on our life experiences, we can replay patterns of relating in situations far removed from when life's difficulties may have moulded how we behave. There is significant research that links difficulties in relationship in early life with adult life behaviours.

For many clients, the TR offers an opportunity to replay and work through unhelpful patterns of relating. It is not surprising, therefore, that therapists can find themselves at times in strange territory with their client. In some sense the client *needs* to work through this pattern; they are driven to make good an uncomfortable pattern with which they in some way are encumbered. Where the problem is in parenting or in the early years of life, the client may not be conscious of the nature or cause of the problem. Many people find themselves repeating patterns of relating over and over again in different relationships. Or they may find themselves turning a partner into a parent. They then come to therapy to try to sort it all out. The therapist then becomes a potential guide to making sense of relational patterns in the here-and-now and can, in session, help the client work through and understand the nature of the problem. This is why for some people therapy can be a long-term experience as problems can be deep and complex.

T

THEORY CLIP 8.1 RELATIONAL PATTERNS IN THE THERAPEUTIC RELATIONSHIP

Within the TR, when dynamics relating to attachment arise, such as the client treating the therapist like a parent or the client projects on to the therapist, it is important to reflect on what relational patterns may be at play.

- The therapeutic space becomes a fertile ground for working through childhood patterns in relationship with the therapist.
- The client approaches the relationship with thoughts and feelings from earlier times of which they are unaware.

These play out in time and space of the relationship.

- The therapist notes these and over time feeds back to the client these behaviours.
- The therapist maintains a stance of positive regard and non-judgement and remains internally authentic.
- The client is thus able to develop insight into their behaviours and find new, healthy ways of relating in the here-and-now.

The therapist is thus enabling what may be called a '*corrective emotional experience*' (Alexander et al., 1946: 17).

For Clarkson this is:

> The (intentional) provision by the therapist of a corrective/reparative or replenishing parental relationship (or action) where the original parenting was deficient, abusive or over-protective. (1995: 11)

In this next section we outline challenges to the TR which include working with shame and guilt, working with resistance, stuckness and ruptures.

WORKING WITH SHAME AND GUILT

REFLECTION POINT 8.2 COMPETENCIES IN RELATION TO WORKING SHAME, GUILT, STUCKNESS AND RESISTANCE

- What competencies are important in working with issues such as shame and guilt, resistance, stuckness and ruptures?

On entering therapy, clients may be experiencing a range of uncomfortable emotions, including shame and embarrassment about thoughts, feelings or actions. Such experiences may be the root of a set of symptoms. In effect, one part of the psyche of the client is at odds with another, causing internal incongruence or conflict.

It is important in these situations for the therapist to show equal respect and value to each different part so the client can feel safe with both and be able to look at these different feelings in a non-threatening environment. The client can then integrate both aspects and move forward in their lives.

P

PRACTITIONER CLIP 8.4 WORKING WITH SHAME

Kat, 14, came to see me (Steve) because she had anxiety and panic attacks at school. She wanted to run out of school assemblies but was fearful of doing anything, so she just froze and felt very uncomfortable. When we explored together what was behind

(Continued)

(Continued)

this, she was able to reveal that she did not like the way she looked. In assembly she felt highly visible and believed people were looking at her and 'seeing her'. This caused her to go red, which made her even more self-conscious and panicky.

Developmentally, this was a period of change for Kat as she grew from a child to a young woman. By telling me what was going on, she experienced a shift in herself. She had told someone what she was, literally, ashamed of. She was then able to address her thoughts and feelings about how she looked and she became more accepting of herself. As the therapist, I worked with her at her pace and was mindful about offering any judgements on how she looked. She could then freely explore her feelings.

In working with anxiety and panic attacks from a RA approach, the therapist works within the here-and-now of the anxiety. This enables the individual to develop insight into how the anxiety and panic attacks, as they manifest now, relate to difficulties in the past. Furthermore, the client learns how the present therapeutic relationship offers the possibility of discovering or rediscovering their own internal natural tendencies to make positive changes.

Sometimes a person is traumatized by an event and unable to come to terms with it. This may be the case when they do something or something happens to them that is perceived as out of character or out of their own *frame of reference*. This may necessitate the re-evaluation of the self to incorporate this life-changing event. The individual may ultimately need to accept something about themselves that they may in another sense be rejecting. This leads to a sense of turmoil and conflict.

P

PRACTITIONER CLIP 8.5 ACCEPTING CONFLICTING FEELINGS

Tamsin was referred because she had difficulties with a sexual relationship. She had been diagnosed with vaginismus (an inability to have penetrative sex) and had not had any luck with medical treatments. Over a number of sessions she shared that she had been sexually assaulted while on a college trip overseas. She had been drunk at the time and a fellow student had had sex with her. At first I (Steve) believed that the telling and retelling of what had happened would be of help to her… and it was very difficult for her to share what had happened. Tamsin then reported dreams and images in her sleep. These were graphically sexual in nature and she was very embarrassed about them. I maintained a warm therapeutic attitude towards her over this time. Then, in one session, she came in very troubled and conflicted. Over the course of a half hour she proceeded to recount what had happened to her again and then emerged the very last element.... She had enjoyed the feelings when she had been assaulted. She had never told anyone this. She then cried and cried....

After two further sessions she reported that her appetite for sex was reawakened and that all was well.

It is important when working with these situations to be very even handed when working with what the client is exploring. There may be a pull to over-empathize (sympathize) with the client's position which may close off for the client the space and permission to share what they are seeking to reject in themselves. In Tamsin's case, the ambivalent feelings she has about the abuse had made it difficult for her to work through her conflicts.

WORKING WITH RESISTANCE, STUCKNESS AND RUPTURES

Resistance

There are times in therapeutic work when the client appears to be resistant to the therapist and their interventions. It can appear that whatever response the therapist makes is rebuffed or incorrect.

P

PRACTITIONER CLIP 8.6 WORKING WITH RESISTANCE

In a first session working with Sal, a young woman who had come to me (Steve) with relationship problems, I asked her about her family and upbringing. She was quick to respond with the statement: 'I had a great family life, you could not ask for better parents.' In her response there was warmth and feeling. Something about the reply raised a question in me as it was so emotive and seemed out of kilter with her presenting emotional state. However, it was the start of our work together and we had not established the depth of rapport that would have made it possible for me to respond directly to this. So I let it be for the time being.

It was almost as if she was resistant to something else that was arising in her in response to my question.

(Continued)

(Continued)

The session ended well and we arranged to see each other the following week. We duly met for the next session. I summarized where I believed we got to and opened out the session to her. Sal very quickly filled up with sadness, quite overwhelmingly, and amid tears proceeded to tell me that, yes, she had had a lovely childhood but she was adopted. Her adoptive parents were lovely people and she didn't want to criticize them in any way, … but… there was something missing in her life, that she didn't really know how to be with people and in her relationships it was always going wrong. Over the next sessions Sal did significant work over her inner emptiness and her difficulty in giving love.

The resistance had been in her. She had to maintain the self-belief that she had had a wonderful childhood to compensate for her emptiness and sense of loss of her parents and the feeling that something was missing in her life that could not be filled in current relationships.

The role of the therapist here was to be aware of her resistant behaviour and at the same time allow it to be. A direct or badly timed challenge would, in effect, most likely lead her to become entrenched in herself as a defence against the threat the therapist posed in their questioning. By allowing the resistance, it made it possible for it to be safely looked at in due course.

Some therapists may talk about a *resistant client*. Historically, classical psychoanalytical therapists talked about working with the resistance after Freud. For the Freudian therapist, therapeutic resistance can be described as:

> The client's wish not to know, not to remember, that which causes pain and anxiety. The therapeutic process, which is designed to bring about new personal knowledge, can be expected to engender the client's resistance from the start. It follows that the closer the therapeutic work comes to uncovering unconscious material, the greater the resistance which will be expressed. The work of the resistance will often be played out within the realm of the TR and can be thought of as the point where the client withdraws from actively contributing to the therapeutic work. Resistance may take the form of missing sessions, late arrivals, ceasing to contribute material to the therapy, feeling unable to think, dismissing their distress, flights into health, the compulsion to repeat, or aggressive or eroticised feelings towards the therapist. (Howard, 2008: 26)

From a relational perspective, we are concerned with the whole person (which is in some sense composed of acceptable parts and less acceptable or rejected parts). A relational therapist will offer equal care to all parts and over time the client will feel safe enough to explore the difficult areas of themselves. Resistance can be considered a healthy defence mechanism for the psyche against exploring something perceived as threatening. It is therefore protective and valid for the individual and to be treated with care and respect.

Stuckness

Many therapists from time to time report that their client appears 'stuck' or that therapy is not getting anywhere. Of course, when a client comes to therapy they are in some sense stuck in their lives. They come to therapy to resolve this stuckness.

P

PRACTITIONER CLIP 8.7 WORKING WITH STUCKNESS

When I worked with CBT in the 1980s, Andy came to me (Steve) as he was very stuck in his life and his patterns of behaving. Together we tried a range of strategies and homework tasks to help him shift in some behavioural way … all to no avail. There was no possible way to get any 'leverage' on his problems. When we reviewed his progress and the fact he was making none, we realized that one part of the problem was in our relationship. Andy was expecting me to help him change his life and I was expecting and taking responsibility for that. The focus of the work then shifted to his inner world and his upbringing. When some internal conflicts were worked through he was able to change his life in the way he wanted.

Similarly with Monica (Practitioner Clip 8.2), who came to me week after week for 18 months or more. All she talked about was work and her work relationships. In supervision I was working at the time with a classical client-centred therapist as my supervisor. It became apparent that when I took Monica to supervision that the problem was mine. I felt stuck with the pace of the therapy. My client was comfortable with it.

It is, of course, perfectly reasonable for the therapist to share with the client their perceptions of the work together, if this is considered to be in the best interests of the client. To suggest that the client is in some way stuck when in actuality it is the therapist who is experiencing this needs to be very carefully considered.

From a psychodynamic perspective, stuckness can be seen as the conflict the individual feels in themselves. In therapy, the client may be seen as acting out the inner stuckness they experience elsewhere.

Stuckness can also be the perceived symptom for a deep ambivalence. Therefore, care and respect should be given to the client's perception of their situation:

> There is the importance of being satisfied that the patient really is stuck before we introduce facilitating measures. Beware of rushing in to assist the progress. When the patient moves by himself [*sic*], using his awareness of himself or his world, exploring, he is already doing exactly what we hope for. … I am amazed and admiring of how little some people require from me. … Fritz [Perls] is repeating again and again, 'Don't push the river; it flows by itself'. (Daniels, n.d.)

In itself, being stuck is not resistance to therapy, but it can be a very important space for the client to explore.

A client may remain stuck not only because they are struggling on the edge of awareness with something that causes them discomfort, but also because the therapist's behaviour is in some sense causing them to feel unsafe. Maintaining the frame and offering empathy is important.

Warner (1991) stated that clients who have, for example, what she termed the fragile style of processing, tend to experience core issues at very low or high levels of intensity. She argued that some of what appears to be resistance to therapy may be because such clients tend to have difficulty starting and stopping experiences that are personally significant or emotionally connected. A client with a fragile style of processing may struggle to engage with their emotions in sessions and when they do they may struggle to manage them. Warner (1991: 42) stated that:

> In a certain sense, clients in the middle of fragile process are asking if their way of experiencing themselves at that moment has a right to exist in the world. Any misnaming of the experience or suggestion that they look at the experience in a different way is experienced as an answer of 'no' to the question.
>
> They may try to test the therapist with negative behavior to find out if the therapist is likely to leave them before they risk the intense dependence which will occur if they open up fragile processes.

From a relational perspective, a way of working with clients who present as resisting therapy is to offer not only tentative empathic responses, but, as Warner puts it, they need to hear their reactions put into words in such a way that they know that their therapists have grasped what they were feeling and trying to express.

Ruptures and threats to the therapeutic frame

As we have seen, the therapeutic frame is the boundaried arena created and contracted into by the therapist and client in order to create a 'safe space' in which therapy can take place. One of the biggest causes of problems in the therapy process is when the therapeutic frame is threatened. This threatens the foundations of the working alliance and all that it carries. Both parties can act in that way, and the therapist and client can both collude in avoiding some aspect of the work that is arising.

Why do therapists inappropriately change the frame?

Pressures to change the frame can come from the client, the therapist and third parties (for example, the agency, colleagues, professionals, or family/friends of the client).

1 Client factors

On a rational level a client may have practical reasons for changing the frame (to include, for example, work and family demands). In a conscious level, both client and therapist will be able to respond to these 'administrative' issues (Pelham and Stacey, 1999). However, the frame may become the boundary against which the client may play out their own issues which arise in therapy. It can become part of the acting out of their 'script' or 'drama'. In these cases the client may not be aware of what is behind their actions. A request to change times, length of session, repeated missed sessions, and so on may well be due to the client's fears and anxieties around what may be emerging in therapy. Such behaviour may also be to test therapist's willingness to stay with them and be there for them.

P

PRACTITIONER CLIP 8.8 CHALLENGES TO THE FRAME

A common behaviour experience by therapists is 'the doorknob moment', when the client reveals something important at the very end of the session, often as they are leaving. The challenge for the therapist is to maintain the agreed boundary. Many trainee therapists find themselves tested in such ways and report lengthening sessions.

An extreme example of this was a young lady who came to see me (Steve) at my home practice in London. At the end of the session she would disappear into the bathroom for 20 minutes or more.

I also had a client in my early days of practice who would bring a gift. After five sessions, a similar number of plants were sitting comfortably on my window sill. I eventually plucked up the courage to say to her that I really didn't need any gifts.

Therapist's therefore need to consider carefully what is going on and, where appropriate, to raise issues with the client.

2 Therapist factors

The therapist may seek to make changes to the frame. If the frame is seen as a working, administrative arrangement, then they might see little significance in requesting the client to change arrangements. The therapist needs to be mindful of the importance of the frame for the client.

The therapist may find themselves wishing to make changes when the dynamics of the TR evoke strong feelings for them. From the concept of projective identification (Casement, 1985; Gray, 1994), the client can unconsciously project feelings, or parts of themselves on to the therapist as a way of 'parking them'. For example, a client has inner feelings of hostility which they are not accessing; the therapist may pick up on such feelings in the room, perhaps believe them to be their own and then try to manage them by, for example, leading the client into 'easier areas of focus' or, in extreme cases, referring 'a difficult client', and so on. The dynamics here are in fact part of the client's 'drama' which they are enacting.

The therapist, of course, brings their own relational history into the room and if they feel threatened or unresolved issues emerge from them, they may seek to make changes. For example, a therapist who perhaps doesn't feel 'good enough' may work extra hard to help a client in distress, and might offer extra sessions, text their clients after sessions, and so on.

Issues of gender, race and sexuality can also be present. A therapist who has issues around class might offer a special fee, or work extra hard to 'help' their client. Of course the client may unconsciously be drawn into the therapist's own drama and both parties will then play out an adapted relationship.

The importance of supervision needs to be emphasized here. A therapist needs to be able to explore all aspects of their relationship with their client to ensure their client is best served.

3 Third-party factors

In some cases the frame is threatened by arrangements at the agency. For example, appointments are changed to suit the agency, or other professionals may request information, or a relative of the client may wish to speak with the therapist. All of these factors need careful consideration. We have noted the importance of supervision. From the perspective of the RA, we believe that such issues should be appropriately reflected on in therapy so that meaning can be made collaboratively by both parties.

T

THEORY CLIP 8.2 WORKING WITH CHANGES TO THE FRAME

- Changes in the frame carry both conscious and unconscious meaning.
- Whatever course of action is taken involving the frame may affect the subsequent dynamics of the relationship.

- Do not make sudden decisions to change the frame.
- Reflect collaboratively with your client when such issues arise.
- Explore changes to the frame in supervision.
- Consider how issues around the frame may be a playing out of the client's 'script' or 'drama'.
- Reflect on your own feelings which emerge around frame issues. Your own material will give you insights into your client's situation and will also ensure you check on your own motives and unresolved issues.

(Pelham and Stacey, 1999)

The frame – possible problems

When in place the working relationship is clearly delineated, physical and emotional limits of the relationship between client and therapist are defined and understood. When it is altered:

- The relationship can become ambiguous and unfocused.
- There is less chance of the potential therapy being fully realized unless clarity is sought.

The therapeutic frame is fragile.

It involves a trust relationship. Much of the agreement is acted out in trust, in which feelings and trauma can potentially threaten and cloud the boundaries. There is unequal power, especially early in the relationship. Whatever might be said or written, in most cases the therapist, as the professional, 'sets' the rules.

Sessions are held in private, thus there is limited accountability. Who on the outside really knows what goes on in a therapy session?

Therapeutic challenges

The power and intimacy that a TR holds can clearly be transformational. However, if not well boundaried and if the therapist is not managing themselves well, problems can occur. Table 8.1 outlines some of the episodes that can happen.

While there are relatively few cases of therapist malpractice in the UK, and a higher percentage in the USA, the erosion of any aspect of the contract can lead to problems further down the line. This is why it is the responsibility of the therapist to maintain the therapeutic frame for the wellbeing of their client, with whom they have a professional relationship.

TABLE 8.1 The slippery slope – therapeutic challenges (Simon, 1995)

An innocent start…

- Therapist really likes this particular client
  - Changes are made to session timings or session content
    - Therapy becomes mutually sociable
      - Therapist self-discloses
        - Therapist discusses own life or needs with client
          - Physical contact begins
            - Therapist becomes 'out of control' with client over agreed boundaries
              - A special relationship develops
                - Therapist–client intimacy occurs.

P

PRACTITIONER CLIP 8.9 THE SLIPPERY SLOPE... A CAUTIONARY TALE

A therapist was once involved in a professional body complaint which involved a lesbian therapist choosing to hug her lesbian client at the end of sessions. The therapist had in a previous session rejected intimate advances from her client. The therapist was found to have acted unprofessionally and sanctions were imposed.

Another male therapist was once the subject of an internal complaint for hugging a mature female student in an educational seminar who, they believed, needed reassurance. The student complained, citing an abuse of power on their part. The complaint was upheld.

It is worth reflecting on what was happening for both parties in each case and why their complaints were valid. Incidentally, the therapist never hugged a student again, noting paradoxically how many female colleagues hugged him and their students in the years after.

The therapeutic encounter is a meeting in time between two people who lead different lives. There is a clear power dynamic present. The potential for misunderstanding is clearly evident and therapists, with the best will in the world, may find themselves succumbing to personal thoughts and feelings. There are a number of reasons as to why a therapist may find themselves failing to maintain the professional boundary. There could be a number of trigger points. The importance of supervision, self-care and, if appropriate, personal therapy cannot be overemphasized.

The therapist may have personal needs and/or unresolved feelings that may be stimulated in the therapeutic encounter, and this may lead to the therapist often unconsciously seeking personal fulfilment out of their professional work.

TABLE 8.2 Potential therapist causes of rupture

Lowered self-esteem
Family/relationship problems
Power needs
Burnout
Naivity
Childhood trauma and related patterns
Addiction
Isolation
Abuse

TABLE 8.3 Why might a therapist break the frame?

- The need to dominate
- Incestuous longings
- The need to nurture
- Rescue fantasies
- Fantasy that love or sex are curative
- Anger with client
- Client seen as victim
- Defence against therapy ending
- Frame itself seen as legitimate safe space
- Vicarious pleasure/voyeurism

Epstein, 1994; Gabbard and Lester, 2008)

While it is not possible to consider all the possible signs of therapist over-identification with their clients, areas for consideration by therapists in their own self-monitoring may include:

- You really like your client. They feel like a friend or you want to be friends.
- You have sexual feelings in response to a client that you keep to yourself.
- Sessions frequently run overtime or you change them regularly.
- You self-disclose personal material and accept gifts without consideration.
- You allow your client to owe you money.
- You sometimes feel like controlling or punishing a client.
- Your client flirts with you and you don't know how to handle it.

- You become emotionally affected by a client's material and it reduces your effectiveness. You may feel distress or identify with your client's problems. You can't stop thinking about it in between sessions.
- You find yourself doing extra things for a particular client.
- You hold sessions in non-traditional settings. You may agree to meet in a café one week, for example.

The list above is neither definitive nor extensive. In fact, many therapists may find themselves responding to some clients differently from others. It is quite common, for example, for the therapist to report sexual feelings or feelings of intimacy towards a client. This may well be useful material to work with and reflect on, to enable the therapist to be even more effectively present with their client. It is not necessarily anything to do with a private feeling to be kept to oneself. Full use must be made of supervision. If you find yourself not wanting to tell your supervisor thoughts, feelings and actions, such as those listed above, you may be losing your ability to maintain the therapeutic frame.

TABLE 8.4 Possible consequences for clients (Sarker, 2004)

- Exacerbation of problem
- Dependency
- Anxiety
- Depression
- Sexual /relationship problems
- Sleep problems
- Confusion
- Substance abuse
- Mistrust of professionals
- Not attending sessions

REFLECTION POINT 8.3 POSSIBLE CONTRIBUTORY FACTORS TO RUPTURES

- When do you think clients may be most vulnerable to possible ruptures to the therapeutic frame?

The potential outcomes to clients of therapists' inept behaviour, however naïve and innocent, may be severe. Given that this may lead to a re-stimulation of unresolved issues that brought the client to seek therapy in the first place, therapists need to maintain clear professional boundaries, follow their relevant code of ethics and practice, and make full use of supervision.

Prevention guidelines

- Keep to your professional body's ethical code of practice boundaries.
- Keep to your organization's policies and procedures.
- Use supervision.
- Use peer and support networks.
- Report to your line manager as necessary.
- Keep full notes.
- Ensure you act professionally in the same way with each client.
- Recognize and reflect on your clients' reactions to you and yours to the client.
- Manage your thoughts and feelings.
- Keep to agreed contract and/or review progress with your client openly.
- Consider referral and discuss with colleagues.
- Do not keep a secret – discuss private feelings with a trusted colleague.
- If you are stimulated to the degree that it is affecting your personal life, explore in personal therapy.

TABLE 8.5 Summary of competencies necessary in working with clients to manage potentially challenging situations (adapted from Roth et al., 2009)

Practical
Ability to help clients reflect on and develop and articulate their emotions, experiences and personal meanings.
Ability to foster and maintain and develop a good relational therapeutic relationship in the here-and-now.
Personal
Ability to recognize and address own prejudices.
Ability to respond non-defensively to client feedback.
Ability to work with difficult and complex processes.
Professional
Knowledge of, and ability to operate within, professional and ethical guidelines.
Ability to recognize own limitations in professional practice.

RESOURCE BOX 8

Gutheil, T.G. and Brodsky, A. (2011) *Preventing Boundary Violations in Clinical Practice*. New York: Guilford Press.

A guide to safe practice.

(Continued)

(Continued)

Proctor, G. (2002) *The Dynamics of Power in Counselling and Psychotherapy: Ethics, Politics and Practice*. Ross-on-Wye: PCCS Books.
Issues of power in the TR are discussed in depth.

Roth, A., Hill, A. and Pilling S. (2009) *The Competencies Required to Deliver Effective Humanistic Psychological Therapies*. London: University College of London.
Competencies central to ethical, competent practice.

Warner, M.S. (1991) 'Fragile process', in L. Fusek (ed.), *New Directions in Client-Centered Therapy: Practice with Difficult Client Populations*. Monograph Series 1. Chicago, IL: Chicago Counseling and Psychotherapy Center. pp. 41–58.
Explores working with a client's fragile process which may manifest as resistance to the therapy or being negative to the therapist.

WEBSITES

http://nrepp.samhsa.gov/Norcross.aspx summary of Norcross

CHAPTER SUMMARY

To help the reader to explore possible challenges to the relationship we have outlined and discussed the following:

- The dynamics that can emerge in the TR and different ways of responding, including interpretation, interruption, confrontation, empathic and dialogical responses.
- How attachment patterns can play out their own difficult relational patterns in the therapeutic frame with their therapist.
- Shame and guilt – it is important for the therapist to show equal respect and value to each different part of the client so they can feel safe and able to look at these different feelings in a non-threatening environment.
- How resistance can be considered a healthy defence mechanism for the psyche against exploring something perceived as threatening. It is protective and valid for the individual and needs to be treated with care and respect.
- Stuckness and its causes.
- How ruptures can occur and what can threaten the therapeutic frame.
- The importance of using supervision and adhering to professional codes of conduct.

9

Ending the relationship

The aims of this chapter are for the reader to understand what is involved in ending therapeutic work. We consider the following:

- Preparing for endings.
- Reviewing the contract.
- Unplanned endings.
- Referral on to other services.
- Therapist issues and ending.

We have seen in Chapters 6 and 7 how to establish and maintain the TR. In the last chapter we looked closely at challenges to the TR. Different clients have patterns of relating (or attachment patterns) and it is generally accepted that they will respond differently to the therapeutic process and to the ending phase of therapy. The successful ending of therapy is an important phase in any therapeutic modality. Although clients and therapists know that their TR will end at some point, a host of uncertainties and processes can occur to stop a successful ending to therapy. In this chapter we therefore aim to address the key issues around endings. These include the importance of preparing for ending, reviewing the therapy contract, and client and therapist issues around ending. We also address working with therapeutic ruptures that result in unplanned endings and considerations on referring to other services. Besides therapy goals that clients set at the onset of therapy, successful preparation and ending of therapy can be seen as a distinct ingredient of therapy in itself.

P

PRACTITIONER CLIP 9.1 CHALLENGES OF ENDING FOR CLIENT

I (Divine) worked with Constanza for 24 sessions. Through the therapy it emerged that her parents had died in a tragic car accident. She shared how she remembered that they had just had an argument an hour before the accident. She explored the emotional pain she had about this, and the feeling that she had not had the chance to say goodbye. Through the sessions she also explored how she struggled with saying goodbye in any situation. As the sessions progressed, Constanza also explained how her marriage ended without it being her choice. After returning from work she found her husband had taken a few belongings and left.

We started to talk about preparing to end our sessions in our 15th session. I explored with her how we would start to work towards an ending and she became very angry, stating she could not believe that I was thinking about the end of our sessions already.

On looking it this closely, it is clear that from the client's experience, endings had been an area which cause anxiety. It is therefore important for the therapist to be aware of how clients may play this out in the therapy room. The client's anger at me for suggesting that we plan for ending triggered for her other feelings of anxiety she has about being left and abandoned.

PREPARING FOR ENDINGS

Preparing for endings is an essential therapeutic process which requires the therapist and client to collaborate. It is important that the therapist takes responsibility in initiating this process as clients are often engrossed in working through their experiences. Even though clients know the time limitations of the therapeutic frame, the transference dynamics in therapy may mean that the client's unconscious defences, fantasies and anxieties protect them from awareness of endings or any feelings associated with endings.

T

THEORY CLIP 9.1 ESSENTIAL THERAPIST KNOWLEDGE AND SKILLS IN PREPARING FOR ENDINGS

Knowledge

- Knowledge that preparation for endings is an integral part of the process from the outset, and not just a distinct phase.
- Knowledge of the dynamics of attachment, separation, loss and mourning as the basis for understanding the client's subjective experience of endings/separations.

Skills

- An ability (throughout the therapy) to help the client become aware of their subjective experience of separations as they occur in the context of the therapy and in their life. This serves the aim of helping them work through their relational patterns and the feelings associated with dealing with endings, separations and loss.
- An ability to draw on relational theory and how clients may manifest their experience of separation and loss.
- An ability to utilize the ending phase of therapy as an opportunity to revisit initial goals and to refocus on what has been achieved and what still has to be worked on.

Professional

- An ability to use supervision effectively in relation to the client's difficult processes, unexpected/unplanned endings and to reflect on working through endings with clients.

Context- or setting-specific

- An ability to formulate a professional, accurate discharge letter/notes (highlighting relevant interventions employed, the progress of the client, any challenges and therapeutic goals achieved).
- An ability to formulate referral letters or psychotherapy reports at the end of therapy in settings where these are required.

(adapted from Roth et al., 2009)

REFLECTION POINT 9.1 PLANNING FOR ENDING

- What competency is important for therapist to have in place in relation to the ending of the TR?
- How long before the last session do you talk to the client about ending?
- How do you explore how they relate to endings in their life with the current therapy relationship ending?

This is perhaps a little misleading as from the point of establishing the contract both parties will be talking about goals, the frequency and number sessions, reviewing and ending. Some trainee and beginning practitioners report difficulties in maintaining session times (see 'doorknob moments' in Chapter 8). When, therefore, do we start preparing for ending? In reality, we do this from the first session onwards. If both client and therapist are mindful of the agreed frame, then both will be focused on the work that is needed within this time boundary.

REVIEWING THE CONTRACT

The contract agreed provides permission and a forum for the discussion of the progress of therapy. In relation to the goals of therapy, consideration of endings should be brought into awareness where both parties are at the point of reviewing. It is therefore beneficial to build a process for review into any contract made. A review which reminds both parties of the time left, or the possibility of ending therapy early, or negotiating for another series of sessions will help the client and therapist bring to the fore the aims of therapy and how far it has gone. It is important that planned reviews are adhered to. Allowing therapy to drift on or to be so centred on dynamics or heavy material without reference to the agreed frame may not be at all helpful.

T

THEORY CLIP 9.2 REVIEWING THE CONTRACT

Reviewing is helpful for both parties in order to:

1. Reflect on the relationship.
2. Address current dynamics and issues.
3. Refocus on the original goals.
4. Explore current material in relation to the original goals
5. Explore the practicability of the contract itself.
6. Have a safe space to address issues not out in the open in therapy.
7. Discuss any needs for onward referral.
8. Get feedback from the client about their experience of the therapeutic process.

C

CLIENT CLIP 9.1 CLIENT ISSUES AROUND ENDING

Emily had been attending for psychotherapy for six months. She explored how she was struggling with the ending of her relationship and, through the course of therapy, she finally left her violent husband. Although leaving him was her choice, she often went through phases of doubting whether she had done the right thing. Through therapy, she started to notice that she had always been in violent relationships and struggled to end them. On the therapist evaluating the therapy sessions with her and establishing that they had six sessions left before ending, Emily became upset and asked how the therapist could do this to her after making her feel safe, loved and accepted. She stated there was no point continuing with the sessions and she would not return for the rest.

This Client Clip shows how clients can interpret endings as the therapist letting them down. It is therefore important, as noted in Table 9.1, for the therapist to have an ability to systematically draw attention to, and address, the client's defences, feelings, unconscious fantasies and anxieties about the ending of therapy and perceived loss. It is also important for the therapist to manage their own feelings that may be triggered around endings and separation. Furthermore, the therapist can utilize the ending phase of therapy as an opportunity to revisit initial goals and to refocus on what has been achieved and what still has to be worked on. This leaves the client with a clear sense of the work that they have done as well as what they still have to do.

In Chapter 4 we presented the basic assumptions for change in therapy. These assumptions highlighted that problems are resolved in therapy through:

1. A relationship which offers the right conditions for healing and transformation.
2. A relationship which helps clients work through issues from their past in relation to the therapist.
3. A meeting with the therapist which enables growth, nurturing and transformation.

Alongside these relational assumptions, therapists also endeavour to offer unconditional, undivided attention to their clients in the therapeutic frame. This is often very different from what clients would have experienced in their day-to-day lives. These conditions (which we also encapsulated as 'love' in Chapter 4) often impact on clients in profound ways, to the extent that working through the termination phase of therapy can be a painful experience for clients. It can also often result in ruptures in the TR as clients try to make sense of how to 'move on' from a TR in which they felt accepted, understood and empowered to explore their experience.

Drawing from Client Clip 9.1, the impact of multiple violent relationships in which Emily felt unloved and unable to leave is clear. Having now engaged in a therapeutic process for six months, a time in which she felt accepted, valued and safe, she inadvertently communicated how she was struggling with the reality of therapy ending. Although on face value she stated she would leave and not return to further sessions, her expression in a relational context can be considered in different ways. These include:

1. That she was experiencing some anger about therapy ending and hence reacts in a way that reflects an insecure/ambivalent attachment pattern.
2. That she was communicating a need to be reassured to confirm her feelings and experience that she is lovable, a person of worth, etc., in line with what she felt of the therapist. This relates directly to what she said about having felt safe, loved and accepted in the TR.
3. It can also be said that although it may not be present to her awareness, the client was manifesting something about the dynamics of her unconscious fantasies, and anxieties about separation and loss of a meaningful relationship. This was in relation to the therapist.
4. Another perspective is that she was communicating defences which she had used in the past to protect herself from feelings associated with endings, loss and the fear of working through the termination phase of a relationship.

Emily's case highlights these issues around ending. However, as clients respond differently to the ending of therapy, there are other issues that may emerge around ending.

In Practitioner Clip 8.2, we referred to Monica, who attended a private therapy clinic and continued to come to therapy week after week and month after month. The agreed aim of the therapy was to explore issues at work. These continued for her and she recontracted at every review session for further therapy. To my mind (Steve), therapy provided an unspoken space for her to have support and succour, ending was only achieved when she changed jobs and moved away. Each ending is unique and must be understood as such. Meaning must be owned by the client and not the subject of a theoretical interpretation.

UNPLANNED ENDINGS

In therapeutic work, it is inevitable that some of our endings with clients will be unplanned. This can often leave the therapist questioning their own competence. Wosket (2009) stated that because we rarely see clients again, often we do not know exactly what it was that we provided that was helpful. Unplanned endings can be caused by many factors, including:

- Client extra-therapeutic factors/dynamics, i.e. inability to afford therapy.
- Client fears about being 'confined' in a therapy relationship as they start to experience new feelings and to face difficult aspects of their experiencing, resulting in their failure to return.
- Therapists doing something that the client is unhappy with.
- Therapist incompetence or lack of professionalism.
- A rupture in the TR.

- Therapists initiating an unplanned ending due to client behaviours, i.e. an abusive or inappropriate client.
- Therapist conflict of interest, i.e. it emerges that the therapist is has an association with someone who is close to the client.

(adapted from Wosket, 2009)

This list is not exclusive and we believe reflecting on unplanned endings can illustrate for the therapist areas in which they need to improve and develop to ensure that, where possible, they minimize unplanned endings.

For clients, endings are an area which can cause anxiety. It is therefore important for the therapist to be aware of how clients may play this out in the therapy room. From a relational perspective, endings can trigger emotions relating to past relational and attachment patterns. The role of the therapist is to offer a containment of these emotions as well as a reparative relationship in which the client can work through their ending as a new experience in a secure relationship.

REFLECTION POINT 9.2 ENDINGS WITH CLIENTS

- How do you explore how your clients relate to endings in their life with the here-and-now ending of the therapy relationship?

REFERRAL TO OTHER SERVICES

When working in different contexts it is important for therapists to recognize their own limitations, as well as when it may be important to refer clients on to other services. The decision to refer a client on to other services must not be made as a solution to resolve the therapist's stuckness or to avoid the uncomfortable feelings of a rupture in the TR. It needs to be a process in which therapists and clients collaborate and openly explore the challenges and limitations of their current therapy work.

In different services there are referral pathways which have to be followed and these are often informed by referral criteria. It is therefore important for therapists to:

1. Be open to clients when they recognize their own limitations.
2. Prepare the client for ending and for further referral.
3. Evaluate their sessions with the client, including what went well in the therapy and what the challenges encountered were.

4. Support the client to be clear about the goals or therapeutic aims to be worked on in the consequent service.
5. Collaborate on what goes into the referral letter/psychotherapy reports.

THERAPIST ISSUES AND ENDING

In Chapters 4 and 5 we explored the importance of the therapist being aware that their own relational patterns will have an impact on their own internal reaction to their client and/or on their way of relating to their client. This is applicable too when it comes to working through endings with clients. If therapy is to end successfully and in a planned way, the therapist aims to be mindful of their own patterns in relation to loss, separation, endings and to ensure they do not negatively affect the therapy process.

There may be circumstances where it is difficult to see how clients will progress post-therapy, especially when clients vocalize their distress at the prospect of the TR ending. It may even be that the therapist is tempted to extend the sessions where possible. From a relational perspective, we believe that the therapist trusts that the client is doing the best they can in their present circumstances, even when the client becomes negative and feels the whole therapeutic encounter has been unhelpful. The therapist trusts that the client will find their own resolution to their problems and helps the client to work through the feelings associated with loss, separation and ending.

In continuing to work through the client's experience moment by moment, a competence that is required by the therapist when responding to a client's expressed wish to terminate a therapy before its agreed end, is an ability to critically appraise whether the therapy may have reached an irresolvable impasse. Ending and/or referral onwards may be the most helpful way forwards (Roth et al., 2009). Again, supervision will be helpful for the therapist.

Listening and responding

Careful and respectful listening is founded on the fact that it is impossible to know the client's world unless we put in meticulous effort moment by moment to build up our comprehension of what the client says to us (Worsley, 2002). From a relational perspective, we know that the client's worldview and experiences are made up of different elements. These include different degrees of thoughts, feelings, beliefs, cultural and religious contexts, scripts, way of looking at relationships and relational patterns. Often it is difficult to listen and respond to clients when they give negative feedback and state that they are going to stop attending. Clients may talk about ending therapy and therapists may be tempered to respond defensively to feedback. It is therefore important that therapists recognize their own script to endings and respond *non-defensively* to client feelings about endings, as we have seen in the last few chapters. Often, when clients feel listened to, it may even repair the rupture in a way that minimizes the chances of unexpected or unplanned endings. Exploring thoughts and feelings about endings in the here-and-now of therapy may in fact be transformational.

P

PRACTITIONER CLIP 9.2 RESPONDING TO A CLIENT'S PERCEIVED REJECTION NON-DEFENSIVELY

Rasheba had been coming to therapy for about 18 months and had been working through very difficult feelings about serial sexual and psychological abuse in her family. After a very difficult period of time, she abruptly stopped therapy and wrote me (Steve) a letter explaining why I was not a good enough therapist for her. I replied and wished her well, with an invitation to return to therapy in the future should she wish.

Two years later she returned to therapy. After another 18 months, when the work was particularly intense for her, I received another letter from her almost exactly the same as the previous one. I wrote back and explained this. She booked in for therapy the next week, when I showed her the two letters.

She realized the process she was going through and that she was repeating a cycle of rejection. We then worked together through some very difficult material. About a year later she completed therapy and met and married a new person in her life.

For Rasheba, the expression of an ending meant something to her in relation to her own problems. The ability of the therapist to work through this non-defensively proved very helpful to her and enabled the work she needed to do to progress.

The different therapist issues can therefore be summarized as:

- The therapist's prejudice.
- The therapist's inability to deal competently with an impasse.
- The therapist's perceptions about countertransference, therapist fantasy and unresolved issues around endings.
- The therapist's lack of power to advocate for clients where necessary in short-term therapy services (in our experience, even in services where therapy is provided in the short term, extenuating circumstances may be made to extend therapy for some clients).

ORGANIZATIONAL ISSUES AND ENDINGS

Organizational contexts can impact on how the client experiences therapy. A series of counselling sessions in a GP's surgery may not provide the client with the same experience as open-ended sessions in a voluntary service which is established explicitly to support individuals with specific trauma. The therapist needs to be aware of how the organizational context may impact on their client and, as necessary, address this with the client.

Many agencies will operate time-limited therapeutic services. This can often prove a challenge to the therapist, who is committed to doing the best for their client. Furthermore, the client may find it difficult to do the work they need to do in a limited time frame. In the original contracting process, the limitations of therapy, including duration and frequency of therapy, need to be made explicit. Both parties can then address progress collaboratively. It may be possible to negotiate a further term of therapy, referral to another agency or to address ways in which the client may work through issues that they are still experiencing in other ways in their everyday lives. It is therefore the responsibility of the therapist from the outset to ensure that both parties remain aware of the time limits of therapy as the sessions progress.

ENDINGS AND NEW BEGINNINGS

Recently, my (Steve) daughter left school for the last time. The last few days were very emotional. The teachers were, in some sense, sad to see the students go, without knowing what lay ahead for them, while they were also pleased at the work they had done and, no doubt, were happy to see the back of them, have a break and welcome new students next year. My daughter, for her part, was very sad to leave, glad that all that work was over and had little idea as to what lay ahead.

Similarly, as therapists, we are regularly the receptacle for people's problems, their struggles, rage, sadness and fears. They work it through in therapy, and then, we hope, go off to lead happier and fuller lives … and we are left, not knowing and not seeing any of it. We then welcome another client with another set of life problems. We looked at Rogers' continuum of the process of therapy in Chapter 7 (Figure 7.2). Rogers noted that when people reach the last stage, in which they are more fully functioning, they have in most cases left therapy. So we don't see the results of our work.

It is important, therefore, as professionals, that we have clear, clean endings with our clients, make full use of supervision, and have good fulfilling lives for ourselves outside our work. We can then bring the best of ourselves into our next session with our next client. (See self-care in Chapter 10.)

In this chapter we have outlined the different dynamics and challenges that come up in planning for and working through endings with clients. We have identified the importance of reviewing the contract, and addressing client and therapist issues around ending. We have also looked at unplanned endings and referrals on to other services. The ability to end therapeutic relationships is an important part of any successful therapeutic relationship.

In Theory Clip 9.1 we looked at the skills that are essential for the therapist to practice in working with endings. We therefore conclude this chapter on endings with the following therapists' skills related to the competency of the therapists.

TABLE 9.1 Competencies relating to ending the therapeutic relationship (adapted from Roth et al., 2009)

Practical
Ability to help clients reflect on, develop and articulate their emotions, experiences and personal meanings in relation to endings.
Ability to help the client to reflect on previous experiences of endings in relation to the ending of the therapeutic relationship.
Ability to conclude the therapeutic relationship.
Personal
Ability to recognize and address own prejudices around unplanned endings.
Ability to respond non-defensively to client feedback and their decision to end before the agreed number of sessions are complete.
Ability to work with difficult and complex processes which may trigger therapists' negative emotions about their own experiences of endings or separation.
Professional
Knowledge of, and ability to operate within, professional and ethical guidelines.
Ability to recognize own limitations in professional practice. For example where the therapist may need to initiate an unplanned ending in order to refer to more appropriate/specialist services.

RESOURCE BOX 9

DeYoung, P. (2003) *Relational Psychotherapy: A Primer*. New York: Brunner-Routledge.
Useful for both trainee and experienced practitioner. Readable and practical.

Roth, A., Hill, A. and Pilling, S. (2009) *The Competencies Required to Deliver Effective Humanistic Psychological Therapies*. London: University College of London.
Outlines the specific competencies that relate to therapists' abilities to end a TR.

(Continued)

(Continued)

Teyber, E. (2006) *Interpersonal Process in Psychotherapy: A Relational Approach* (5th edn). California: Brooks/Cole.
A chapter in this book looks at ending as a stage with client–therapist examples.

Tolan, J. (2012) *Skills in Person-Centred Counselling & Psychotherapy*. London: Sage.
Clearly written, including case examples.

CHAPTER SUMMARY

To help the therapist understand and work with endings we discussed in this chapter:

- Preparing for endings.
- Reviewing the contract.
- Issues around ending.
- Unplanned endings.
- Referral on to other services.

Part III

The Relationship in Context

This part explores the relationship in a range of therapeutic practices and professional roles. Issues of diversity are further developed. In the final chapter, areas for developing practice and a critique of the Relational Approach are discussed.

10

The therapist's self in relationship

The aims of this chapter are for the reader to develop an understanding of:

- The importance of the self-awareness of the therapist in the helping relationship.
- The relationship between personal awareness and professional effectiveness.
- The place of personal therapy and personal development.
- The use of self in the relationship and the appropriate use of self-disclosure.
- Models of supervision and the supervisory relationship.
- Models of self-assessment and their relational components.

INTRODUCTION

In this chapter the links between personal awareness, development and therapeutic effectiveness are clarified and explored. The place for personal therapy is also illustrated. We propose that from a relational perspective the use of self and awareness of the impact and degree of appropriate self-disclosure are important aspects of the TR.

Supervision is central to practice: we draw and expand on it because it has a huge impact on the TR and therapists' self-awareness. Ideas for self-assessment and their relational components are presented and further explored. Towards the end of the chapter we focus on the importance of reflexive practice and self-care, thereby encouraging therapists to become committed to being a self-reflective, self-aware and self-caring therapist.

WHY IS SELF-AWARENESS IMPORTANT IN A RELATIONAL APPROACH?

Therapists who have an awareness of themselves within and without the therapeutic relationship may be more effective in working with a wide range of clients. In line with the relational competencies we have proposed in this book, self-awareness enables therapists to maintain good therapeutic relationships in the here-and-now. Where therapists are aware of their own experiences and worldviews, and the impact these have on the therapeutic relationship, they are more likely to work collaboratively and respectfully with clients.

As we have seen, the TR is central to change in therapy. Forming a good working relationship at an early stage, along with agreement on the task of therapy, is linked to positive outcomes.

Central to all aspects of these processes is the being and self-awareness of the therapist. It is therefore important for the therapist to have awareness of how their theoretical framework impacts on their self, and vice versa, as well as on the formulation and maintenance of the therapeutic relationship.

Burnout

The professional work of therapists is fraught with different risks, including 'burnout', which has been noted also in wider healthcare settings (Christopher and Maris, 2010). Another risk is 'compassion fatigue', which is a form of burnout in which the therapist can experience physical, emotional and even spiritual exhaustion.

T

THEORY CLIP 10.1 RELATIONAL FATIGUE

From our experience of working with individuals who have been experiencing this, we have termed it '*relational fatigue*', a sense of being 'fed up or tired of working with clients in the therapeutic relationship'. This can then lead to feelings of guilt, which are often self-soothed by trying to work even harder and then even harder.

Central to **relational fatigue** is a lack of balanced self-awareness and self-care. Stress particularly affects therapists in training as it reduces their capacity to be empathic, be present and pay attention to the therapeutic process (Shapiro et al., 2000).

Self-traumatization

Self-awareness and care are also important in order to avoid '**vicarious traumatization**' (Christopher and Maris, 2010). This could result from continuously working with clients who have experienced diverse levels of suffering, hurt, pain, etc. From a relational perspective, it may be caused by the cumulative effect of being fully open to the other, with all they bring. This includes offering congruent, empathic responses, creating and holding a safe space in which clients' learned/previous patterns of interaction are inevitably enacted in the TR. At this point, it is important to consider the impact of the social context within and without the relationship.

SOCIAL CONTEXT

As we have noted, we are not in isolation in relation to our client. Factors such as power, age, gender, colour, ethnicity, class, culture, belief system, sexuality and ability/disability may all be present to one degree or another (Moodley, 2005; Vontress 2012a). It is important for therapists to be aware of how their relationship with these influences impacts on each session and moment in the TR.

As practitioners, we have explored our identities and how we have developed through our encounters with others. One of us (Divine), a black male psychotherapist, acknowledges how at times in his work with refugees and asylum seekers his identity is often questioned. Clients may want to know his heritage or at times they assume that he understands their experiences of discrimination or racism. Clients may also assume/project their thoughts about his social class, understating of culture, or beliefs. Self-awareness, development and resolution of the therapist's own identity is important as it clearly impacts on the TR.

If a therapist's own experiences of racism, discrimination, prejudice or identity are unresolved and not in their awareness, then this will impact on the client and will affect the therapeutic process (Mackenzie-Mavinga, 2009). This may be through an over-identification with clients' experiencing or prejudice.

We also state that for Steve, as a white male psychotherapist, it is also important for him to be aware of his experiences and how his identity development is important when working with clients. Writers have started to focus on the importance of white therapists being white-aware (Jacobs, 2005). Lago and Haugh (2006) and Ryde (2011) argued that white counsellors' racial identity is the unacknowledged, unknown, unaware aspect of self in TR. It is thus important for all therapists to be aware of, and comfortable with, their racial identity in order to be open to working with clients from all cultural spheres of society.

Singh and Tudor (1997) concurred that awareness involves the therapist's knowledge of their own race, culture and the world. They proposed that congruence is central to awareness. This is about therapists not only living their awareness for themselves but also reflecting this in their day-to-day lives outside their professional setting and in challenging incongruence in themselves.

PERSONAL AWARENESS AND THERAPEUTIC EFFECTIVENESS

We would now like to explore why it is important for therapists to have self-awareness? We start by posing the following questions, which we encourage you to explore.

REFLECTION POINT 10.1 ON SELF-AWARENESS

- How do I impact others in my day-to-day life and in therapeutic relationships?
- How do I know when I am working at my best and when I am not?

For each therapist answering these questions, there is a plethora of answers which may emerge. These include aspects of identity, gender, beliefs, values, abilities, competencies, self-perceptions/concepts and reflections. Many of the responses given when we explore these questions, with both trainee and qualified therapists, relate to self-awareness and aspects of being in relationship.

Therapist empathy

Empathy is considered vital for the therapist to be able to understand the client's frame of reference and to respond helpfully. We have earlier seen the components that make up empathic responses. Given that, in order to help the client, we need not only to accurately understand their situation, but also to be able to respond accurately to unspoken or unclear elements of what is communicated.

As with the analogy of the Johari window, which we saw first in Chapter 7, a therapist who is clear and congruent in themselves will be able to see more of their client and thus be in a position to work with a fuller understanding of their situation (Figure 10.1).

The therapist can 'see' the blind spot in the client and thus, by helping bring that into the client's awareness by sensitive and tentative responding, can help

	Known by Self	Unknown by Self
Known by Others	**OPEN ARENA**	**BLIND SPOT**
Unknown by Others	**FACADE**	**UNKNOWN**

FIGURE 10.1 Johari's window of self in relation to others

enable the client to become more fully self-aware and empowered to use their internal resources. We need to be careful in empathic responding that we perceive all the material the client is presenting. The problem with one-dimensional or zero-sum responding was noted earlier in this book.

In Gestalt psychology, practitioners talk about the figure and ground (Kohler, 1947/1970). In our immediate experiencing, a primary form, or 'figure', stands out and appears prominent against its background, or 'ground'. The ground itself, in contrast to the figure, appears unbounded and formless (Polster and Polster, 1973). It includes past experiences, beliefs, pre- and unconscious material, constructs, social and cultural factors. This is therefore the context for our immediate experience.

In the world of the client, as the figure emerges from the ground, it gathers the attention and focus of the client. Over time, when it no longer holds the focus (because it is resolved or due to the emergence of another figure), it recedes back into the ground.

In the case of considering a client's issue, what is emerging is an inner response, the summative experiencing of their life situation in the present moment. When attended to, it is able to resolve itself and no longer be in the foreground of thinking as a 'problem', but melt back into the self (the ground).

For the therapist, the task, therefore, is to be able to accurately respond to all that the client is presenting rather than simply to focus on what they are overtly telling us.

P

PRACTITIONER CLIP 10.1 AWARENESS OF CLIENT'S BODY LANGUAGE AND COMMUNICATION

A client is sitting in front of me with his arms tightly crossed while looking away from me to the floor. He is saying: 'I have no issues being here and feel a lot better.' A good empathic response may be to reflect both on what the client says and how they are holding themselves. From a relational perspective, the therapist may also comment on how their body posture has changed in the past few exchanges as the client is talking about their feelings around intimacy.

The therapist must be as clear in themselves to perceive all that the client is consciously and unconsciously communicating. This may be a word, a feeling, something in the way they are holding themselves, a smell, a half-expressed sound, and so on.

Fully understanding the meaning for the client

REFLECTION POINT 10.2 FULLY UNDERSTANDING THE MEANING FOR THE CLIENT

- What relational competencies does the therapist need to demonstrate in order to clearly and accurately perceive the client's reality?

The main consideration here is in the ability of the therapist to clearly and accurately perceive the client's reality. In order to be as clear as possible, the therapist needs to be freed up from their own internal thoughts and feelings that distract them from fully experiencing what the client presents. Like a clear body of water responds to a stone falling into it, and ripples out as a direct response, so the therapist can truly respond to the client's communications.

This requires listening deeply to the client with heightened awareness and using all the therapist's senses to experience the client's presentation. All the different words, gestures and movements communicate to us the client's state of mind. Demonstrating to the client our attention to all the detail enables the client to get a clearer sense of their internal world. Another way of putting it is – listening to the harmony that the different elements of the music make up. Reik (1948) talked about listening with the *third ear*: listening to hear the subtleties and the different combinations that make up the whole.

Of course it is very easy to think we have heard what someone has said or to partially understand and formulate a response as a result. This may be due to association of ideas or concepts. For example, in everyday conversation people commonly assert 'I know what you mean' when in reality they mean 'I have my understanding of what you mean and I believe it to be the same as yours'.

P

PRACTITIONER CLIP 10.2 DIFFERENT MEANINGS

For a number of years when teaching a class on empathy to groups of students, I (Steve) would ask students to write down three words that they associated with the word 'angry'. I would then offer to give a sum of money to any charity if any two course participants, and there were sometimes up to 30 in these classes, had the same words on their lists. In the 30+ times we did this exercise, only once did two people have the same three words. The purpose of this exercise is to show that it is very easy to assume we know what another person means when we say something, but in effect we can be very wrong.

It is important, therefore, to move awareness as much as possible into the client's frame of reference and put aside one's own internal dialogue while seeking to fully understand the meaning for the client. This enables the therapist to be more fully present.

We note here that there are three relational competencies that it is important to consider in the ability of the therapist to clearly and accurately perceive the client's reality. They are as follows:

- An ability to work collaboratively with the client, understanding their experiences and 'world view'.
- An ability to help clients reflect on, develop and articulate their emotions, experiences and personal meanings.
- An ability to be reflexively self-aware in relation to the client.

When the therapist is more present in the relationship and reflexively self-aware there is less therapist interference impacting into the relationship. In working collaboratively with the client, the therapist is more able to accurately understand the meaning for the client and to communicate this with clarity. Through this process, the client is able to reflect on and develop the meaning of their subjective experience.

PERSONAL THERAPY AND PERSONAL AWARENESS

It now accepted by training and accreditation organizations that personal therapy is a requirement for trainees. There is debate as to the right timing for this.

Many people become therapists or helping professionals because of difficult life experiences. Where someone has had such experiences and worked through them, trainers will often see this as helpful to the trainee. As professionals, they will have experienced some psychological problem which has enabled a developing of self-awareness in relation to this. It might be argued that to have had some experience of, for instance, bereavement, will help a developing therapist as they will have worked through some of their own issues in this area.

However, as indicated above, it may be a little easy for the therapist to make assumptions about the bereavement which are not in line with the client's experience. The therapist may link sadness with the loss whereas the client may be experiencing release and may be feeling some guilt. It is therefore very important, in most cases, not to use one's own experiences as the basis for relating when responding to the client.

P

PRACTITIONER CLIP 10.3 ADDRESSING PREJUDICE

Nikki (Practitioner Clip 8.3) was going through reconstructive surgery as a result of a gender reassignment. This client would discuss in great detail the operations and the progress. I (Steve) found this personally very difficult to sit with, as the notion of a sex-change operation was challenging to me at that time. This resulted in my being able to be less present and to be a little held back from my client. I discussed these feelings regularly in supervision and this helped me to be more empathic in the sessions.

In some sense I 'bracketed' my own thoughts and feelings and put them to one side. In order to do that I needed to work through any live issues for me to minimize them impeding on my ability to be present and empathic with my client.

Many therapists perceive themselves as being non-judgemental and accepting people. However, when presented with various scenarios or types of client they will 'draw away' from feeling able to be fully present with their client. Classic scenarios include working with serious criminal behaviour, abortion and fetishist behaviour. To be a good therapist, a person needs to be as level-headed as possible in relation to their own personal development and have an ability to respond without partiality to their client.

For these reasons, a period of personal therapy when experiencing conflicts and difficulties, coupled with regular supervision, are recommended for all trainee therapists. We propose a therapist in training have therapy in the same modality as the model of therapy in which they are training. In order to practise as a relational therapist, working with clients typically over anything up to 30 sessions of therapy, a practitioner needs to have an experience of this form of therapy as a client. Clearly, it is important to be self-aware and to have worked through or be addressing one's own issues.

People may have gone through this process in a wide variety of ways, including, for example, travel, group experiences, personal relationships, art, music, personal journeys, spirituality, and so on. Most people who do not need to attend therapy in their lives, experience fulfilment and personal growth in such ways.

Some therapists may be vicariously attracted to the personal struggles of others as a way of reaching personal inner satisfaction. It is important to be mindful of this and to reflect on one's own inner processes. Therapists need to attend to their own personal development perhaps more consciously than the general population.

T

THEORY CLIP 10.2 BENEFITS OF PERSONAL THERAPY

From a relational perspective, engaging in personal therapy enables (trainee and practising) therapists to:

1. Process habitual patterns of interaction/ways of being, which are drawn from previous primary relationships (which are inevitably enacted in the therapeutic relationship). Personal therapy therefore enables reflexive self-awareness.
2. Develop a new meaningful self-understanding/way of being. Through management of transference, countertransference, projection and other dynamics, the trainee therapist can experience first-hand, feelings, emotions and have a felt sense of the challenge and benefit of the relational encounter.
3. Relate the here-and-now experience of relational dynamics to their work with clients.
4. Develop an understanding of commitment to a long-term intimate therapeutic relationship.
5. Experience ending and the concluding process of a therapeutic relationship.

Of course, the issue of therapy is not just for trainees. It is important for all therapists to have an openness and awareness of when they may need to access therapy themselves, for example, when facing existential challenges in their own lives.

THE USE OF SELF IN THE RELATIONSHIP AND THE APPROPRIATE USE OF SELF-DISCLOSURE

What the therapist brings to the meeting, their willingness to meet and work with the other, their openness and their non-defensiveness can all enhance the forming of a positive working relationship and good outcomes.

Being congruent in the relationship

When the therapist is more fully present in therapy, they have more capacity to work with their client's material in a way not affected by their own inner thoughts and feelings. In order to do this effectively the therapist must be as clear as possible in their self. A developing and active self-awareness is important here.

When an organism is integrated in itself, then it can respond more effectively and holistically to life. Where we are hampered by internal conflicts and splits, we are not best placed to help others.

As indicated in Chapter 2, the TR is considered as central to therapeutic change in therapy, and the therapeutic conditions variously described as empathy, positivity and therapist authenticity are generally accepted as key therapist behaviours. The person of the therapist is therefore a major component in therapy.

REFLECTION POINT 10.3 THERAPIST'S PERSONAL QUALITIES

Think of someone you would or have turned to in the past for support and guidance.

- What qualities do they possess and what was it about them that made it safe for you to approach or be with them?

Appropriate self-disclosure

With the issue of any therapy, however, comes the question of **self-disclosure**. We are often asked this by both therapists in training as well as seasoned therapists. We now address this from a relational perspective.

C

CLIENT CLIP 10.1 CLIENT REQUEST FOR THERAPIST SELF-DISCLOSURE

Sasha is a client who comes for therapy. She is a professional woman, but feels she is struggling since the ending of her last relationship. She states she is increasingly 'putting on a front' to cover up how she is feeling. She thinks she did everything she could and blames her ex-partner for being less open and not working at the relationship in order to take things 'to the next level'. Through the therapeutic relationship, although she becomes increasingly aware of a pattern that she has a part in her relationship ending, she still maintains she tried everything and blames her ex-partner. In the therapy she asks the therapist if they have ever been in a relationship that ended, one in which they felt they had done everything they could and feel it was really the other's issues.

In this Client Clip, the client is clearly asking the therapist for personal information about their life. The therapist's self-awareness is important in order to manage this dynamic and not act unhelpfully.

Different therapeutic modalities may approach self-disclosure very differently, with some not responding or disclosing anything at all. Wilson and Syme (2006) note that ambiguity on the part of the therapist, especially when starting working with a client, is unhelpful. They state that often clients ask questions about how therapy will work and sometimes this is met with an ambiguous response from the therapist (Wilson and Syme 2006).

As supervisors we have often had dialogue with supervisees from different modalities who when asked questions by their clients will give responses such as 'I wonder what makes you ask that question', or 'This process is not about me, it's about you'. Such responses are not always helpful because they often inadvertently show the lack of the therapist's awareness of power in the relationship. This could be seen as an arrogant stance of 'I am the therapist and you are the client and I am not willing to disclose anything about myself'. Self-disclosure, however, is subjective to the therapist and we encourage the therapist to explore their own practice and reflect on their ability to work through instances when the issue of self-disclosure comes up.

Rucker and Lombardi (1998) suggest that therapist self-disclosure is increasingly seen to be a powerful intervention in the therapeutic process, especially with regards to working with client resistance. It could be argued that in Client Clip 10.1, Sasha is being resistant to exploring something about herself and is therefore blaming her ex-partners as well as looking for the therapist to agree with her.

Resistance is noted within the analytic tradition as everything in the words and behaviours of the client that prevents access to unconscious material (Ivey et al., 2012). Within the relational encounter, however, resistance is the client's struggle with change, because of the security provided by what is familiar (Evans and Gilbert, 2004). Sasha's resistance is about being more trusting of others: to do so may mean being fully open to love, which from her previous experience means eventually getting hurt.

Guidelines for self-disclosure are as follows:

1. The therapist needs to consider the client's intention.
2. The therapist needs to be aware of their own intentions when they decide to disclose. Will their self-disclosure help the client in any way? Whose need is it to self-disclose?
3. The therapist needs to be mindful about what they disclose and of the possible impact this can have on the TR.

The therapist ensures that the focus remains on the client's material. This can enable new meanings to emerge which the client can relate to their experience.

Given the complexity of the therapist's use of self and of self-awareness, the use of supervision is important.

A RELATIONAL MODEL OF SUPERVISION

The ability to make use of supervision is one of the professional competencies we noted in Chapter 4. Supervision aids the therapist's ability to be self-reflexive and become more self-aware.

As the RA maintains, the client has the capacity to find resolution to their life problems. A relational approach to supervision similarly holds that the supervisee has the resources to effectively develop as a therapist. The supervisor is not seen as an expert, but rather serves as a 'collaborator' with the supervisee. The supervisor's role is to provide an environment in which the supervisee can be open and congruent to their experience, both in themselves in supervision and in relation to all aspects of their relationship with their client (after Lambers, 2000).

As in person-centred therapy, 'the attitudes and personal characteristics of the therapist and the quality of the client–therapist relationship are the prime determinants of the outcomes of therapy' (Haynes et al., 2003: 118). A RA to supervision embraces this principle, in which the supervisor–supervisee relationship is the vehicle which facilitates effective reflection, learning and growth in supervision. The goals of supervision need to make explicit that the supervision relationship, the therapist's needs, and the supervisor's role and functions.

For relational supervision to be successful there needs to be an open collaborative relationship. Both parties need to be able to work non-defensively with all the material the supervisee brings. Often, the blocks or obstacles the therapist may bring to supervision will be founded in their personal reaction to their client. The therapist needs to be facilitated to explore such reactions and their meaning both towards understanding the world of the client and their own relationship with their client.

T

THEORY CLIP 10.3 BENEFITS OF SUPERVISION

For supervision to be successful:

- The supervisor needs to respect the person and autonomy of the therapist.
- The supervisor needs to be able to work with relational principles from the therapist's locus of evaluation.
- The supervisor works to enable the internal supervisor of the supervisee to develop.

- The supervisor does not offer interventions to impress the therapist with their knowledge and experience, but 'minds the developmental gap' between the supervisee and themselves. This fosters an environment in which the internal supervisor of the supervisee can develop.
- The therapist needs to able to be open and honest in dialogue with the supervisor.
- Both parties need to respect the autonomy and needs of the client.

A relational model of supervision

There are eight domains in this model (developed from Hawkins and Shohet, 2007). Each domain is an aspect of relational experience that is present in the therapy session and in the supervisory space:

1. The client's life and experience.
2. The therapist's interventions and techniques.
3. The process and relationship between the client and the therapist.

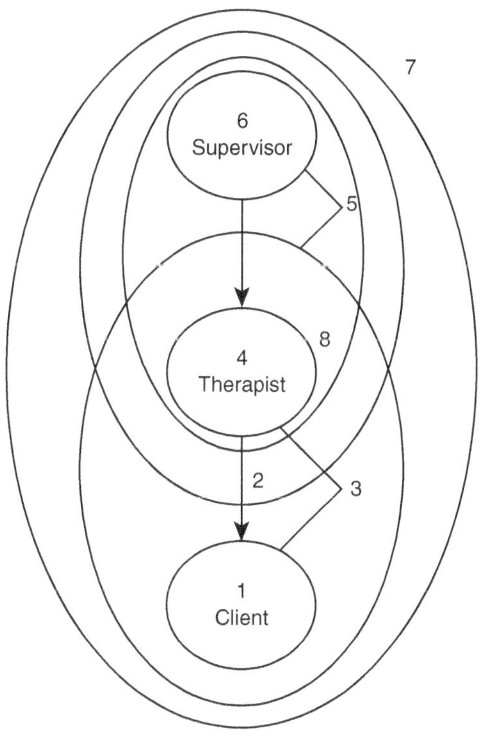

FIGURE 10.2 A RA to supervision

4. The internal experience of the therapist.
5. The here-and-now relationship and process between the therapist and the supervisor.
6. The internal experience of the supervisor.
7. The social, cultural and organizational contexts.
8. The principles of relational practice.

Attending to the domains as they arise in each session keeps the supervision process relational. *Attending* to what is going on in the here-and-now is an important focus.

While for beginning therapists much of the work may focus on the therapist–client relationship, relational supervision enables exploration of any issues relating to practice. Above all, supervision must be creative and have meaningful value for the supervisee.

P

PRACTITIONER CLIP 10.4 DIFFERENCES IN SUPERVISION SESSIONS

For a number of years I (Steve) have supervised a manager of a statutory service. Supervision sessions have included:

- The need for self-care and a good work–life balance
- Client material
- Working with severe abuse and trauma
- Theory
- Research findings
- Areas for continuing professional development
- Dealing with management and service demands
- Record keeping

With another supervisee, approximately half of every session will be spent walking and talking to enable the therapist to reflect on their work outside their normal working environment.

The practice of supervision has been a common feature of therapy for many years, where it is used to offer a facilitative space for therapists to share their practice, their difficulties and to experience the support and feedback of other professionals to enhance and inform that practice.

PRACTITIONER CLIP 10.5 INTEGRATED MODEL OF SUPERVISION IN PRACTICE

I (Divine) offer supervision to a diverse range of individuals in different organizations. I work with individuals and groups, drawing on a relational integrationist model which highlights the importance of a collaborative process between supervisor and supervisee. Emphasis is also placed on issues of difference between the client and therapist, as well as exploring transference, countertransference issues in the therapeutic relationship and in the supervisor–supervisee relationship (Charura and Wallace 2012; Charura, 2012c).

We emphasize the importance of relational supervision as a collaborative endeavour with a focus on professional and personal development. Ultimately, it serves to enable the therapist to be the best they can be with their client, as well as a space to celebrate what's going well and to work on areas that may be challenging for the therapist.

FACTORS IMPACTING ON THE THERAPEUTIC FRAME

As we saw in Chapter 6, the initial meeting and contracting process are fundamental to the establishment of a secure TR with good outcomes. We emphasized the importance of creating a secure frame as a container for the therapeutic work. Given that the client is literally bringing into the room all the people in their lives past and present – their work, their home, their pets, their god(s), and so on – it is important for the therapist to be able to provide a container for the work which will ensue.

The therapist will additionally be bringing into the room their life with all its relationships and significant others, which need to be appropriately managed. There is the potential, therefore, for a multiplicity of communications, internal and external. For example, see Client Clip 10.2.

CLIENT CLIP 10.2 EXTERNAL FACTORS IMPACTING ON THE THERAPEUTIC CONTEXT

Padmeena is coming to counselling. Her parents have recommended that she attends. Her friends don't know she is seeing a therapist and she would come under a lot of pressure if they knew. Her grandfather wants her to marry a young man in Pakistan. In

(Continued)

(Continued)

therapy, she is clarifying that she does not want this. Her parents become angry with the effect of therapy on her. Therapy is the only space she has to herself. She is barely coping. She wants to break free of their influences. Her cousins are telling her she should follow her grandfather's wishes as he knows best for the family. A student of a different cultural background at university has befriended her and asked her to go away with him over the vacation. She can't tell her family as they will forbid this. Her father is visiting Pakistan and has asked her to travel with him for a holiday. She doesn't want to go.

Padmeena's problems are wound up with external factors. Her parents want therapy to 'straighten her out' to do the right thing for her family. For her, what is emerging is what she wants to do for herself, which may create more problems for her.

Often therapists may be faced with challenges and tensions between the client's cultural-familial expectations and what the client feels they really want for themselves. It is important for the therapist to be competent in working with the client in order to help them benefit from therapy. We will explore competencies that are essential in working with such challenges later in this chapter.

The therapeutic frame is the container that is co-created by the client and the therapist and in which therapy can safely take place (Figure 10.3). There is a multiplicity of factors at play in any context. External factors will impact on the frame uniquely, depending on the setting in which therapy is situated.

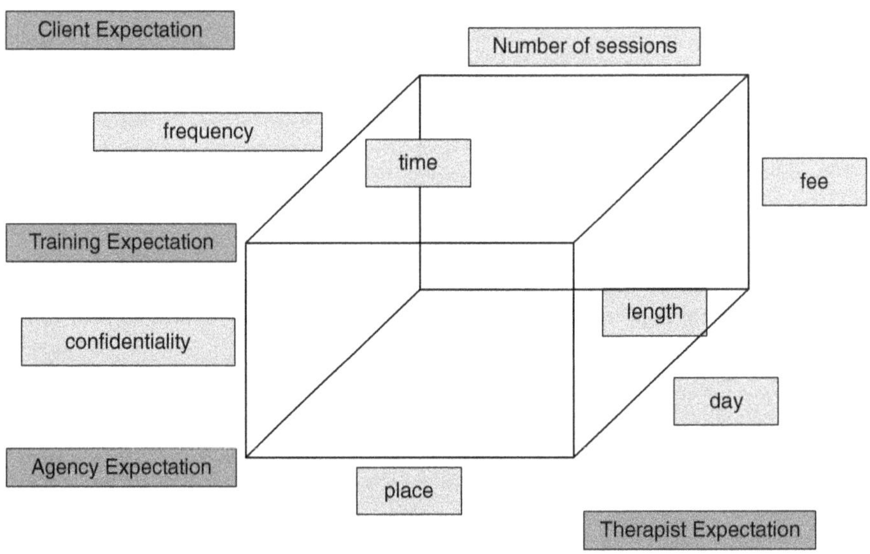

FIGURE 10.3 The therapeutic frame

Additionally, as well as client and therapist factors there will be the institutional factors that need to be addressed and managed, in the main by the therapist.

The basic elements of the frame include a specific setting as well as other components, such as the individual therapist's philosophy and modality. It also includes the therapist's competencies and the client's frame of reference. These factors all meet in the therapeutic encounter. The modality of therapy *and* the context of practice will therefore determine the contours of the therapeutic frame.

THE NEED FOR SELF-CARE

We believe that living a healthy and fulfilling life and addressing life's issues as they emerge are a very important part of being an effective and congruent therapist. A RA bases so much of its practice on the person of the therapist. A RA therapist therefore needs to be able to:

1. Reflect on their practice and their impact on others.
2. Explore the balance between caring for others and caring for self.
3. Explore ongoing ways of self-nurturing and developing both personally and professionally.

We propose a model for self-care based on five domains, as proposed by Higgins (2004), which therapists can use to ensure that they take time to reflect on their practice before, through the encounter, and afterwards. The five domains are:

- Physical
- Emotional
- Spiritual
- Professional
- Psychological

It is important to achieve a balance in these five domains. In order to be the best that they can be in their work with others, a therapist needs to nurture themself.

Reflective practice

It is important that, as therapists, we are consciously aware from moment to moment of our practice, our internal thoughts, our conflicts, what we need to take to supervision and how we respond to our clients in relationship. All these factors impact on the TR. Reflective practice is based on an openness to unique and different perspectives instead of holding on to a rigid or manualized, theoretical and practice 'expert stance' (Barger-Charleson and Van Rijin, 2011).

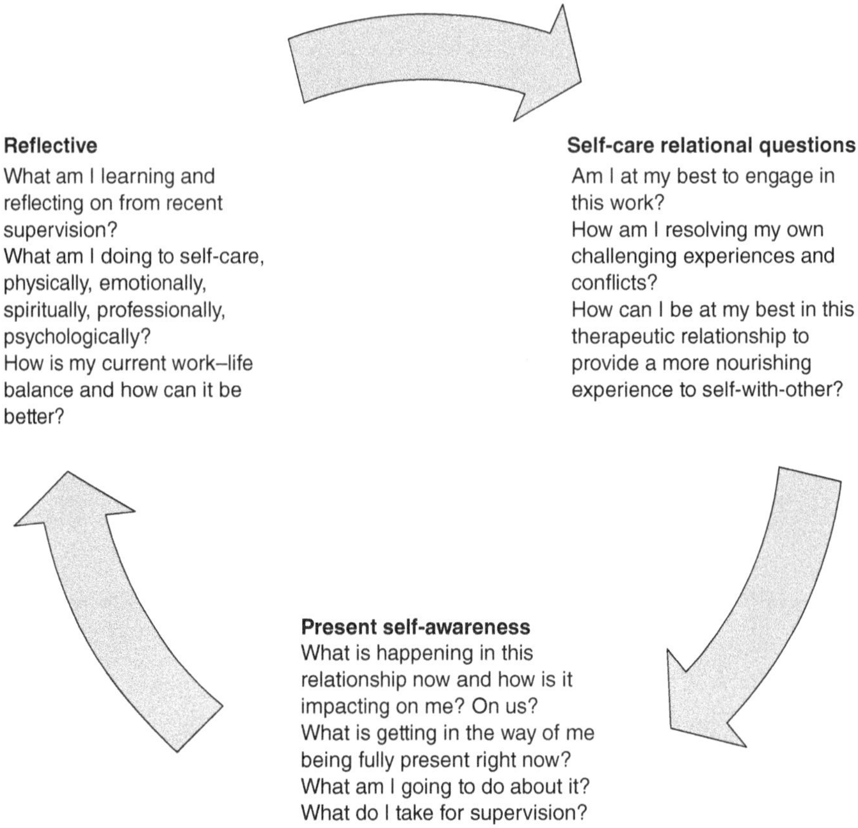

FIGURE 10.4 Relational practice and self-care – a reflective model

REFLECTION POINT 10.4 THE THERAPIST'S AWARENESS OF WORKING ENVIRONMENT

- What do I do in my role as a therapist to foster an environment that is nurturing and to work collaboratively with clients in the therapeutic process?
- Do I have capacity to take on more clients?

There are further useful questions which may relate to ethical practice. These include, for example, when considering for oneself the ethical principle of non-maleficence (doing no harm), to ask oneself: 'What impact does my working environment have on the clients I work with?' (Barger-Charleson and Van Rijin, 2011).

We encourage therapists to reflect on the quality of the TR that they will be offering. A central question for this, for example, would be: 'Am I fully present with those that I see later in the day when I compare it to those I work with at the start of the day?' Such a key question reflects, for us, the importance of a healthy relationship with oneself, and where therapists are self-reflective in monitoring their own practice they can extend their relational capacity to working ethically and effectively with clients.

We would now like to draw on the importance of continually developing our skills and capacities to effectively work with a wide range of clients.

RA effectiveness and the therapist self

The therapist's self is therefore the tool of therapeutic effectiveness. It enables the therapist to be available in the best possible way to the client and to be committed in the TR. It also buffers the therapist from some avoidable ruptures around inadvertent discriminatory practice which may result from a lack of knowledge or sensitivity. Furthermore, it protects the therapist from burnout, compassion/relational fatigue or vicarious trauma. It is, in fact, good and ethical practice for therapists to be self-aware and to self-care. It is important to access regular supervision as well as to be open to access therapy in order to ensure that there is continual self-awareness of the therapist's self.

TABLE 10.1 Competencies relating to therapists' self-awareness

- Ability to work collaboratively with the client, understanding their experiences, and 'world view'.
- Ability to help clients reflect on and develop and articulate their emotions, experiences and personal meanings.
- Ability to be reflexively self-aware in relation to the client.
- Ability to make use of supervision
- Ability to recognize and address prejudice.

RESOURCE BOX 10

Gilbert, M. and Evans, K. (2000) *Psychotherapy Supervision: An Intergrative-Relational Approach.* Maidenhead: Open University Press.
A well-written and informative, yet easy-to-read text on supervision.

Skovholt, T.M. and Trotter-Mathison, M. (2011) *The Resilient Practitioner* (2nd edn). New York: Routledge.
This includes a wide range of self-care and self-awareness tools.

CHAPTER SUMMARY

To help the reader to understand the therapist's self in relationship, in this chapter we explored the following:

- The importance of the self-awareness of the therapist in the TR and the ability of the therapist to use their own understandings and internal responses helpfully.
- Using self-awareness to remain effective and avoid vicarious traumatization, burnout, or relational fatigue.
- The place of personal therapy and personal development in relation to the ability to respond to clients without partiality, acknowledging that people may develop in a wide variety of ways, including, for example, relationships, art, music, personal journeys and spirituality.
- The use of self in the relationship and the appropriate use of self-disclosure, ensuring that the focus remains on the client's material.
- A model of supervision. From a relational perspective, the supervisor is not an expert but rather serves as a 'collaborator' with the supervisee.
- An approach to evaluative self-assessment. Emphasis has been placed on the importance of therapists engaging in self-assessment in five domains – of the physical, emotional, spiritual, professional and psychological – to provide the most nourishing experience of self-with-other.

11

Working with difference within the therapeutic relationship: A relational perspective

The aims of this chapter are for the reader to develop an understanding of:

- The importance of being aware of and exploring difference from a relational perspective.
- The relationship and society.
- Cross-cultural relationships and the challenge that can emerge in the therapeutic relationship.
- Transcultural approaches and theories to therapy.
- Empowerment in the relationship.
- Effective anti-oppressive and competent practice.

In this chapter we explore difference and diversity. As mentioned elsewhere in this book, ethical practice, power dynamics, diversity and anti-oppressive practice are central themes to all aspects of the TR.

We invite you to reflect on your awareness of issues of difference in your practice with the clients you work with. As the chapter progresses, some of the challenges of working with difference and diversity are explored. 'Working with difference' is a blanket term which in this chapter will encompass different therapeutic theories, including 'working with diversity', 'transcultural working', and 'cross-cultural theory and practice'. Alongside this notion of working with difference is the concept of anti-oppressive practice, which we believe is central to a RA and to client empowerment in the therapeutic process.

For the therapist in their consulting room, one-to-one therapy cannot be simply an encounter in a vacuum. Many people and forces impact on what is happening.

1. Intrapsychic forces
2. Interpersonal dynamics
3. The client's external world and social influences
4. The therapist's external world and social influences
5. The therapy setting
6. General social influences
7. Socio-cultural contexts

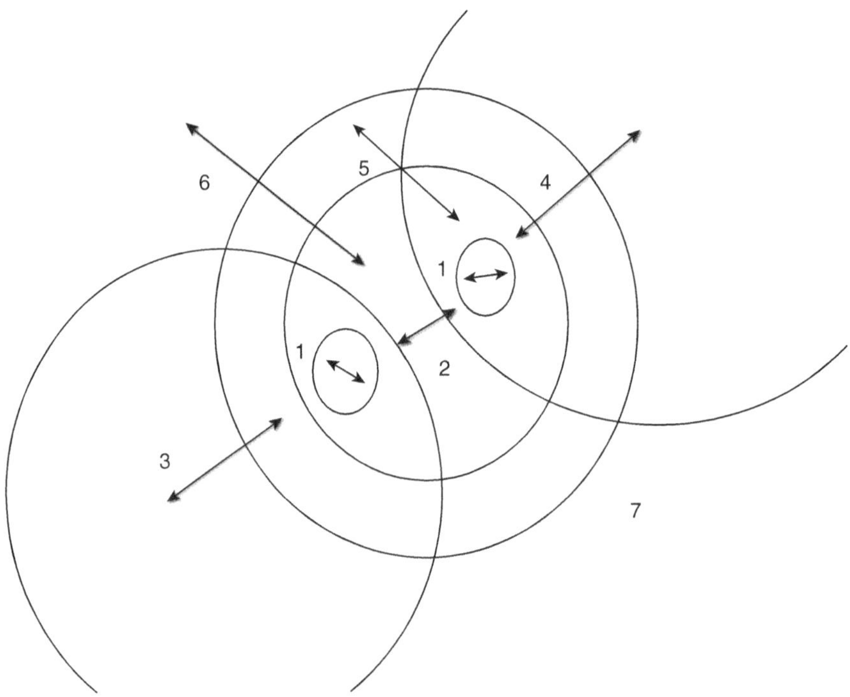

FIGURE 11.1 Forces impacting on a therapeutic encounter

Social context

Within a RA, consideration of the client's social context is an important influential factor on the therapeutic frame. The social context includes the way in which the client relates to other members of the community and the impact of the following:

- Cultural factors – these include collective ideas, values, beliefs, attitudes and behaviours which the client shares with a particular group.
- Political factors – these relate to laws, policies and other governing influential structures on the client's life in society.
- Economic factors – these relate to the client's experience of the impact of financial and other material resources in society.

These social factors all impact in relation to client outcomes. As the relationship is the most significant in-therapy factor, as related to positive outcomes (Paul and Haugh, 2008), the therapist needs to be willing and able to explore factors, implicit or explicit, that may impact on the TR.

REFLECTION POINT 11.1 DIFFERENCE AND DIVERSITY

- What do we mean by difference and diversity?
- What does it encompass in therapy?

In working within a relational paradigm we understand that difference is not just about skin colour or visible features but includes an awareness of all dimensions which influence the therapist and client. In this chapter we use Moodley's (2005) synonymously inclusive definition, which extends difference and diversity to seven major categories. These are named as race, gender, class, sexual orientation, disability, religion and age (Moodley, 2005). We believe that these areas contribute to the dynamics of the relational encounter, when considering working with difference, and we make reference to them throughout this chapter.

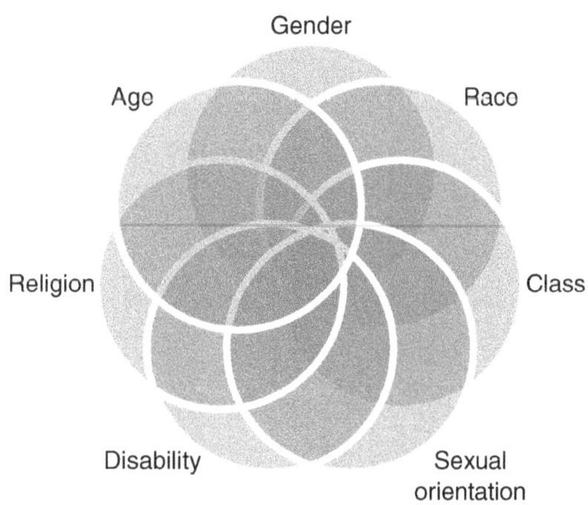

FIGURE 11.2 The seven diversity issues in therapy (Moodley, 2005)

THE THERAPEUTIC RELATIONSHIP AND SOCIETY

Pelham (2008), in his writing on the TR from a relational perspective, suggested that the therapist and client meet in a cultural context which influences their relationship and encounter. Within a relational approach, each therapeutic encounter is cross-cultural, intercultural and transcultural. This is primarily because the therapist's and client's experiences are embedded and influenced by different socio-politico, economic and cultural backgrounds as well as by different life experiences.

We often ask counselling and psychotherapy training groups to consider these two questions:

> **REFLECTION POINT 11.2 DIFFERENCE, DIVERSITY, SOCIETY AND PREJUDICE**
>
> - In relation to me, who are those I consider to be in different and diverse groups in society?
> - What are the differences between me and others in terms of power, privileges and advantages within society?

The questions in Reflection Point 11.2 enable the therapist to identify areas in which they need to work and, consequently, they need to be prepared for times when issues of difference may be challenging to the TR.

To help us further explore answers to these questions we draw on the definitions given by the Equality and Diversity Forum of the British Association for Counselling and Psychotherapy in (2004), as noted in Table 11.1.

Another dimension of extreme importance to consider in working with difference and diversity is current legislation in the UK. This includes The Equality Act (2010) and The Public Sector Equality Duties (2011), which both inform practice. In the Public Sector Equalities Duties (2011) the importance of eliminating discrimination, promoting equality of opportunity and promoting good relations is noted as necessary in working with specific population groups. These

TABLE 11.1 Advantaged and disadvantaged people in society

Advantaged/normal people in society
This group includes white people, heterosexual people, able-bodied people, men, and people who are working (income-generating).
Disadvantaged/different people in society
This group includes disabled people, lesbian, gay and bisexual people, black and minority ethnic people, women, young people, older people, and unemployed people.

include current equality-protected characteristics, which are age, disability, gender reassignment, pregnancy and maternity, race, religion or belief, gender and sexual orientation.

Traditionally, the social context has been often overlooked in psychotherapy and counselling. Omitting the social-environment context communicates an underlying assumption that the problems that clients bring to therapy reside within themselves rather than being influenced by society (Vontress, 2012b). Awareness of potentially marginalized groups and of difference therefore enables us to explore not only our position, but also those of the clients and colleagues we work with (Pelham, 2008).

T

THEORY CLIP 11.1 RA AND A CONSIDERATION OF SOCIAL CONTEXT AND ENVIRONMENT

Within a RA consideration of the social context and environment is important because:

1. The social context impacts on the client's development, experience and self-concept.
2. The clients' problems and limitations are associated to primary relationships within society.
3. Therapeutic goals and change should take into consideration clients' social context in order to help them best.
4. The therapeutic relationship is embedded within a social context and both client and therapist need to be open to explore the impact of the therapeutic relationship and change in relation to this social context.

An awareness of how clients may face prejudice, have prejudice, marginalize others or be marginalized is important for the therapist. Furthermore, self-awareness of the therapist's own position within society is important. Overall knowledge of societal position, dynamics and strata enables us to be effective in the therapeutic relationship.

P

PRACTITIONER CLIP 11.1 AWARENESS OF THE CLIENT'S SOCIETAL POSITION AND DIFFERENCE

I (Divine) have been working with refugees and asylum seekers. In my work with Zack, an asylum seeker from Iraq, it is important for me to know how his position in society and my position impact on our therapeutic relationship. For example, Zack

(Continued)

(Continued)

is unemployed, he speaks very little English, often faces racism, is paid £36 a week (2013) in vouchers, is housed in a property with no gas or heating, and is disabled following serious torture when he was in prison in Iraq. As a wheelchair user, travelling seven miles to come for therapy is difficult, for many reasons. These include the discrimination he faces because of his disability, limited funding for travel, his difficulty in communicating because of his limited English, and his needs for wheelchair access to different buildings not always being met etc.

A different client is James, a white, British middle-class man, whom I see for weekly therapy in private practice. He is a merchant banker, educated at one of the top universities in the country, he drives a new Mercedes, lives in an affluent area and pays for weekly therapy. He describes his position in society as 'well-off', he does not feel discriminated against and states he has always had well-paid jobs.

Consideration of the different clients already highlights how a client's societal position and difference in relation to the therapist can influence the therapeutic relationship. It is important for therapists to reflect on each client and to consider what the issues of client–therapist difference are, and how they may be impacting on the client's experience and self-concept.

Other important questions to ask ourselves in working with difference in practice include:

- Am I aware of my own prejudice?
- How do I respond to these factors when they are named or unnamed in the therapeutic relationship?

These questions can enable therapists to start to be aware of their own positions in relation to their views on issues of difference and of others, such as their clients in society.

IMPORTANCE OF AWARENESS OF DIFFERENCE WITHIN THE THERAPEUTIC RELATIONSHIP

Lago and Haugh (2006) suggested that our attitudes are learned and become so smoothly incorporated, owned, affirmed and an unquestioned part of the self. Therefore, not to address our attitudes and prejudices to 'other' groups puts us, as therapists, at risk of repeating discriminatory practices within the therapeutic setting.

Not to address our awareness of difference and power often results in therapists feeling stuck in their work with clients and in some cases results in incompetent practice. The therapist can have a blind spot to aspects of the world of the client and consequently be less empathic. On reflecting on working with clients similar to those in Practitioner Clip 11.1 can therapists identify their own prejudices or behaviours and how they differ between particular clients? Failure to address and change this can lead to a client's lack of therapeutic engagement and serious ruptures in the TR which may consequently result in clients dropping out of therapy.

The relational process: Working with difference and diversity

In reflecting on the different TRs that we engage in with clients, there are nearly always moments when therapists feel challenged or even hesitant to work with particular clients. We now explore how the relational therapeutic process can enable therapists to be more competent.

REFLECTION POINT 11.3 THE CHALLENGE OF WORKING WITH DIFFERENCE

Consider a client you would dread/avoid working with. Consider a client you have worked with in which issues of difference seriously challenged you and the therapeutic relationship.

- What are the factors that impact on you in each of these cases?

C

CLIENT CLIP 11.1 WORKING WITH RACE, GENDER AND SEXUALITY

Jo is a 60-year-old woman of dual heritage. She accesses therapy following a referral from her GP. She recently resigned from her work in the banking industry because she felt 'bullied' and 'unwanted'. She gave examples of times she was told by colleagues that she was too emotional and neurotic. She has also recently come out of a relationship which ended after nine months because her partner said that she was 'too dramatic and emotional'. She stated that before this the last relationship she was in had lasted nearly a year.

Jo also said that she was adopted and was bullied in school and felt that she did not fit in because she was not like the other children. 'I wasn't white or clever, you see.'

She also states that she finds it hard to open up but does not want to offend. She would prefer to be referred to a black, female, gay therapist because then she would not have to 'go into all of it'.

Exploration of difference in encounter: Consideration of relational perspectives and themes

In reflecting on Client Clip 11.1, we highlight relational perspectives. First, we acknowledge that different therapists may respond differently. A RA does not prioritize a manualized, dogmatic way of therapy as this can be very damaging to the client. Instead, the therapist is open to work with whatever emerges in the therapy room and offers empathic responses which are *idiosyncratic*. Idiosyncratic responses depend on the therapeutic context at the time (Bozarth, 1984/2001). Any responses need to be centred on the therapist having a sense of what will help at that particular time with that particular client (Purton, 2004).

T

THEORY CLIP 11.2 IDIOSYNCRATIC EMPATHY

We propose five characteristics of **idiosyncratic empathy** (adapted from Bozarth, 1984/2001):

1. The transparency of the therapist in the relationship to the other person.
2. The person-to-person encounter in the relationship.
3. The intuition of the therapist.
4. The awareness and actions of the therapist towards their empathic responding in relation to the client's difference and socio-cultural context.

> Empathy is not merely about the therapist being in the client's world, nor is it merely about the therapist reflecting the client's feelings or repeating the last thing that the client has said. What idiosyncratic empathy emphasises is the congruence of the therapist and of the relationship. … The meaning-making which emerges in this meeting is unique to the two people involved. (Keys, 2003: 8)

Singh and Tudor (1997) highlighted the importance of what they called cultural conditions of therapy and they reworked Rogers (1957) six conditions from a cultural perspective. The therapist needs also to have awareness of their own culture, difference and themselves in relation to it and to the world (Singh and Tudor, 1997). A therapist needs also to be integrated in themselves as much as possible.

From Client Clip 11.1 of Jo, it is easier to note the issues of difference, such as age, gender, ethnicity, class, as well as the client's historical socio-cultural experiences, etc. However, the more complex questions arise in what approach the therapist would take in working with her.

First, knowledge of some of the relational assumptions which apply here are important if work with this client is to progress. These are outlined and discussed as follows:

1. The client's intrapsychic structure, i.e. what they believe about themselves, others and the world, is influenced by their experience of their primary relationships. It is therefore important to be tentative in exploring the development of Jo's 'concept-of-self', based on her socio-economic and cultural experiences. Within the therapy room she re-enacts her responses to the difficulty of this difference.

   Of equal importance is the impact and dynamics of the issues of subtle and obvious differences between the therapist and client. So in Jo's case, the therapist's responses to the client's need to be referred to a black, female, gay practitioner denotes something of the client's feelings about difference. When the clients name issues of difference it is the opportunity (the relational window) to explore the difference that has been named.

   Some of the issues of difference, for example the therapist's sexuality, may not be evident to the client. The therapist therefore needs to be open to approach, and where appropriate, *name* the other unspoken issues of difference within the TR.

2. Another relational assumption is that clients resist change because of the security provided by ways of coping and behaviours that are familiar. The therapist's knowledge of why clients may be resistant to change in therapy is important.
3. The therapist also has to be mindful of a relational assumption, as outlined in Chapter 4, that *clients will enact their experience and way of being in the therapy room.* The therapist may also, where appropriate, tentatively explore the client's pattern of relating in the here-and-now of the therapeutic relationship. What this can illuminate for both client and therapist is an emerging view of the clients, experiencing and problematic areas in relating to others in their day-to-day life.

Client therapist matching

While it may appear that Jo's request for a therapist that she perceives to be similar to her was extraordinary, there is working with difference and diversity literature which explores the argument for this. Matching theories explore the pros and cons of matching clients and therapists (Lago, 2011; Sue and Sue, 1990). Schechter (1992), for example, postulated the concept of 'associative identification', which is the establishment of matching aspects of the client and therapist, such as in relation to gender, race, sexuality, etc.

From a relational perspective, we concur with the possibilities of instances when client matching may be prioritized, for example in specialist services dealing with trauma, rape, religion, etc. There may also be occasions when, because of language barriers, clients may seek bi/multilingual therapists to work with them. However, there are guidelines on working with interpreters/translators within the therapeutic arena (Tribe and Raval, 2003).

It is important to distinguish between client resistance to engage in therapy and openness to embrace working with difference. So, in the case of Jo, she stated her reason for wanting a different therapist was so that she did not have 'to go into all of it'. This suggests some anxiety/hesitation to engage in the TR rather than an exception where client–counsellor matching may be therapeutic.

Identity development

The fact that Jo named her cultural-historical heritage and sexuality suggests the centrality of identity to the TR.

T

THEORY CLIP 11.3 DEVELOPMENT MODELS: RACE, SEXUALITY, GENDER AND DISABILITY

Lago (2011) listed some of the developmental models that explain various aspects of identity, including:

- Racial/ethnic identity (Atkinson et al., 1993; Cross, 1995; Helms, 1990).
- Biracial identity (Kerwin and Ponterotto, 1995; Poston, 1990; Vontress 2012b).
- Homosexual/gay/lesbian/bisexual identity (Coleman, 1982; Marszalek and Cashwell, 1999; McCarn and Fassinger, 1996).
- Womanist identity (Downing and Roush, 1985; Ossana, Helms and Leonard, 1992).
- Disability identity (Gill, 1997; Vash, 1981).

Different models of identity development seek to describe the human developmental pathways and stages through which persons may journey in relation to their own (and their group's) identity. This journey is contrasted with and frequently determined by the values of the dominant group within society. These models frequently have a series of six developmental stages in which a person's identity in relation to their ethnicity, gender or other aspect is described (see Helms and Piper, 1994).

Through the relational therapeutic encounter, the individual's awareness of themselves grows (for example, awareness regarding their sexuality, disability, ethnicity, etc.) and they are hypothesized to move through a series of stages. These range from an internalization and acceptance of the majority group's attitudes towards them, through to struggling with their identity and eventually changing into a more balanced self-relationship.

It is therefore important for the therapist to have gone through their own identity development and to be non-defensive when clients present with requests that may appear discriminatory. Identity and identity development are therefore central to the relational arena because, after all, therapy often brings about identity change.

The proxy self, difference and the I–Thou relationship

Thomas (1992, 1999) stated that when working with difference, clients do not always present their real self in the first encounters with therapists. He argued that clients may present what he termed a **proxy self**, which is the presentation of an 'acceptable' front/persona by a person of diversity that helps them manage life relating to those persons and attitudes of the dominant group. Given this assumption, therefore, we note that it is only through the therapist's attitudinal qualities that the client comes to feel safe. Consequently, this helps the client to begin to show parts of their real selves. This relates to all areas of difference, including disability, sexuality, race, gender, age, religion, spirituality, and so on.

We therefore emphasize the importance in a RA of meeting: the therapist meets the client as they are; both the therapist and the client work with whatever comes up in the therapeutic space.

As we have seen, the philosopher Martin Buber postulated the I–Thou quality of relating rather than an I–it relationship in which the other is an object (Buber, 1958). The I–Thou relationship is a process of authentic encounter and dialogue between the therapist and client. Any issues regarding client/therapist differences are explored through dialogue and authentic encounter. However, there may be other moments when working with difference is more complex and challenging for the therapist. In such cases there is a need for the therapist to extend their relational capacity.

P

PRACTITIONER CLIP 11.2 WORKING WITH GENDER DIFFERENCES

When working with a client who in the first session informed me (Divine) that she was a radical feminist and that she hated men, my initial reaction was to be surprised, and frustrated. I asked the client why she had chosen to come for therapy with me. She stated that she wanted to 'face her issues'. As we explored whether we could work together I felt that I was really being pushed to my relational limits. As the therapy progressed, more facts emerged about her three failed relationships, which had also been abusive.

Working with such a client as a male therapist brought up many challenges for me and it would have been easier to end therapy. However, as we continued to work together, we explored through often difficult processes her self-professed hatred for men. Eventually, at the end of therapy, she stated that the best thing that had happened for her was me as a male therapist staying with her, working through a difficult process without becoming defensive and abusing my power. On reflection, while this example says something about the client, it also confirms how working with difference can be challenging to our relational capacities.

Importance of the quality of relationship

> In my early professional years I was asking the question: How can I treat, or cure, or change this person? Now I would phrase the question in this way: How can I provide a relationship which this person may use for his own personal growth? (Rogers, 1961: 32)

We would like to draw on the importance of continually developing our capacity to effectively work with difference. Rogers' conditions, empathy, congruence and unconditional positive regard (UPR) (1959) inform the interplay of the different dynamics of the TR.

REFLECTION POINT 11.4 THERAPEUTIC CONDITIONS AND DIFFERENCE

- What are the challenges of effectively communicating these conditions with the client when working with difference?

C

CLIENT CLIP 11.2 WORKING WITH RELIGION AND AGE DIFFERENCES

Akim is a 62-year-old man who was released from prison a few months ago. He was imprisoned following multiple counts of domestic violence and, consequently, for attempting to murder (he felt it would be a sacrifice/honour killing) his 18-year-old daughter. She had denounced what Akim termed a 'religious way of the truth', running away from her arranged marriage and having an affair with 'one of the local boys'.

Akim was released before completing his full term, owing to his good behaviour and conformity with the prison system. He was also advised to seek psychological therapy to help him with his anger and feelings about his actions in the last 15 years, which had consequently led to imprisonment. He attends for his first session of therapy, which he also hopes will help him with his 'anger management issues'. He states that he is willing to engage in therapy but wants to ask you how old you are, what your beliefs are and how you feel therapy could help him.

As therapists, in our endeavour to illuminate the complexity of working with difference there are key questions which emerge immediately.

REFLECTION POINT 11.5 RESPONDING TO CLIENT ABOUT THERAPY AND DIFFERENCE

- What feelings come up for you?
- What do you notice about your and Akim's differences?
- Would you tell him about your beliefs?
- How would you communicate how therapy would help him?

There is a range of dynamics which becomes evident when sitting with Akim in the therapy room. Therapists, both trainee and experienced, may respond in a number of ways to challenging dynamics in the TR. Clearly, Akim is a client who challenges the therapeutic frame in many ways. We have heard the phrase 'working with a difficult client' on many occasions. We do not believe that there is a difficult client as such, because therapy is relational and it takes two parties. However, we appreciate that there can often be difficult processes within the therapeutic frame.

What is often meant, then, when therapists refer to a 'difficult client' is that the client has challenged the therapist and is somehow not conforming to the perception of the therapist's theoretical and therapeutic practice frame. It is in these moments that it is most helpful for therapists to extend their relational capacity.

EXTENDING OUR RELATIONAL CAPACITY

What do we mean by *extending the relational capacity?* This entails working towards a therapeutic engagement or any successful therapeutic outcomes by collaboratively working with the client through difficult and challenging processes. We need to consider our capacity to offer empathy, congruence/genuineness and UPR.

> Thinking about congruence implies difference. You cannot reflect on being congruent if you don't experience and consider diversity. If there was no difference, there would be no process and progress. (Schmid, 2001: 218)

In Akim's case, for example, in working with therapist–client religious and age differences, the therapist has to do more than just offer empathy, congruence and unconditional positive regard. There are evident differences between the therapist and client as well as wider social differences in belief systems, gender, age, inequality and injustice. There is also a difference evident in acculturation to the therapeutic process. It is clear that, as therapists, we often overlook that there are many clients who come to the therapy room who have no idea about how therapy works or what we are going to do in order to help them.

Therapists working with clients (such as Jo and Akim) need to be aware of the impact of cultural and socio-politico influences. And therapists need to be competent, demonstrating:

- Knowledge and understanding of how the particular context in which the therapist works impacts on the client–therapist relationship.
- Ability to work collaboratively with the client in exploring potential barriers to change or challenges when considering the client's social context.
- Ability to work with difficult and complex processes.
- Ability to help clients reflect on, develop and articulate their emotions, experiences and personal meanings.
- Ability to recognize and address their own prejudice.

These competencies ensure effective therapeutic practice with a client like Akim as they enable an opportunity to:

1. Approach particularly sensitive matters regarding issues of difference, such as religious beliefs, differences in gender, age, etc., within the therapeutic encounter.
2. Choose when to bring the sensitive issues to the client's awareness/therapeutic frame – a challenge too soon could result in a rupture of the TR, consequently resulting in the client dropping out.

Schmid (2004) explained that one way of working with such challenging dynamics is through working with therapist presence and immediacy. Each moment within the TR, whether there are difficult matters arising or not, is a moment of opportunity for a client–therapist meeting. Encounter means 'to meet the unexpected'. In many cases of working with difference, the unexpected may be to do with any of the dimensions we have focused on in this chapter (such as around issues of difference in race, gender, class, sexual orientation, disability, religion or age). To encounter another person first of all means recognizing that the other really 'stands counter', because he or she is essentially different from me (Schmid, 1998, 2004).

Working with difference, like any other skill, requires dedication and openness to taking risks and being willing to learn about ourselves and from our clients. It also requires a continual willingness to work even with clients/processes we would often consciously/unconsciously avoid because of fear of difference. Speight, Myers, Cox and Highlen (1991) used the terms 'emic' and 'etic' to postulate the assumption that when therapists have mastered skills of working with difference they will be effective multicultural therapists.

T

THEORY CLIP 11.4 ETIC AND EMIC APPROACH

The **etic approach**, developed by Vontress (1988), is an external or outsider's view on the client's beliefs and customs.It sees them as 'culturally universal'. The assumption, therefore, is that all clients should be treated the same in every setting regardless of their culture. The etic approach highlights the importance of focusing on the commonalities rather the differences between people

The **emic approach** is an insider's view about their own customs and beliefs. This view is more about seeing clients as 'culturally specific'. The emic view is based on the assumption that many factors can influence psychological disease, especially in regards to the client's culture (Sue and Sue, 2003).

When considering working with difference it is therefore important from the emic view to place importance on the emic and etic perspectives.

From a relational paradigm, it can therefore be stated that understanding the emic and etic is important for successful therapeutic practice. For when a client is accepted as an individual with needs like any other human being (etic), and also as a unique being with culture and difference (emic), then a TR that is relational and potentially growthful emerges.

Working with difference in this way ultimately aligns itself with an effective RA which empowers the client. We now explore relational competencies for the successful empowerment of clients.

EMPOWERMENT, RELATIONAL COMPETENCIES AND IMPLICATIONS FOR PRACTICE

As already explored, an underlying assumption of the RA is that the therapeutic encounter facilitates empowerment. Through a relationship that fosters positive changes, clients can start to be aware of their own power and potential as they become aware how their primary relationships and societal context had limited them.

In order to meet the relevant professional competences, as detailed in Chapter 4 and in this chapter, we propose the following considerations:

1. Therapists address the issue of power in the therapy room. This entails working collaboratively with clients rather than taking the expert position in which the therapists pathologize the client's experiences.
2. Therapists commit to working with the client's experiences that they may find challenging because of issues of difference.
3. Therapists gain knowledge about how oppressive '*isms*' (ageism, sexism, racism, etc.) within society impact on their clients and influence their own personal prejudices.
4. Therapists are open to develop further in cultural awareness.
5. Therapists use supervision to ensure that there is no inadvertent discrimination within the relationship due to a lack of self-awareness.
6. Therapists address their own assumptions and prejudices on a personal level (see Chapter 10).

We anticipate that, gaining further knowledge and skills to deal with the multi-faceted complexities of difference around the issues of race, gender, class, sexual orientation, disability, religion and age, as noted in this chapter, will enable therapists to be effective in their practice.

TABLE 11.2 Competencies relating to working with difference (adapted from Roth et al., 2009)

- Knowledge and understanding of how the particular context in which the therapist works impacts on the client–therapist relationship.
- Ability to work collaboratively with the client in exploring potential barriers to change or challenges when considering the client's social context.
- Ability to work with difficult and complex processes.
- Ability to help clients reflect on, develop and articulate their emotions, experiences and personal meanings.
- Ability to recognize and address own prejudice.

RESOURCE BOX 11

Lago, C. (ed.) (2011) *The Handbook of Transcultural Counselling & Psychotherapy.* Maidenhead: Open University Press.

Contains a wealth of information from different cultural heritage perspectives and theoretical orientations. All contributors focus on transcultural issues and anti-discriminatory practice, and how to best work with different clients in the TR.

Proctor, G. (2002) *The Dynamics of Power in Counselling and Psychotherapy: Ethics, Politics and Practice*. Ross-on-Wye: PCCS Books.

Explores issues of power in the therapeutic process.

CHAPTER SUMMARY

To help the reader to understand working with difference within the therapeutic relationship, this chapter has discussed the following:

- The relationship and society – how difference impacts on the therapeutic relationship when we consider race, gender, class, sexual orientation, disability, religion and age.
- Cross-cultural relationships and the challenge that can emerge in the therapeutic relationship.
- The importance of socio-cultural awareness and a therapist's openness and competence to work with difference.
- Transcultural approaches to therapy through the use of idiosyncratic responses, empathy, working with the proxy self and client identity development.
- Extending our relational capacities when working with challenging issues of difference.
- Empowerment in the relationship that fosters positive changes in clients and raises awareness of their own power and potential. This happens as they become aware how their primary relationships and societal context has limited them.
- Effective anti-oppressive practice through relational competencies for working with difference.

12

Developing your practice: A relational perspective

This aims of this final chapter are to introduce the reader to areas for practice development:

- Professional contexts.
- Statutory, voluntary and private practice contexts.
- Working online.
- Short-term approaches.
- Applying the relationship in other settings.
- Developments in theory and practice.
- Developing transtheoretical approaches.
- Mindfulness and neuroscience.
- CBT.

We conclude with:

- Criticisms of RA.
- Future directions in theory and practice.

PROFESSIONAL CONTEXTS

In this section we consider the practice of therapy in a number of different modes and settings. We then explore the use of the therapeutic relationship where the primary role of the practitioner is not that of a psychological therapist.

Statutory, voluntary and private practice contexts

Individuals access different services for therapy depending on their distress, need, age and societal setting. The availability of specific services within their area is a factor too. Given the diverse services, it is undoubtedly the case that the practice of therapy is context-dependent. There are many settings in which different therapeutic approaches are offered to clients. Each setting has different challenges and the interplay between the agency, type and length of therapy impacts on the therapeutic relationship.

NHS psychotherapy services

In the NHS, particular approaches may be used in different services. Currently in the UK, short-term and CBT approaches may be favoured. This presents a challenge for relational therapists.

Working within multidisciplinary teams can be complicated. In many services, data is recorded electronically and other professionals (such as psychiatrists, psychologists, care coordinators, mental health nurses) can access the notes. This means that the boundaries of confidentiality between therapist and client may be extended beyond the therapy session. Within the NHS, different system dynamics therefore impact on the therapeutic frame.

Voluntary agencies

The voluntary sector plays an important part in the therapeutic arena. It is dependent on limited funding and this impacts on service provision. A further consideration in the voluntary sector is its dependency on trainee and volunteer therapists. There are four key issues:

1. **Clarity about the interplay of the organization's setting, purpose and therapeutic relationship**: Volunteer therapists may work from different modalities. Quality of practice needs to be maintained regardless of model.
2. **Therapists' openness to clarify their way of working**: It is important that the organization and therapist work together in relation to assessment, length of therapy and frequency of sessions, particularly where different models of therapy are in operation in the same agency.
3. **Information governance**: Therapists have to be clear about what they do with data from their sessions with clients, for example information from assessments, session evaluations and any matters about risk to self or others.
4. **Working in partnership and need for referral to specialist services**: Where specialist services are required, therapists need to manage confidentiality, referral processes and referral paths.

Private practice

When working in private practice there are many challenges that therapists face. Within private practice, therapists have to be aware of the following issues:

1. Clear contract – frequency of meeting, cost of therapy.
2. Lone working – sometimes therapists are working alone and it is important for them to be clear about their policy on lone working as there are risks to consider as well as issues of potential allegations.
3. Insurance.
4. Power issues.
5. Complaints – how the therapist manages and deals with complaints and ruptures in the TR.
6. Issues of confidentiality.
7. Storage of client notes and the law on keeping client details on computers.
8. Advertising – ensuring that, as a therapist, you offer what you have advertised, and this is safeguarded by clear boundaries and contracting.
9. Managing payments and complexities if a client does not pay or states they forgot to bring some money.
10. Ethical practice and adhering to the professional body.
11. Keeping up CPD and supervision.
12. Procedures in place in the event of illness or death of therapist.

A specialist setting

Working in specialist settings, such as eating disorder, forensic or addiction units, presents different issues for the practitioner to work with. We illustrate this with an example of working in a forensic unit (Practitioner Clip 12.1).

P

PRACTITIONER CLIP 12.1 THE THERAPEUTIC RELATIONSHIP IN PROFESSIONAL SETTINGS – A FORENSIC EXAMPLE

I (Divine) have worked in a forensic mental health service with patients who were detained for committing serious offences and were also deemed mentally ill. The hospital in which I worked had very high security and strict regimes for the patients. Many of the patients I worked with presented with high risks to self and others. Some had committed murder or seriously harmed children. In working therapeutically with these clients, I faced many challenges which related to the context.

There are unique challenges in a forensic setting:

1. **The medicalization of criminality**: This is clearly a controversial issue because working with what are called rapists, paedophiles, murderers and

terrorists in a medical setting signals to them a degree of diminished responsibility because of mental illness (Pilgrim, 2005).

2. **Risk management**: A conflict exists in secure forensic settings between efforts by therapists to encourage responsible relational ways of working and third-party interests which ensure the security of others.
3. **Isolation and indefinite detention**: In forensic settings, there is isolation and the lack of the prospect of liberty affects mental wellbeing. This can also affect motivation to collaborate with the therapeutic goals explored in therapy.
4. **Dual roles, confidentiality and boundaries**: One of the major challenges in forensic settings is that the therapist is often engaged in dual roles: as a therapist and also as a guardian of the law, ensuring that any issues of risk to self or others or any criminal information that emerges is shared with the wider team. This therefore means that in contracting with confidentiality, the boundaries of the therapy must be clear.

In the different therapeutic contexts, it is therefore clear that attention must be paid to:

- Professional role and the relationship
- Ethics and responsibilities
- Dual roles, confidentiality and boundaries
- Awareness of professional and statutory issues

DEVELOPING YOUR PRACTICE IN WORKING ONLINE

> In a few years, it will seem strange to imagine that once our only option to get therapeutic support was to travel to a set location, finding time and transport, making arrangements at home to ensure we could attend. Rather, this model will be one option amongst many, and people will also have access to a range of support online, with many options for therapy available. (Hyatt, 2014: 19)

Here, Hyatt clearly puts forward emerging ideas about how the development of online work is becoming accepted as one of the forms in which therapy is offered to clients. Different authors have shared ideas about how virtual space therapeutic work (anything occurring online, from emails to avatars) presents therapists with both benefits and challenges.

Benefits of online and virtual space working

Sand (2007) argued that as therapists we need to develop and expand our ways of working with these new forms of communicating. Otherwise we risk our profession becoming stagnant and outdated as we lose the interactive richness of what will be an integral part of our clients' experience. From the perspective of considering what matters for the client, Wright (2002) noted the advantages in working online and through texts, stating that it can be less shaming for clients who require therapy for issues such as abuse, and so on. The pace and focus of the work is within the client's control, and this can be attractive to some clients.

P

PRACTITIONER CLIP 12.2 SUPERVISION ONLINE

I (Divine) have been involved in some work with international organizations, offering supervision to therapists and psychologists working in countries with victims of war. Working a few times a month with these different professionals has highlighted the benefits of working online, such as the ability to access therapeutic services from remote locations.

Challenges of online and virtual space working

The following issues are challenges that need to be considered when working online and in virtual space (Weitz, 2014):

1. Jurisdiction – UK law may not apply in some countries and it would be illegal to do therapy or supervision with clients in that country online (see Anthony et al., 2014).
2. Choice of software, methods of encryption and record keeping.
3. The absence of visual cues and complexity of language (Charura, 2014).
4. Challenges in ensuring confidentiality and managing ethical dilemmas.
5. Challenges in assessment, contracting, boundaries, and so on.
6. The dynamics of the work itself, for example, relational issues.
7. When working through video platforms, delayed responses due to connection problems.

(Adapted from Weitz, 2014)

In order to combat this, different authors have suggested ways of working in order to help therapists develop their practice and to be effective.

Maintaining online boundaries

Lago and Wright (2006) have identified key points which are useful in understanding and adopting this relational principle to practice:

1. Have clear boundaries and contracting by informing the client that their message will be responded to at a specific time each week.
2. Set aside an hour (in the same way as you would for face-to-face practice) when engaging in online work. This helps in maintaining traditional boundaries.
3. Spend time carefully composing and reflecting on your replies to the client concerns that need addressing before sending your response.

Importance of language

When working in new media it is extremely important for therapists to choose their language carefully. Charura (2014) stated how meaning can easily be lost, so the therapist really needs to take time in responding, particularly when working asynchronously, that is, in emails or by text. The therapist needs to use language that describes their process openly and that gives the client a visual image of the therapist's process (Charura, 2014). An example, when working via email, in responding to a client's email, the therapist may respond in a way that gives the client a visual image of the therapists body movements, i.e.

> … I have read your email again and even though you stated you are coping I got a sense that you are feeling deeply hurt by the break-up of your relationship. … I find myself reading over and over again the paragraph in which you wrote that you feel that there are people in the world who experience worse things. I have now started looking outside my window thinking how I might respond as I can imagine how 'cut-up' you are right now…

Adlington (2010) highlighted the importance of building rapport when working online through the use of language. He suggested ways in which therapists can work effectively with clients through language without the aid of visual clues. He noted basic skills such as matching the client's language. For example, where a client starts an email with *Hayal…*, or with *Dear so and so…*, then the therapist should match the client's use of language by responding with a parallel reply which also starts with *Hayal…*, or with *Dear so and so*….. Adlington (2010) advised that therapists should be aware that when they respond, a client may no longer be in crisis, as when they initially made contact. It is therefore important to use language that enables clients to re-engage with their process.

A relational approach to working online

As we have seen in this section, working online presents different challenges. A RA can make the work more effective. The therapist can adopt the relational assumptions that we outlined in Chapter 4. We have tailored these to be specific to working online, and they include the following:

- The therapist endeavours to enter into a real relationship with the client rather than seeing it as a therapist to email or virtual world relationship.
- The therapist knows that relational difficulties are likely to come to the fore through the virtual medium as the work develops.
- This relates to the fact that the therapist is aware that clients' difficulties may be relational even if the story they are telling and the words they are using appear to have no other people in it. This is a very important relational underlying principle to understand, especially when working with avatars and other platforms in which clients adopt a personality (such as in *Second Life* forums, etc.).

A RA to working online therefore enhances our capacity as therapists to have meaningful and effective therapeutic relationships.

SHORT-TERM WORK

P

PRACTITIONER CLIP 12.3 SHORT-TERM THERAPY IN PRACTICE

I (Divine) have worked in NHS and voluntary settings where short-term therapy is now required due to limitations in funding and due to long waiting lists. In such work, the therapist has to be competent in developing and maintaining the therapeutic relationship in a short space of time. By the end of the therapy clients and employers expect successful therapy outcomes.

Short-term therapy is based on a specific time scale and is limited. Typically, short-term work is 6–12 sessions. In Chapter 4 we looked at the principles, assumptions and competencies of a RA and in Chapters 6 and 7 we explored in-depth how to develop and maintain the relationship.

REFLECTION POINT 12.1 COMPETENCIES FOR SHORT-TERM THERAPY

- What are the essential competencies for short-term work?

The application of short-term therapy frequently involves assessing the client's problem(s) in collaboration with the client. In some modalities, such as CBT and psychodynamic approaches, this also includes a collaborative approach to the formulation and development of short-term goals.

Appropriate relational competencies will enable the TR to be developed, strengthened and maintained while the client and therapist work on the goals. It is essential that the therapist has the ability to help the client to reflect on and develop and articulate their emotions, experiences and personal meanings.

As the sessions near the end, it is important for the therapists to be competent in endings. As we have seen in Chapter 9, it is the therapist who must take responsibility for the preparation of endings.

In short-term therapy, evaluation of sessions during or at the end of therapy is an important part of the process. The therapist needs to work collaboratively with the client in this evaluation process. In some settings, evaluation tools such as CORE (Clinical Outcomes in Routine Evaluation) or the PHQ9 (Patient Health Questionnaire) may be used.

In summary, the following factors are key ingredients to a successful outcome:

1. Setting clear assessment criteria.
2. Working to a clear formulation and goals set by the second session.
3. Maintaining a collaborative approach to therapy and to the client–therapist relationship.
4. Therapist competency in using specific tools for those settings in which tools are used for interventions (i.e. thought diaries in CBT) or as evaluation tools.
5. Competency in planning and ending the therapeutic relationship.

THE RELATIONSHIP IN ROLES AND SETTINGS IN WHICH THERAPY IS NOT THE FUNCTIONAL ROLE OF THE PRACTITIONER

There are many professionals who work with clients in a non-therapy context, where psychological therapy is not their functional role and their work has a therapeutic component. In education, health care and social care, where the relationship is central, research now indicates the importance of creating and maintaining a good TR (for example, see Freshwater, 2003).

The following elements are helpful in working with clients in these settings:

1. **Empathy**: It is vital for professionals to make efforts to understand their clients' experiences and to demonstrate this understanding through responses which address the client needs (Elliott et al., 2011).
2. **Unconditional positive regard**: In working with clients in any setting, often Rogers' notion of positive regard is illuminated. Rogers posed two questions: 'Do we tend to treat individuals as persons of worth, or do we subtly devaluate them by our attitudes and behaviour? Is our philosophy one in which respect for the individual is uppermost?' (Rogers, 1951: 20). Through this description, Rogers referred to an attitude of respecting our clients and we believe this is essential in any professional relationship.

3. **Congruence**: This quality enables clients to be engaged in an authentic relationship in which they can see that they are engaged in a professional relationship with someone who is not hiding behind a professional façade. There is an endeavour to help and be in a human-to-human encounter. Being 'real' with each other facilitates trust and communication (Rogers, 1961).
4. **Developing rapport**: As we have seen in Chapter 6, developing rapport is key to any successful therapeutic encounter.

C

CLIENT CLIP 11.1 THE CLIENT AS A PERSON

When first working in a secure psychiatric unit in the 1970s as a trainee, I (Steve) was the only staff member not to be attacked by a particularly disturbed patient. He said to me: 'I like you. You see me as a person... not as a patient... with a disorder.'

Trisha Greenhalgh, a GP commissioned to do research into the TR by the King's Fund in the UK, notes:

> Think about your own relationship with your general practitioner (GP). What would you score that relationship on a scale of one to ten, and why? What about your relationship with your practice nurse, counsellor, receptionist, health care assistant, alternative practitioner, and so on? Again, give it a score, and then say why you feel this relationship ranks as high, middle, or low quality.
>
> One of us (TG) did this – not as a scientific exercise, but to see what came up. I would rate my GP nine out of ten for the TR (though I have no idea what she scores on official assessments, such as the Quality and Outcomes Framework or General Practice Patient Survey).
>
> I like her. She is always welcoming. She listens and empathises. When I was pregnant and anxious after some minor complications, she took time to reveal the sound of my unborn baby's heart to me. That 'baby' is now at university and she still asks after him. She is knowledgeable and skilled, but also honest when she is unsure. She saw me through a difficult bereavement. When I was exhausted after an operation, she politely refused to sign me back to work. Whenever I attend for a problem, she deals with that first before offering me 'opportunistic' checks flagged by the computer. I am sure she has never told anyone anything that has come up in the consulting room. My only criticism is that because she's so popular, it's hard to get an appointment with her. (Greenhalgh and Heath, 2010: 4)

TABLE 12.1 Competencies in relation to the professional context (adapted from Roth et al., 2009)

- Knowledge and understanding of a RA, mental health problems, and the ability to understand and employ the model in practice.
- Ability to undertake relevant assessment (relevant history and to identify suitability for therapy).
- Ability to foster, maintain and develop a good therapeutic relationship in the here-and-now.
- Ability to work collaboratively with the client, understanding their experience and their worldview.
- Ability to work with difficult and complex processes.
- Ability to respond non-defensively to feedback.
- Ability to recognize limitations in professional practice.

DEVELOPMENTS IN THEORY AND PRACTICE

In this section we explore further developing a transtheoretical relational model, CBT within a relational paradigm, and mindfulness in therapeutic practice

Developing transtheoretical approaches

Clarkson (1995, 2003) proposed an integrative, transtheoretical approach to therapy. She postulated that there are five dimensions or modes in the TR (Figure 12.1). At any one time in therapy one dimension comes to the fore while the others remain

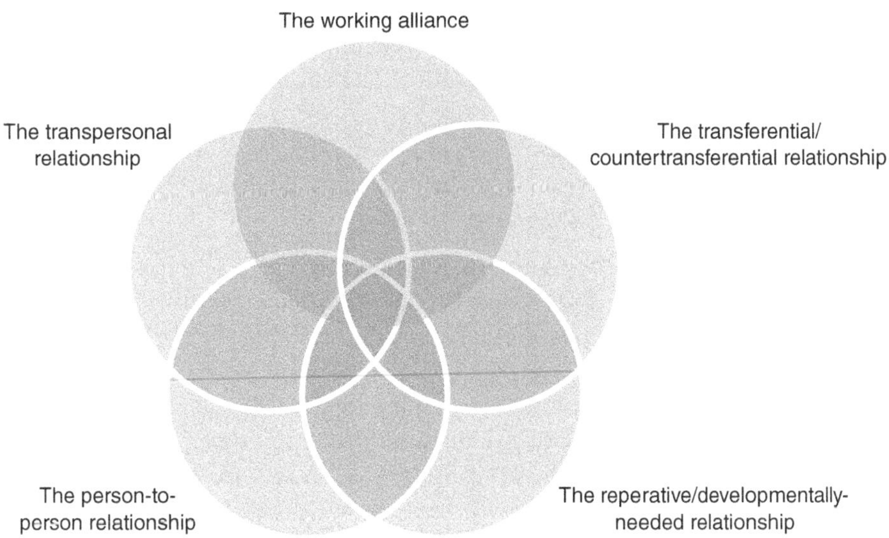

FIGURE 12.1 Clarkson's embedded relational matrix

in the background. For her, it is the relationship that transforms not the model: 'The work lies in the creative space between, in the relationship' (Clarkson, 1995: xiii). This matrix offers insights into the relationship from different perspectives. There are five primary relationship modes present in every relationship:

The working alliance is the mode in which the client and therapist make contact and contract to work together. It waxes and wanes in strength during the course of therapy and may be tested by the client. Clients and therapists vary in their ability to form a strong working alliance. Rogers' therapeutic conditions facilitate the development of the working alliance. It is important to provide clear boundaries for the work of therapy to take place.

The transferential/countertransferential relationship is the mode in which unconscious fears or wishes impact the relationship. For Clarkson, it is the mode that is perhaps most extensively written about and is an essential part of the psychoanalytic process. It can be variably utilized in any model of practice. She differentiates between the classical psychoanalytic transference (1995: 68) versus transference phenomena which manifest and can be addressed in all models of therapy. For Clarkson, transference is 'everywhere', as can be seen in the *Gloria* films (Shostrom, 1965).

It is important to be mindful that transference attitudes lead to transference relationships (Rogers, 1951) and working in this way may be a function of the analyst's pathology. In other words, we find what we look for.

The reparative/developmentally-needed relationship is the mode through which a corrective, healing interaction is played out. The therapist provides the opportunity for the client to work through previous deficiencies or trauma. The client goes back to (or regresses to) that part of their psyche which is somehow stuck in a past experience. This becomes their reality and, in therapy, they work it through. Alexander et al. (1946: 18) call this process a 'Corrective emotional experience'.

The person-to-person relationship is the real human relationship between both parties. This might be called existential relating or the I–Thou authentic relating. This relationship is characterized by 'Autonomous, separate, independent here-and-now feelings and emotions' (Clarkson, 1995: 159). There may be a difficult transition from the developmentally needed/reparative relationship to this mode of relating. This is the deep insight of Fairbairn (1952) and the existential bond of Boss (1963). As Gelso and Carter (1985: 186–7) note: 'The real relationship exists in all therapies … alongside of and intermingled with the "unreal" or transference relationship.' This mode of relating often does not occur until in the later stages of therapy.

The transpersonal relationship is considered the egoless, perhaps spiritual, dimension of human contact:

> Implied is a letting go of skills, of knowledge, of experience, of pre-conceptions, even of the desire to heal. … It is essentially allowing passivity. … It cannot be made to happen, it can only be encouraged in the same way that the inspirational muse of creativity cannot be forced. … What can be prepared are the conditions conducive to the spontaneous or spiritual act. (Clarkson, 1995: 20)

For Clarkson, the unconscious of the client and therapist meet and synergetically interact. She compares it to the space between *Temenos* (Adler, 1979) and what Rogers called a deeper reality beyond the senses (Van Belle, 1980). At this mode of meeting, healing and transformation can happen spontaneously. Clarkson's matrix is presented in Figure 12.1.

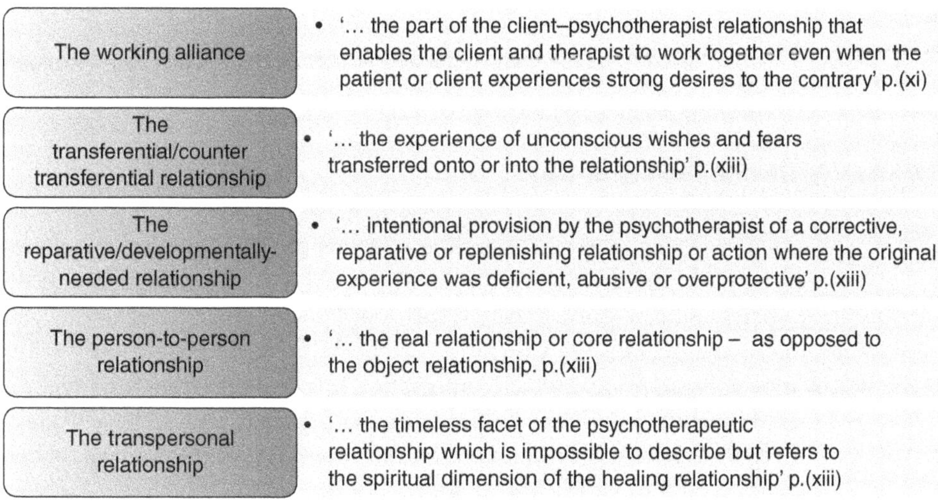

FIGURE 12.2 Dimensions of the therapeutic relationship (Clarkson, 1995)

In the matrix shown in Figure 12.1.

- All modes overlap and interlink.
- They are states not stages.
- When one figures the others form the ground.
- It is a fractal rather than a whole. Each mode is unique, a layer or dimension yet forming part of the whole relational dynamic.
- Different modes can come to the fore or overlap any time in the therapy, even during one session. Modes may even jostle with each other.
- The therapist focuses on the actual relationship with the client and works with each presenting mode to address the client's unique needs.

There are real challenges to the practitioner in working in this way. However, Clarkson's matrix does give the practitioner insight into different dimensions of the relationship which may be present at the same time.

Clarkson's model offers a different insight into and experience of the therapeutic process. She integrates theory and offers a holistic model of the dimensions of the therapeutic relationship which gives relational therapists a coherent template to work transtheoretically.

REFLECTION POINT 12.2 THE CHALLENGES OF CLARKSON'S MATRIX

Clarkson's matrix enables therapists to make sense of work with complex theory across models.

- What might be the challenges and opportunities in working in this way?

Developments in CBT

As a result of research into short-term approaches to therapy, there has been a demand in the UK for therapists to practise CBT in the NHS and other settings. There has been much debate (House and Loewenthal, 2008) about whether short-term and goal-focused therapies are philosophically or ethically compatible with interpersonal and relational approaches. It is quite possible for a relational therapist (if they wish) to work with these forms of therapy, although, as we saw in Chapter 2, there is no clear evidence of better outcomes. We look at elements of working in this way in this section.

Relational Frame Theory and Acceptance and Commitment Therapy

Relational Frame Theory (RFT) of CBT is an approach in which all language and thoughts are dependent on deriving relations among and from events (relational frames). The environment is seen to contain stimulus functions that are dependent on relational frames. RFT therefore seeks a broader understanding of cognition by having a wider scope of focus on developmental, contextual and behavioural links to client experience/presentation. This fits with a relational paradigm, as we have noted throughout this book.

Acceptance and Commitment Therapy (ACT) is one example of further development of CBT and is based on RFT. It was developed by Hayes, Strosahl and Wilson (1999). ACT uses acceptance and mindfulness strategies to help clients to manage psychological distress. It differs from traditional CBT in that instead of trying to teach people to control their thoughts, feelings and experiences, clients are encouraged to be aware of their experiencing, to 'just notice' and accept their private cognitions, especially the previously unwanted ones. The key assumptions of ACT are that psychological processes of what may be called 'normal' are often destructive.

Such psychological distress is caused by experiential avoidance, cognitive entanglement and consequent psychological rigidity in the client (Wills and Sanders, 2013). This leads to the client failing to take the necessary behavioural steps which are congruent with their core values and beliefs. When working with clients, this may manifest as avoidance of what the individual is experiencing and reason-giving or excuses for behaviour. Psychological distress is therefore the product of this incongruence between the client's values/beliefs and their behaviour.

ACT and RFT are a further development of CBT and are commonly recognized as part of **Third Wave CBT** (Wills and Sanders, 2013). Within 'Third Wave CBT' different techniques, which include mindfulness, meditation and the two chair technique, are all designed to help clients relate to their own thinking process in the present moment.

Wills and Sanders (2013) stated that at the core, third wave therapies are about changing the client's relationship to thoughts and experience through acceptance, compassion and mindfulness.

Guided Discovery through Socratic dialogue

Another intervention in CBT which has been noted as effective is **Guided Discovery** (GD). GD is a series of interventions using **Socratic questioning** (Wills and Sanders, 2013). A GD sequence in CBT is based on a common four-sequence process:

1. Asking informational questions to uncover information outside the client's awareness.
2. Accurate listening and empathic reflection.
3. Summarizing information discovered.
4. Asking synthesizing questions that help apply the new information discussed to the client's original thought or belief.

Table 12.2 provides some examples of Socratic questions.

A therapist can offer their client the possibility of discovering or rediscovering their own internal natural tendencies to make positive life choices. Socratic questioning and Guided Discovery may, with care, therefore be explored relationally.

TABLE 12.2 Examples of Socratic questions (Wills and Sanders, 2013)

- What things do you think you could change to make the situation different?
- What would you do differently another time?
- How does thinking that make you feel right now?
- How might we check that out?
- Is there an alternative way of dealing with it?
- What do you conclude from this weighing up?

Mindfulness and the impact of the therapeutic relationship

Mindfulness as a practice originally emerged out of ancient Buddhist meditation traditions. An operational working definition of mindfulness is: 'the awareness that emerges through paying attention on purpose, in the present moment, and non-judgmentally to the unfolding of experience moment by moment' (Kabat-Zinn, 2001: 145).

Kabat-Zinn pioneered work on the use of mindfulness in stress reduction practice (MBSR). He integrated Buddhist meditation in group work in order to help participants (patients with a wide range of physical and psychological problems) to manage their stress, pain or illness. Following the success of MBSR, Segal, Williams and Teasdale (2002) pioneered the use of mindfulness as a therapeutic tool in CBT. They developed an in-depth understanding of why clients who have received treatment and therapy for depression relapse after effective treatment. They argued that relapsing into depression was a result of the relationship between the person and their thinking (Wills and Sanders, 2013). From this, it was formulated that the client's attempts to avoid unwanted moods, thoughts, difficult bodily sensation or experiences only creates secondary suffering and additional layers of problems (Segal et al., 2002). Furthermore, Kabat-Zinn (2004) argued that avoidance reduces the ability to respond effectively to difficult experiences because it takes one away from the qualities of kindness, compassion and interest, all of which hold the potential for literally changing our minds and experience. Given this research, the concluding suggestions were that the ability to connect with all subjective experiences, however difficult, is positively related to good therapeutic outcome (Wills and Sanders, 2013). The implications of mindfulness to therapeutic practice are that the client experiences everything in their awareness rather than ruminating on default narrative patterns which may be negative or unhelpful.

We therefore advocate the importance of positive empathic responses and valuing the exploration of direct experiencing as it enables the client to discover a different way of being to the negative default they may be used to. This consequently fosters change in clients.

Neuroscientific research also supports mindfulness within the TR. As clients learn to be *mindful* and to experience their senses and subjective experiences in each present moment, new neuro-pathways and networks are activated or formed

(Farb et al., 2007). This links to another relational basic assumption that the TR offers the right conditions for healing and transformation (see Chapter 4).

It is now widely accepted that mindfulness and acceptance-based CBT focus on working with the client to move towards experience rather than trying to control or change it (Wills and Sanders, 2013). We can see how this, rather than symptom control, corresponds with relational perspectives of not pathologizing, and of entering a real human-to-human relationship which provides a space for the client to explore the meaning of their subjective experience.

T

THEORY CLIP 12.1 NEUROSCIENCE AND UNDERSTATING THE REPARATIVE IMPACT OF THERAPY

Throughout this book we have seen how neuroscience has been increasingly developing and enabling us to understand the neurological and reparative impact of the therapeutic relationship. We have also seen in this chapter how mindfulness has become one of the practices that has been developed as a result of research. Neuroscientific research is beginning to demonstrate a correlation between the therapeutic relationship and successful personality and physiological change.

New research in mindfulness (e.g. Farb et al., 2007) demonstrates the importance of learning to be mindful in the here-and-now and experiencing the senses and subjective experiences in each present moment. As a result, new neural pathways and networks are activated or formed. By offering empathy, unconditional positive regard and acceptance, these changes will take place, thereby affecting not only the client's subjective experience over time, but also their neurone physiology.

From traditional CBT to third-wave relational CBT

T

THEORY CLIP 12.2 NEW DEVELOPMENTS IN CBT AND IMPLICATIONS OF THE RELATIONAL PARADIGM

1. Further developments in behavioural activation approaches (Martell et al., 2001; Richards, 2010).

   When considering a relational perspective in this approach, the focus in this way of working is on therapists not making assumptions or interpreting what behaviours might prove rewarding for the client. Wills and Sanders (2013) stress

(Continued)

(Continued)

that, rather, the therapist should work in collaboration with the client in order to explore what cognitions and behaviours are affecting their life and how they make sense of their current and past relational patterns.

2. The emergence of a set of acceptance and mindfulness interventions, which focus on helping clients to move towards experience rather than trying to control or change it (Hayes et al., 1999; Linehan, 1993).
3. Further appreciation and consideration of the importance of the therapeutic relationship in CBT. Examples include particular new developments in understanding how the reinforcement and reward process can facilitate the therapeutic relationship (Tsai et al., 2009).

(after Wills and Sanders, 2013)

In summary:

1. A RA to CBT needs to focus on a collaborative approach and on the therapist's use of self as the ultimate tool for facilitating change.
2. Conceptualizations and formulations will be explored in the therapeutic frame context relating client experiences and responses not only to their environment but also to the client–therapist relationship.
3. Rather than pathologizing the client, their behaviours are seen as a creative adjustment to earlier patterns of relating in primary relationships. The therapist needs to be competent in working collaboratively with the client, understanding their experiences, cognitions, behaviours and 'worldview'.
4. The therapist needs to help the client to reflect on and develop and further articulate their cognitions, emotions, experiences and personal meanings. Guided Discovery through Socratic questioning is one way of doing this.
5. There is a movement in working with the client to progress towards experience, as evidenced by further developments, rather than trying to control or change their experience (i.e. Mindfulness-Based Cognitive Therapy (MBCT), Acceptance and Commitment Therapy (ACT).

Through a RA to CBT, the client learns that their difficulties are not pathologized as faulty thinking, but rather are seen as a creative adjustment to social and relational contexts. With this understanding, the client works towards change by working through their experience and relational patterns. They use the therapeutic relationship as a reparative nourishing relationship rather than an interaction to experiment with the best ways of controlling or changing their experience.

CRITICAL PERSPECTIVES ON A RELATIONAL APPROACH

All approaches to therapy, by their nature, are an attempt to conceptualize, using language and cognitive concepts, human nature and the human psyche and, as such, may be limited in their capacity. Additionally, a RA is a fairly recent and developing paradigm. Criticisms of different models of relational therapy may be:

- The model is theoretically complex and confusing.
- The model is difficult to define methodologically and operationally.
- The model seeks to marry conflicting theories.
- The model does not use a coherent language.
- Eclecticism: the model does not operate as a theoretical, coherent whole but invites a pick-and-mix approach of techniques and concepts.
- Shifting modes of practice may be unhelpful to clients.
- The therapeutic frame may not be clearly maintained.

We have in this book drawn from research and theory to present a clearly defined RA. We said in Chapter 3 that this was a book on *a* relational approach as opposed to *the* relational approach. We have set out key concepts for a relational paradigm and have drawn from a range of models to illustrate theory and practice. As Pelham (2008) noted, the notion of a paradigm rather than an approach is more fitting to describe the position of relational therapeutic concepts in contemporary therapy (Paul and Pelham, 2000). A paradigm (Kuhn, 1962) is not a unified theory or model, but rather a set of basic assumptions that allow for a variety of concepts, approaches and practices.

Within the relational paradigm, perspectives have been taken on various aspects of the psychological development of the person and the implications of this for the TR (Clarkson, 1995; Mitchell, 1988, 2000). An example of the differences from the psychoanalytic modality are given in Theory Clip 12.3.

T

THEORY CLIP 12.3 DIFFERING PSYCHOANALYTIC PERSPECTIVES ON A RA

- Some writers (Kohut, 1984; Stolorow et al., 1987; Winnicott, 1965) propose a 'developmental arrest' position, i.e. that the growth of the client has been interrupted in childhood, and that the aim of therapy is to provide the environment that will address this deficit. This involves working towards the growth needs of the client.
- Other therapists explore the notion of 'relational needs' (Erskine et al., 1999).
- Others, such as Ehrenberg (1992), focus on an interpersonal stance. They argue that the therapeutic relationship is co-created in the present moment by the client and therapist and that therapeutic change comes through exploration of that relationship in the here-and-now.

Given the examples in Theory Clip 12.3, the account offered in this book is not a fixed model; rather it is a way of conceptualizing and drawing upon the resources of the wider relational paradigm.

It is quite possible to practise *a* core model of relational therapy, as outlined in Chapters 3 and 4, and use theory from differing modalities to contextualize our practice. We expect that this will differ from practitioner to practitioner.

Having said this, we wish, however, to advise caution to individual practitioners and trainers, who draw from the body of knowledge to suit their own interests and needs. An approach to therapy which works with a fluid living relationship needs to be grounded in a clear conceptualization of model, method and practice. As De Young (2003) suggested, there is potential for much eclectic practice within relational approaches.

While we and other relational theorists do not advocate one way to practise, we caution against a *pick-and-mix* eclecticism in practice.

P

PRACTITIONER CLIP 12.4 ECLECTICISM OR COHERENCE

I (Steve) have on occasion seen therapists for supervision who say, for example, that they are person-centred or relational. In the course of supervision they talk about 'using CBT this week' or 'I worked in a person-centred way in the last session'.

While this is not a common occurrence, it seems to be the case for therapists whose training is lacking in a solid philosophical and theoretical base. It is of course quite practicable for a relational therapist to practise CBT, or to practise according to person-centred principles, for example. We do advise therapists to develop practice based on a clear philosophical perspective and theoretical model which is consistent and coherent.

FUTURE DIRECTIONS IN THEORY AND PRACTICE

Personal reflection

I (Steve) once worked in Bhutan and would walk over mountain passes from one valley to another to visit different staff in their projects. Local villagers would say to me 'Watch out for the people in the next valley, they will poison you.'

With roads, electricity, education and the internet reaching further and further across the globe, how we make sense of each other and how we operate as human beings is changing and developing: 'Today, after more than a century of electric technology, we have extended our central nervous system in a global embrace, abolishing both space and time as far as our planet is concerned' (McLuhan, 1964: 3).

As the world we live in moves closer and closer to the 'global village' envisioned by Marshall McLuhan in the 1960s, the differences between people diminish and common languages and concepts are shared. Psychology has similarly moved a long way from the times of Freud, Skinner and even Maslow. In this new era there is a move to relating, commonality and, in many ways away, from the sectarianism of the past. However, the psychological therapies are subject to economic and political pressure.

While attempts to foresee the future of therapy are likely to be confounded, we believe we can predict:

- The development of relational therapies and relational approaches in established therapies with more understanding of the effective components of the TR.
- More accurate research methodologies which are less susceptible to bias.
- Developments in research (including neuroscience) which detail what goes on during, in and post therapy.

Out of this research, we do expect therapists to be able to practise more effectively and collaboratively with their clients.

RESOURCE BOX 12

THERAPY IN DIFFERENT SETTINGS

Barger-Charleson, S. and Van Rijin, B. (2011) *Counselling and Psychotherapy Practice: Understanding Assessment in Counselling and Psychotherapy*. Exeter: Learning Matters.

Explores aspects of assessment.

Freshwater, D. (2003) *Counselling Skills for Nurses, Midwives and Health Visitors*. Buckingham: Open University Press.

Applying therapeutic skills in health settings.

Harvey, J. and Smedley, K. (2010) *Psychological Therapy in Prisons and Other Settings*. Cullompton, UK and New York: Willan Publishing.

Examines a range of therapeutic approaches used in prisons and other secure settings and explores the challenges in such work.

(Continued)

(Continued)

Hemming, A. and Field, R. (2007) *Counselling and Psychotherapy in Contemporary Private Practice*. Hove: Routledge

Focuses on managing the dilemmas faced by therapists in private practice and their impact on the TR.

McLeod, J. and McLeod, J. (2011) *Counselling Skills: A Practical Guide for Counsellors and Helping Professionals*. New York: McGraw-Hill.

An excellent book for health and social care professionals with chapters on skills, dual relationships and the therapeutic relationship.

WORKING ONLINE

Weitz, P. (ed.) (2014) *Psychotherapy 2.0: Where Psychotherapy and Technology Meet*. London: Karnac Books.

Incorporates chapters which explore the benefits and challenges of working online.

DEVELOPING TRANSTHEORETICAL APPROACHES

Clarkson, P. (2003) *The Therapeutic Relationship* (2nd edn). London: Whurr.

In-depth description of her model.

CBT

Dryden, W. and Branch, R. (ed.) (2012) *The CBT Handbook*. London: Sage.

Wills, F. and Sanders, D. (2013) *Cognitive Behaviour Therapy: Foundations for Practice*. London: Sage.

These two books explain the central concepts of CBT and its new developments. They illustrate with numerous case examples how to put these concepts into practice.

Segal, Z.V., Williams, J.M.G. and Teasdale, J.D. (2002) *Mindfulness-Based Cognitive Therapy for Depression: A New Approach to Preventing Relapse*. New York: Guilford Press.

This book is a good introduction to mindfulness-based CBT interventions when working with depression.

NEUROSCIENCE

Cozolino, L. (2010) *The Neuroscience of Psychotherapy: Healing the Social Brain* (2nd edn). New York: W.W. Norton.

Research findings and theories in neuroscience.

FUTURE DEVELOPMENTS IN PSYCHOLOGY AND THERAPY

Charura, D. and Paul, S. (eds) (2014) *The Therapeutic Relationship Handbook: Theory and Practice*. Maidenhead: Open University Press.

Explores and develops many of the themes in this book.

Frisch, S., Hinshelwood, R.D. and Gauthier, J.M. (eds) (2001) *Psychoanalysis and Psychotherapy: The Controversies and the Future*. London: Karnac.
Debates on the future developments in psychoanalysis.

House, R., Kulich, D. and Maidman, J. (eds) (2013) *The Future of Humanistic Psychology*. Ross-on-Wye: PCCS Books.
An edited book with a number of forward-looking chapters from many leaders in the field.

CHAPTER SUMMARY

To help the reader to understand how the RA can develop your practice, in this chapter we outlined and discussed the following:

- Working therapeutically in statutory, voluntary, private practice and a specialist setting.
- The factors involved with working online and short-term approaches.
- Applying the relationship settings in which the functional role of the practitioner is not a therapist.
- A transtheoretical approach which enables the relationship to be explored from a number of different dimensions.
- Working relationally with CBT and new developments such as Third Wave CBT, including ACT and mindfulness.

We concluded with:

- Key criticisms of the RA.
- Future directions in theory and practice.

Glossary

Actualizing tendency Innate movement towards realizing one's full potential.

Agape Selfless love towards another.

Authenticity Being true to and living from one's own self, despite external conditions.

Behaviourism A modality which is deterministic and assumes that people's behaviour and self-concept is entirely controlled by their environment and their prior learning. The 'second force' in psychology.

Common factors The core factors that research has found to be effective in all forms of therapy, regardless of theoretical model. These include extratherapeutic change, hope/expectancy, model or technique and the therapeutic relationship. The TR is considered to be the most powerful in-therapy factor.

Conditions of worth As the child develops, they learn that some behaviours attract more positive regard than others. When they actively choose or avoid a self-experience because of the need for positive regard they are said to have acquired a condition of worth.

Configurations of self A 'configuration' is a construct made up of a pattern of feelings, thoughts and behavioural responses which represent to the person different aspects or parts of their self.

Congruence The ability to be present, open and genuine in relationship with the client.

Consensual validation Comparing our experience with the feedback of others through interpersonal therapy.

Containment Therapist's ability to work and maintain the therapeutic frame with whatever the client brings.

Core model The coherent theoretical discipline the practitioner works from, for example, psychodynamic, Gestalt, cognitive-behavioural, psychosynthesis.

Countertransference This is the process by which an individual is stimulated by the behaviour of their client and responds personally from their own material.

Dasein Literally meaning *being there*, to be truly present with another.

Dodo effect Relates to the idea of psychotherapeutic equivalence – that all psychotherapies are equally effective regardless of modality. It originates from Lewis Carroll's *Alice's Adventures in Wonderland* where the Dodo said after a race, 'Everybody has won and all must have prizes.'

Drive theory Relates to the idea that humans are born with particular psychological needs and that human functioning is based upon the interaction of drives and forces within the person. A negative state of tension is created when these needs are not met.

Eclectic A mix of theory and practice drawn from a range of models of therapy.

Eclecticism A multi-modal approach to working effectively with clients. It mainly refers to the drawing on of a range of different techniques to get the best result for the client.

Ego Is the sense of our conscious '*I*' which regulates our inner drives and our social self.

Emic approach An approach based on the unique insider's perspective and customs and beliefs; a 'culturally-specific' way of relating with others.

Empathy The ability to enter the perceptual world of the client and have an accurate understanding of that perceived reality.

Etic approach An approach based on an outsider's view of another and seeing them as 'culturally universal'. The assumption, therefore, is that all should be treated in the same way in every setting regardless of their culture. It is critiqued as a dominant, likely Eurocentric, perspective.

Eurocentricism Focused on Europe or European/western people's ideas concepts and values.

Existentialism A philosophical school of thought that proposes that the personal meaning of life is central to existence and that there is no objective ultimate Truth.

Existential-humanistic A modality of psychotherapy which focuses on individual responsibility and self-determination. The existential-humanistic therapist is typically engaged in helping the client take responsibility for their situation and operates as a catalyst for growth. A term for the 'third force' in psychology including incorporating both humanistic and existential psychologies.

Frame of reference The perspective an individual has of their reality.

Fully-functioning person A state of psychological adjustment when all conditions of worth are dissolved or removed. The individual is living fully in the moment.

Guided Discovery A process that a therapist uses to help the client reflect on the way that they process information. The therapist asks the client Socratic questions which enable the client to reflect on their thinking processes.

Humanistic Associated with humanistic psychology, the 'third force' in psychology concerned with personal growth and self-actualisation.

I–Thou relationship Buber's concept of the I–Thou relationship relates to a way of being in the therapeutic relationship. It is essentially about a human-to-human relationship in which there is a process of authentic encounter and dialogue.

Id The Freudian *unconscious*; senses and thoughts below the surface of our awareness; the id is the home of our instinctual drives.

Idiosyncratic empathy Empathic responses that are unique to an individual client.

Incongruence A mismatch between self-concept and experience which results in a feeling of anxiety.

Interactive coordination This is the joint collaboration by both parties in the work of therapy.

Internal working model A cognitive conceptual framework that an individual uses to make sense of the world, the self and others.

Interpretation Possible explanations of a meaning in dream, behaviour, action, thoughts or feelings. Interpretation may be used to explain how the client's presenting issues are embedded in old relationships and conflicts.

Interruption A strategy to stop the client in mid-process to enable them to reflect on their behaviour.

Intersubjectivity There is not one reality (the client's) and an objective observer (the therapist) in the therapy room, but two subjective realities.

Introjected, introjection The psychological process in which the standards and values of others are unconsciously and symbolically taken within oneself.

Locus of evaluation (LOE) With internal LOE, self-assessment is independent of others, while with external LOE, there is a dependence on the judgement of others.

Magnetic Resonance Imaging (MRI) A test using a magnetic field and pulses of radio wave energy to 'see' internal structures in the body.

Meta-analysis A comprehensive independent review of a number of studies which identifies factors that are measurably significant. A meta-analysis employs standardized methods to evaluate, compare and review many different studies.

Mirror neurons A type of brain cell activated when doing an action, and similarly when watching someone else perform the same action. Mirror neurons have been associated with our ability to be empathic. The communication of empathy by the therapist triggers and activates new mirror neurons within the client.

Neuroplasticity The brain's ability to reproduce new neurones and reorganize itself by forming new neural connections throughout an individual's life.

Neurotransmitters Chemicals that are exchanged between neurones.

Object Relations theory Object Relations theory proposes that people relate to others and situations in their adult lives as shaped by family experiences during early childhood. Significant experiences are internalized as objects which form part of the self-structure.

Organismic valuing process A process in which all action is directly motivated towards immediate inner gratification and fulfilment of the self.

Paradigm A holistic way of viewing or conceptualizing; a worldview.

Parataxic distortions Perceptions of others based on our own (distorted) inner experiences.

Philosophy The study of the fundamental nature of knowledge, reality and existence.

Pluralistic approach A way of practising, researching and thinking about therapy which is embedded in humanistic, person-centred and postmodern values, but also fully embraces a whole range of effective therapeutic methods and concepts.

Positive regard The valuing of the other and their perceptual world.

Postmodern Psychology A branch of psychology which questions whether there is an ultimate or singular version of truth. Reality is considered to be multi-dimensional and practitioners seek to avoid reducing human experiencing to a model based on past social perspectives. It reflects current social and cultural values and contexts.

Projection The act of locating one's own thoughts and feelings on to another person.

Projective identification The projection of unconscious feelings/impulses on to another in such a way as to evoke, in the other, those feelings/impulses projected.

Proxy self The presentation of an 'acceptable' front/persona by a person of diversity that helps them manage life relating to those persons and attitudes of the dominant group.

Psychiatry The medical specialty dedicated to the study, diagnosis, prevention and treatments of mental disorders.

Psychoanalysis The first 'force' of psychology, a psychological theory and therapy which aims to understand and treat psychological problems by examining the interaction of conscious and unconscious elements in the psyche and bringing repressed fears and conflicts into conscious awareness.

Psychodynamic The interaction of conscious and unconscious processes and emotions that determine motivation and personality; a form of therapy using psychoanalytic theory relationally.

Psychology The scientific study of the human mind and its functions, especially those affecting behaviour in a given context.

Randomized control trial A study that randomly assigns subjects to two groups: a control group in which members are not subjected to any interventions, or may in some cases be treated with a placebo effect; and an experimental group in which members are subject to one or more interventions that the experimenter wants to investigate. The results are then compared to determine any significant change.

Relational approach A paradigm which overarches modalities and schools. In the RA, our self is formed through relationship with others. We grow and develop through relationship, and problems are solved through relationship. A relational therapist is a facilitator and full participant in the TR. A relational approach can also be a core model of therapy.

Relational depth Describes feelings of connectedness and relating between therapist and client. They may be moments of encounter or refer to a particular *quality* of relationship.

Relational fatigue A sense of being 'fed up' or tired of working with clients in the therapeutic relationship.

Researcher allegiance A risk of bias in psychotherapy outcome research. An example is research funded by those who want to prove that their preferred way of working is best.

Resistance Considered a healthy defence mechanism for the psyche against threats to the self-structure. Traditionally considered within the analytic tradition as everything in the words and behaviours of the client that prevents access to unconscious material.

Rupture A break in the agreed working alliance.

Self-concept The image a person has of themselves based on experiences, beliefs, perceptions and thoughts.

Self-disclosure The revelation of personal rather than professional information about the therapist to the client.

Self Psychology Self is a central structure of the personality. It is formed over time in relation to impressions from parents or significant others.

Selfobject A part of the infant's experiencing that becomes an element of the developing self-structure.

Socratic questioning A systematic combination of questions which facilitates the client's ability to look at things from alternative angles that they may not have considered before.

Super-ego In psychodynamic psychology, the element of our psyche which is concerned with our place in society and how we behave in relation to the expectations of others.

Theorem of reciprocal emotion We gain or suffer as our needs are met in relationships.

Therapeutic alliance A component of the therapeutic relationship; the agreement between client and therapist on goals, tasks and the boundaries of the TR which helps form the frame in which therapy takes place.

Therapeutic frame The container in which therapy takes place and is held. This will include the context, the contract and the therapeutic relationship.

Therapist facilitativeness A generic term to describe relational behaviours of the therapist to enable change.

'Third Wave' CBT A range of therapies, including acceptance and commitment therapy, dialectical behavioural therapy, metacognitive therapy, mindfulness-based cognitive therapy and schema therapy. The focus is on accepting and understanding thought and feelings and inner psychic relations rather than changing or controlling them.

Transference A term used by therapists to describe feelings, thoughts or memories that a client has from their past that they project on to another person. This is done out of conscious awareness and can be quite innocuous or can have more complex dynamics.

Transmuting internalizations The process by which aspects of the selfobjects are absorbed into the child's self.

Transpersonal The fourth 'force' of psychology which focuses specifically on the development of *being*, spirituality and a holistic view of the individual. A transpersonal therapist undertakes a guiding role in the client's journey.

Unconditional positive regard An accepting, valuing attitude to another person without condition or judgement.

Unitary paradigm A way of conceptualizing that includes all perspectives.

Vicarious traumatization (VT) The cumulative effect of the therapist working with clients who are traumatized or distressed. This results in the therapist becoming traumatized.

Working alliance This is the working relationship between the therapist and the client based on agreed goals and ways of working together.

'Zero-sum' responding A global generic response as opposed to responding empathically and non-selectively to all the different aspects of the client that present.

Appendix

Conclusions and Recommendations of the Interdivisional (APA Divisions 12 & 29) Task Force on Evidence-Based Therapy Relationships (John C. Norcross, PhD, Chair, 2 January 2011)

CONCLUSIONS OF THE TASK FORCE

- The therapy relationship makes substantial and consistent contributions to psychotherapy outcome independent of the specific type of treatment.
- The therapy relationship accounts for why clients improve (or fail to improve) at least as much as the particular treatment method.
- Practice and treatment guidelines should explicitly address therapist behaviours and qualities that promote a facilitative therapy relationship.
- Efforts to promulgate best practices or evidence-based practices (EBPs) without including the relationship are seriously incomplete and potentially misleading.
- Adapting or tailoring the therapy relationship to specific patient characteristics (in addition to diagnosis) enhances the effectiveness of treatment.
- The therapy relationship acts in concert with treatment methods, patient characteristics, and practitioner qualities in determining effectiveness; a comprehensive understanding of effective (and ineffective) psychotherapy will consider all of these determinants and their optimal combinations.

	Elements of the relationship	Methods of adapting
Demonstrably effective	• Alliance in individual psychotherapy • Empathy • Collecting client feedback	• Reactance/resistance level • Preferences • Culture • Religion and spirituality
Probably effective	• Goal consensus • Collaboration • Positive regard	• Stages of change • Coping style
Promising but insufficient research to judge	• Congruence/genuineness • Repairing alliance ruptures • Managing countertransference • Expectations • Attachment style	

PRACTICE RECOMMENDATIONS

1. Practitioners are encouraged to make the creation and cultivation of a therapy relationship, characterized by the elements found to be demonstrably and probably effective, a primary aim in the treatment of patients.
2. Practitioners are encouraged to adapt or tailor psychotherapy to those specific patient characteristics in ways found to be demonstrably and probably effective.
3. Practitioners are encouraged to routinely monitor patients' responses to the therapy relationship and ongoing treatment. Such monitoring leads to increased opportunities to reestablish collaboration, improve the relationship, modify technical strategies, and avoid premature termination.
4. Concurrent use of evidence-based therapy relationships and evidence-based treatments adapted to the patient is likely to generate the best outcomes.

POLICY RECOMMENDATIONS

1. APA's Division of Psychotherapy, Division of Clinical Psychology, and other practice divisions are encouraged to educate its members in the benefits of evidence-based therapy relationships.
2. Mental health organizations as a whole are encouraged to educate their members about the improved outcomes associated with using evidence-based therapy relationships, as they frequently now do about evidence-based treatments.
3. We recommend that the American Psychological Association and other mental health organizations advocate for the research-substantiated benefits of a nurturing and responsive human relationship in psychotherapy.
4. Finally, administrators of mental health services are encouraged to attend to the relational features of those services. Attempts to improve the quality of care should account for treatment relationships and adaptations.

PRODUCTS OF THE TASK FORCE

Norcross, J.C. (ed.) (2010) Evidence-based therapy relationships. Module on SAMHSA's National Registry of Evidence-based Programs and Practices: NREPP/SAMHSA Website.

Norcross, J.C. (ed.) (2011) *Psychotherapy Relationships that Work: Evidence-Based Responsiveness* (2nd edn). New York: Oxford University Press.

Norcross, J.C. (ed.) (2011) 'Evidence-based therapy relationships', *Psychotherapy*, 48(1).

Norcross, J.C. and Wampold, B.E. (eds) (2011) 'Adapting psychotherapy to the individual patient', *Journal of Clinical Psychology*, 67(2).

References

Adler, G. (1979) *Dynamics of the Self.* London: Covenuture.

Adlington, J. (2010) 'Rapport in cyberspace', *Therapy Today*, 21.

Ainsworth, M.D.S., Blehar, M.C., Waters, E. and Wall, S. (1978) *Patterns of Attachment: A Psychological Study of the Strange Situation.* Hillsdale, NJ: Lawrence Erlbaum.

Alexander, F., French, T.M., et al. (1946) *Psychoanalytic Therapy: Principles and Application.* New York: Ronald Press.

Alleyne, A. (2011) 'Values and principles underpinning good practice in working with issues of difference and diversity', in C. Lago (ed.), *The Handbook of Transcultural Counselling and Psychotherapy.* Maidenhead, UK: Open University Press/McGraw-Hill.

Allport, G.W. (1950) *The Individual and his Religion.* New York: Macmillan.

American Psychiatric Association (1994) *Diagnostic and Statistical Manual of Mental Disorders* (4th edn). Washington, DC: American Psychiatric Association.

American Psychological Association (2011) *Conclusions and Recommendations of the Interdivisional (APA Divisions 12 & 29) Task Force on Evidence-Based Therapy Relationships.* Springfield, MO: American Psychological Association.

Angyal, A. (1965) *Neurosis and Treatment: A Holistic Theory.* New York: Wiley.

Anthony, K., Goss, S. and Nagel, D. (2014) 'Developing ethical delivery of cross-border services', in P. Weitz (ed.), *Psychotherapy 2.0: Where Psychotherapy and Technology Meet* (Vol. 1). London: Karnac.

Aron, L. (1996) *A Meeting of Minds: Mutuality in Psychoanalysis.* Hillsdale, NJ and London: The Analytic Press.

Arvey, M.J. (2000) 'Shattered beliefs: reconstituting the self of the trauma counselor', in R.A. Neimeyer (ed.), *Meaning Reconstruction and the Experience of Loss.* Washington, DC: American Psychological Association.

Asay, T.P. and Lambert, M.J. (1999) 'The empirical case for the common factors in therapy: quantitative findings', in M.A. Hubble, B.L. Duncan and S.D. Miller (eds), *The Heart and Soul of Change: What Works in Therapy.* Washington, DC: American Psychological Association. pp. 33–56.

Asay, T.P. and Lambert, M.J. (2001) 'Therapist relational variables', in D.J. Cain and J. Seeman (eds), *Humanistic Therapies: Handbook of Research and Practice.* Washington, DC: American Psychological Association. pp. 531–57.

Association of Family Therapy and Systemic Practice (2013) Website, www.aft.org.uk/about/view/about.html (accessed 13 July 2013).

Atkinson, D.R., Morten, G. and Sue, D.W. (1993) *Counseling American Minorities: A Cross-Cultural Perspective* (4th edn). Madison, WI: Brown and Benchmark.

Atwood, G. and Storolow, R. (1984) *Structures of Subjectivity: Explorations in Psychoanalytic Phenomenology.* Hillsdale, NJ: Analytic Press.

AuBuchon, P.G. and Malatesta, V.J. (1998) 'Managing the therapeutic relationship in behaviour therapy: the need for a case formulation', in M. Bruch and F.W. Bond (eds), *Beyond Diagnosis: Case Formulation Approaches in CBT*. Chichester, UK: Wiley.

Bachelor, A. and Horvath, A. (1999) 'The therapeutic relationship', in M.A. Hubble, B.L. Duncan and S.D. Miller (eds), *The Heart and Soul of Change: What Works in Therapy*. Washington, DC: American Psychological Association. pp. 133–78.

BACP (2010) *Ethical Framework for Good Practice in Counselling & Psychotherapy*. Available at: www.bacp.co.uk/ethical_framework/ (accessed 13 January 2014).

BACP Equality and Diversity Forum of the British Association for Counselling and Psychotherapy (2004) *Issues of Difference and Equality*. Available at: www.bacp.co.uk/equality/accessibility.php (accessed 13 January 2014).

Baker, E.K. (2003) *Caring for Ourselves: A Therapist's Guide to Personal and Professional Well-Being*. Washington, DC: American Psychological Association.

Balick, A. (2014) 'How to think about psychotherapy in a digital context', in P. Weitz (ed.), *Psychotherapy 2.0: Where Psychotherapy and Technology Meet* (Vol. 1). London: Karnac.

Barden, N. and Williams, T. (2007) *Words and Symbols: Communication in Therapy*. Maidenhead, UK: Open University Press.

Barger-Charleson, S. and Van Rijin, B. (2011) *Counselling and Psychotherapy Practice: Understanding Assessment in Counselling and Psychotherapy*. Exeter: Learning Matters.

Barkham, M., Margison, F., Leach, C., Lucock, M., Mellor-Clark, J., Evans, C. and McGrath, G. (2001) 'Service profiling and outcomes benchmarking using the CORE-OM: towards practice-based evidence in the psychological therapies', *Journal of Consulting and Clinical Psychology*, 69: 184–96.

Barr, J. (1987) 'The therapeutic relationship model: perspectives on the core of the healing process', *Transactional Analysis Journal*, 17: 168–73.

Batmanghelidjh, C. (2010) 'Child centred practice', in C. Lago and B. Smith (eds), *Anti-Discriminatory Practice in Counselling and Psychotherapy* (2nd edn). London: Sage.

Beail, N. (2010) 'The challenge of the randomized controlled trial to psychotherapy research with people with learning disabilities', *Advances in Mental Health and Intellectual Disabilities*, 4: 37–41.

Beck, A.T. (1976) *Cognitive Therapy and Emotional Disorders*. New York: International University Press.

Beck, D.F. (1988) *Counselor Characteristics: How They Affect Outcomes*. Milwaukee, WI: Family Service Association of America.

Begley, S. (2007) *Train your Mind, Change your Brain: How a New Science Reveals our Extraordinary Potential to Transform Ourselves*. New York: Ballantine.

Bentall, R.P. (2003) *Madness Explained: Psychosis and Human Nature*. London: Penguin.

Berne, E. (1961) *Transactional Analysis Psychotherapy*. New York: Grove Press.

Beutler, L.E., Malik, M., Alimohamed, S., Harwood, T.M., Talebi, H., Noble, S. and Wong, E. (2004) 'Therapist variables', in M.J. Lambert (ed.), *Bergin & Garfield's Handbook of Psychotherapy and Behavior Change* (5th edn). New York: Wiley. pp. 227–306.

Bion, W.R. (1970) *Attention and Interpretation*. London: Tavistock Publications.

Bohart, A., Elliott, R., Greenberg, L.S. and Watson, J.C. (2002) 'Empathy', in J. Norcross and M. Lambert (eds), *Psychotherapy Relationships that Work*. Oxford: Oxford University Press. pp. 89–108.

Bordin, E.S. (1979) 'The generalizability of the psychoanalytic concept of the working alliance', *Psychotherapy*, 16: 252–60.

Bordin, E. (1994) 'Theory and research on the therapeutic working alliance: new directions', in A. Horvath and L. Greenberg (eds), *The Working Alliance: Theory, Research and Practice*. New York: Wiley. pp. 13–37.

Boss, M. (1963) *Psychoanalysis and Daseinsanalysis* (Trans. L.E. Lefebre). New York: Basic Books.

Bowlby, J. (1951) *Maternal Care and Mental Health*. World Health Organization Monograph (Serial No. 2). Geneva: World Health Organization

Bowlby, J. (1969) *Attachment and Loss (Vol. 1), Attachment*. New York: Basic Books.

Bowlby, J. (1973) *Attachment and Loss (Vol. 2), Separation: Anxiety and Anger*. New York: Basic Books.

Bowlby, J. (1980) *Attachment and Loss (Vol. 3), Loss: Sadness and Depression*. New York: Basic Books.

Bowlby, J. (1988) A *Secure Base*. New York: Basic Books.

Bozarth, J. (1984/2001) 'Beyond reflection: emergent modes of empathy', in R. Levant and J. Shlien (eds), *Client-Centered Therapy and the Person-Centered Approach*. Westport, CT: Praeger. pp. 59–75. Reprinted in S. Haugh and T. Merry (eds) (2001) *Rogers' Therapeutic Conditions, Volume 2: Empathy*. Ross-on-Wye: PCCS Books. pp. 131–54.

Bozarth, J. (1998) *Person-Centred Therapy: A Revolutionary Paradigm*. Ross-on-Wye: PCCS Books.

Bozarth, J. and Wilkins, P. (eds) (2001) *Rogers' Therapeutic Conditions. Volume 3: Unconditional Positive Regard*. Ross-on-Wye: PCCS Books.

Brazelton, T.B. and Cramer, B.G. (1991) *The Earliest Relationship*. London: Karnac Books.

Bretherton, I. and Munholland, K.A. (1999) 'Internal working models revisited', in J. Cassidy and P.R. Shaver (eds), *Handbook of Attachment: Theory, Research, and Clinical Applications*. New York: Guilford Press. pp. 89–111.

Brody, A.L., Saxena, S., Stoessel, P., Gillies, L.A., Fairbanks, L.A. and Alborzian, S. (2001) 'Regional brain metabolic changes in patients with major depression treated with either paroxetine or interpersonal therapy', *Archives of General Psychiatry*, 58: 631–40.

Brown, F. and Webb, S. (2005) 'Children without play', *Journal of Education*, 35, March special issue: 'Early Childhood Research in Developing Contexts'.

Buber, M. (1950) 'Urdistanz und Beziechung' ['Distance and relation'], in *Knowledge of Man* (1965). New York: Harper Collins. pp. 59–71; cited in Schmidt, P.F. (2001b) *Comprehension: The Art of Not-knowing: Dialogical and Ethical Perspectives on Empathy as Dialogue in Personal and Person-centred Relationships. Volume 2: Empathy*. Ross-on-Wye: PCCS Books. pp. 53–71.

Buber, M. (1958) *I and Thou* (2nd rev. edn). Trans. R.G. Smith. New York: Scribner.

Buber, M. (1988) *The Knowledge of Man: A Philosophy of the Interhuman*. Trans. M.S. Friedman and R.G. Smith. Atlantic Highlands, NJ: Humanities Press International.

Burckell, L.A. and Goldfried, M.R. (2006) 'Therapist qualities preferred by sexual-minority individuals', *Psychotherapy: Theory, Research, Practice, Training*, 43(1): 32.

Burlingame, G.M., Fuhriman, A. and Johnson, J.E. (2002) 'Cohesion in group psychotherapy', in J.C. Norcross (ed.), *Psychotherapy Relationships that Work: Therapist Contributions and Responsiveness to Patients*. New York: Oxford University Press. pp. 71–88.

Burlingame, G.M., MacKenzie, D. and Strauss, B. (2004) 'Small group treatment: evidence for effectiveness and mechanisms of change', in M.J. Lambert (ed.), *Bergin and Garfield's Handbook of Psychotherapy and Behavioral Change* (5th edn). New York: Wiley. pp. 647–96.

Burns, D.D. (1989) 'Foreword', in J.B. Person, *Cognitive Therapy in Practice: A Case Formulation Approach*. New York: W.W. Norton and Co.

Burton, A. (1967) *Modern Humanistic Psychology*. San Francisco, CA: Jossey-Bass.

Carnelley, K.B., Pietromonaco, P.R. and Jaffe, K. (1994) 'Depression, working models of others, and relationship functioning', *Journal of Personality and Social Psychology*, 66: 127–40.

Carr, A. (2000a) 'Evidence-based practice in family therapy and systemic consultation', *Journal of Family Therapy*, 22(1): 29–61.

Carr, A. (2000b) 'Evidence-based practice in family therapy and systemic consultation', *Journal of Family Therapy*, 22(3): 273–96.

Carroll, M. (1996) *Counselling Supervision: Theory, Skills and Practice*. London: Cassell.

Carter, R.T. (1995) *The Influence of Race and Racial Identity in Psychotherapy: Toward a Racial Inclusive Model*. New York: John Wiley & Sons.

Carter, R.T. and Helms, J.E. (1992) 'The counselling process as defined by relationship types: a test of Helms's interactional model', *Journal of Multicultural Counselling and Development*, 20: 181–201.

Casement, P.J. (1985) 'The internal supervisor', in P.J. Casement, *On Learning from the Patient*. London: Tavistock Publications.

Cass, V.C. (1979) 'Homosexual identity formation: a theoretical model', *Journal of Homosexuality*, 4: 219–35.

Charura, D. (2011) 'The effects of an African heritage', in C. Lago (ed.), *The Handbook of Transcultural Counselling & Psychotherapy*. Maidenhead, UK: Open University Press.

Charura, D. (2012a) 'Demystifying the curative factor of group psychotherapy in rehab', *Addiction Today*, 23(135): 22–3.

Charura, D. (ed.) (2012b) 'Love in the therapy room: a theory of love', *The Psychotherapist*, 52: 21–31.

Charura, D. (2012c) *Can three do the tango? Reflections on the challenges of supervision where diversity is involved*. British Psychological Society: Building Bridges – East & West Psychology & Psychotherapy in Practice conference paper. British Psychological Society, London.

Charura, D. (2014) 'Lost in translation: meeting the challenges of language and regional customs when working online, cross-border, without visual cues', in P. Weitz, (ed.), *Psychotherapy 2.0: Where Psychotherapy and Technology Meet* (Vol. 1). London: Karnac. pp. 109–31.

Charura, D. and Lago, C. (2012) 'Transcultural perspectives on love and hate: the yin and yang of relationships, within and without therapy', *The Psychotherapist*, 52: 28–9.

Charura, D. and Wallace, L. (2012) 'Group Supervision when working with complex issues in addiction work', *Addiction Today*, 23(137): 25–7.

Charura, D., Pattison, S. and McAndrew, T. (2015) 'Diversity', in S. Pattison, M. Robson and A. Beynon (eds), *The Handbook of Counselling Children & Young People*. London: Sage.

Chilvers, C., Dewey, M., Fielding, K., Gretton, V., Miller, P., Palmer, B. and Harrison, G. (2001) 'Antidepressant drugs and generic counselling for treatment of major depression in primary care: randomised trial with patient preference arms', *British Medical Journal*, 322(7289): 772.

Christopher, J.C. and Maris, J.A. (2010) 'Integrating mindfulness as self-care into counseling and psychotherapy training', *Counselling and Psychotherapy Research*, 10(2): 114–25.

Chugani, H.T., Behen, M.E., Muzik, O., Juhasz, C., Nagy, F. and Chugani, D.C. (2001) 'Local brain functional activity following early brain deprivation: a study of post institutionalized Romanian orphans', *Neuroimage*, 14: 1290–301.

Clark, D. and Turpin, G. (2008) 'Improving opportunities', *The Psychologist*, 21: 700–701.

Clark, D.M. (2011) 'Implementing NICE guidelines for the psychological treatment of depression and anxiety disorders: the IAPT experience', *International Review of Psychiatry*, 23: 375–38.

Clark, D.M., Layard, R., Smithies, R., Richards, D.A., Suckling, R. and Wright, B. (2009) 'Improving access to psychological therapy: initial evaluation of two UK demonstration sites', *Behaviour Research and Therapy*, 47: 910–20.

Clarke, D.M. and Fairburn, C.G. (2005) (eds) *Science and Practice of Cognitive Behavioural Therapy.* Oxford: Oxford University Press.

Clarkson, P. (1995) *The Therapeutic Relationship*. London: Whurr.

Clarkson, P. (2003) *The Therapeutic Relationship* (2nd edn). London: Whurr.

Coleman, E. (1982) 'Developmental stages of the coming out process', *Journal of Homosexuality*, 7: 31–43.

Conte, H., Ratto, R., Clutz, K. and Karasu, T. (1995) 'Determinants of outpatients' satisfaction with therapists', *The Journal of Psychotherapy Practice and Research*, 4: 43–51.

Cook, A., Spinazzola, J., Ford, J., Lanktree, C., Blaustein, M., Cloitre, M., ... Van der Kolk, B. (2005) 'Complex trauma in children and adolescents', *Psychiatric Annals*, 35(5): 390–98.

Cooper, M. (2005) 'Therapists' experiences of relational depth: a qualitative interview study', *Counselling and Psychotherapy Research*, 5(2): 87–95.

Cooper, M. (2008) *Essential Research Findings in Counselling and Psychotherapy: The Facts are Friendly*. London: Sage.

Cooper, M. and McLeod, J. (2010) *Pluralistic Counselling and Psychotherapy*. London: Sage.

Corey, G. (2013) *Theory and Practice of Counselling and Psychotherapy* (9th edn). Belmont, CA: Brooks Cole.

Corsini, R.J. and Wedding, D. (eds) (2010) *Current Psychotherapies* (9th edn). Pacific Grove, CA: Brooks Cole.

Cottone, R.R. (1988) 'Epistemological and ontological issues in counseling: implications of social systems theory', *Counselling Psychology Quarterly*, 1(4): 357–65.

Cozolino, L. (2002) *The Neuroscience of Psychotherapy: Building and Rebuilding the Brain.* New York: W.W. Norton & Co.

Cozolino, L. (2010a) *The Neuroscience of Human Relationships: Attachment and the Developing Social Brain.* New York: W.W. Norton & Co.

Cozolino, L. (2010b) *The Neuroscience of Psychotherapy: Healing the Social Brain* (2nd edn). New York: W.W. Norton & Co.

Cross, W.E. (1995) 'The psychology of Nigrescence: revising the cross model', in J.G. Ponterotto, J.M. Casas, L.A. Suzuki and C.M. Alexander (eds), *Handbook of Multicultural Counseling.* Thousand Oaks, CA: Sage.

Dallos, R. and Draper R. (2010) *An Introduction to Family Therapy: Systemic Theory and Practice* (3rd edn). Maidenhead, UK: Open University Press.

Daniels, V. (n.d.) *Transitions in Gestalt Therapy.* Available online at: www.sonoma.edu/users/d/daniels/Gestalt%20transitions.htm (accessed 22 January 2014).

Davis, C.G. (2000) 'The tormented and the transformed: understanding responses to loss and trauma', in R.A. Neimeyer (ed.), *Meaning Reconstruction and the Experience of Loss.* Washington, DC: American Psychological Association.

De Young, P. (2003) *Relational Psychotherapy: A Primer.* New York: Brunner-Routledge.

Department of Health (2012) 'Improving Access to Psychological Therapies (IAPT): supporting "No health without mental health"'. London: Department of Health. Available at: www.iapt.nhs.uk/silo/files/iapt-3-year-summary-leaflet.pdf (accessed 20 May 2013).

Deuraseh, N. and Talib, M.A. (2005) 'Mental health in Islamic medical tradition', *The International Medical Journal*, 4(2): 76–9.

Downing, N. and Roush, K. (1985) 'From passive acceptance to active commitment: a model of feminist identity development for women', *The Counseling Psychologist*, 13: 695–709.

Dowrick, C. (2004) *Beyond Depression: A New Approach to Understanding and Management.* Oxford: Oxford University Press.

Dryden, W. (2008) *Rational Emotive Behaviour Therapy: Distinctive Features.* London: Routledge.

Dryden, W. (2012) 'Adapting CBT to a broad clientele', in W. Dryden and R. Branch (eds), *The CBT Handbook.* London: Sage. pp. 214–30.

Dryden, W. and Branch, R. (eds) (2012) *The CBT Handbook.* London: Sage.

Ehrenberg, D. (1992) *The Intimate Edge.* New York: W.W. Norton & Co.

Elkin, I., Shea, M.T., Watkins, J.T., Imber, S.D., Sotsky, S.M., Collins, J.F., ... and Parloff, M.B. (1989) 'National Institute of Mental Health treatment of depression collaborative research program: general effectiveness of treatments', *Archives of General Psychiatry*, 46(11): 971.

Elliott, R., Bohart, A.C., Watson, J.C. and Greenberg, L.S. (2011) 'Empathy', in J.C. Norcross (ed.), *Psychotherapy Relationships that Work* (2nd edn). New York and Oxford: Oxford University Press.

Elliott, R. and Freire, E. (2008) 'Person-centred/experiential therapies are highly effective: summary of the 2008 meta-analysis ', *Person-Centred Quarterly*, November: 1–3.

Elliott, R., Watson, J., Goldman, R. and Greenberg, L.S. (2004) *Learning Emotion-Focused Therapy: The Process-Experiential Approach to Change.* Washington, DC: American Psychological Association.

Ellis, A. (1962) *Reason and Emotion in Psychotherapy.* New York: Lyle Stewart.

Ellis, A. (1977) 'The Basic Clinical Theory of Rational-Emotive Therapy', in A. Ellis and R. Grieger (eds) *Handbook of Rational-Emotive Therapy.* Springer: New York.

Epstein, R.S. (1994) *Keeping Boundaries: Maintaining Safety and Integrity in the Psychotherapeutic Process.* Washington, DC: American Psychiatric Press.

Erskine, R.G. (1997) *Theories and Methods of an Integrative Transactional Analysis: A Volume of Selected Articles.* San Francisco: TA Press.

Erskine, R.G., Moursund, J.P. and Trautmann, R.L. (1999) *Beyond Empathy: A Therapy of Contact-in-Relationship*. London: Routledge.

Erskine, R.G and Trautmann, R.L. (1996) 'Methods of an Integrative Psychotherapy', *Transactional Analysis Journal*, 26: 316–29.

Equality Act (2010), www.legislation.gov.uk/ukpga/2010/15 (accessed 22 October 2013).

Equality and Human Rights Commission (EHRC) (2010). *How Fair is Britain? A Report on Discrimination and Disadvantage in British Society*. London: EHRC.

Etherington, K. (2000) *Narrative Approaches to Working with Adult Male Survivors of Child Sexual Abuse: The Client's, the Counsellor's and the Researcher's Story.* London: Jessica Kingsley.

Evans, C., Mellor-Clark, J., Margison, F., Barkham, M., Audin, K., Connell, J. and McGrath, G. (2000) 'CORE: Clinical Outcomes in Routine Evaluation', *Journal of Mental Health*, 9(3): 247–55.

Evans, G. (2004) 'The environment of childhood poverty', *American Psychologist*, 59: 77–92.

Evans, K. and Gilbert, M. (2004) *An Introduction to Integrative Psychotherapy*. Basingstoke: Palgrave Macmillan.

Fairbairn, W.R.D. (1952) *Psychoanalytic Studies of the Personality*. Abingdon, UK: Psychology Press.

Fairbairn, W.R.D. (1954) *An Object-Relations Theory of the Personality.* New York: Basic Books.

Farb, N.A., Segal, Z.V., Mayberg, H., Bean, J., McKeon, D., Fatima Z., et al. (2007) 'Attending to the present: mindfulness meditation reveals distinct neural modes of self reference', *Social Cognitive and Affective Neuroscience*, 2(4): 313–22.

Farber, B.A. and Doolin, E.M. (2011) 'Positive regard', *Psychotherapy*, 48(1): 58.

Farmer, R.L. (2009) *Neuroscience and Social Work Practice: The Missing Link*. Thousand Oaks, CA: Sage.

Feltham, C. (1997) 'Challenging the core theoretical model', *Counselling*, 8(2): 121–5.

Ferenczi, S. (1932) *The Clinical Diary of Sandor Ferenczi*. Ed. J. Dupont. Cambridge, MA: Harvard University Press; in Hayal, A. (1993) *Psychoanalysis and the Sciences: Epistemology – History*. Trans. Elizabeth Holder. Berkeley, CA: University of California Press.

Fielding, R.G. and Llewelyn, S.P. (1986) 'Applying the social psychology of groups in clinical settings', *British Journal of Psychotherapy*, 2(4): 281–91.

Figley, C.R. (ed.) (1995) *Compassion Fatigue: Coping with Secondary Traumatic Stress Disorder in Those Who Treat the Traumatized*. New York: Brunner/Mazel.

Fisher, H., Aron, A. and Brown, L.L. (2005) 'Romantic love: an fMRI study of a neural mechanism for mate choice', *Journal of Comparative Neurology*, 493: 58–62.

Frankl, V.E. (1963) *Man's Search for Meaning: An Introduction to Logotherapy*. New York: Washington Square.

Freshwater, D. (2003) *Counselling Skills for Nurses, Midwives and Health Visitors.* Buckingham, UK: Open University Press.

Friedlander, M.L., Escudero, V. and Heatherington, L. (2006) *Therapeutic Alliances with Couples and Families: An Empirically-informed Guide to Practice*. Washington, DC: American Psychological Association.

Friedlander, M.L., Escudero, V., Heatherington, L. and Diamond, G.M. (2011) 'Alliance in couple and family therapy', in J.C. Norcross (ed.), *Psychotherapy Relationships that Work* (2nd edn). New York: Oxford University Press.

Friedman, M.S. (1985) *The Healing Dialogue in Psychotherapy*. New York: Jason Aronson.

Friedman, M.S. (1995) 'Constructivism, psychotherapy, and the dialogue of touchstones', *Journal of Constructivist Psychology*, 8(4): 283–93.

Gabbard, G.O., Lazar, S.G., Hornberger, J. and Spiegel, D. (1997) 'The economic impact of psychotherapy: a review', *American Journal of Psychiatry*, 154(2): 147–55.

Gabbard, G.O. and Lester, E.P. (2008) *Boundaries and Boundary Violations in Psychoanalysis.* Washington, DC: American Psychiatric Press.

Gask, L. (2004) *A Short Introduction to Psychiatry.* London: Sage.

Gaston, L. (1990) 'The concept of the alliance and its role in psychotherapy: theoretical and empirical considerations', *Psychotherapy*, 27: 143–53.

Gelso, C.J. and Carter, J.A. (1985) 'The relationship in counseling and psychotherapy components, consequences, and theoretical antecedents', *The Counseling Psychologist*, 13(2): 155–243.

Gerhardt, S. (2004) *Why Love Matters: How Affection Shapes a Baby's Brain.* London: Brunner Routledge.

Gilbert, M. and Evans, K. (2000) *Psychotherapy Supervision: An Integrative-Relational Approach.* Maidenhead, UK: Open University Press.

Gilbert, P. and Leahy, R.L. (eds) (2007) *The Therapeutic Relationship in the Cognitive Behavioural Psychotherapies.* Abingdon, UK: Psychology Press.

Gill, C.J. (1997) 'Four types of integration in disability identity development', *Journal of Vocational Rehabilitation*, 9: 39–46.

Gill, M.M. (1982) *Analysis of Transference. Vol. 1: Theory and Technique.* New York: International Universities Press.

Gilligan T. (2008) 'The therapeutic relationship: Gestalt therapy', in S. Haugh and S. Paul (eds), *The Therapeutic Relationship: Perspectives and Themes.* Ross-on-Wye: PCSS Books.

Goldfinch, M. (2009) '"Putting Humpty together again": working with parents to help children who have experienced early trauma', *Australian and New Zealand Journal of Family Therapy*, 30: 284–99.

Gray, A. (1994) *An Introduction to the Therapeutic Frame.* London: Routledge.

Greenberg, J. and Mitchell, S.A. (1983) *Object Relations in Psychoanalytic Theory.* Cambridge, MA, and London: Harvard University Press.

Greenberger, D. and Padesky, C. (1995) *Mind over Mood.* New York: Guilford Press.

Greenhalgh, T. and Heath, I. (2010) *Measuring Quality in the Therapeutic Relationship.* London: The King's Fund.

Guntrip, H. (1953) 'The therapeutic factor in psychotherapy', *British Journal of Medical Psychology*, 26(2): 115–32.

Gutheil, T.G. and Gabbard, G.O. (1993) 'The concept of boundaries in clinical practice: theoretical and risk-management dimensions', *American Journal of Psychiatry*, 150: 188–96.

Hammen, C.L., Burge, D., Daley, S.E., Davila, J., Paley, B. and Rudolph, K.D. (1995) 'Interpersonal attachment cognitions and prediction of symptomatic responses to interpersonal stress', *Journal of Abnormal Psychology*, 104: 436–43.

Hansen, N.B., Lambert, M.J. and Forman, E.M. (2002) 'The psychotherapy dose–response effect and its implications for treatment delivery services', *Clinical Psychology: Science and Practice*, 9(3): 329–43.

Hargaden, H. and Sills, C. (2002) *Transactional Analysis: A Relational Perspective.* Hove: Brunner-Routledge.

Haugh, S. and Merry, T. (eds) (2001) *Rogers' Therapeutic Conditions. Volume 2: Empathy.* Ross-on-Wye: PCCS Books.

Haugh, S. and Paul, S. (eds) (2008a) *The Therapeutic Relationship: Perspectives and Themes.* Ross-on-Wye: PCCS Books.

Haugh, S. and Paul, S. (2008b) 'The therapy is the relationship?', *Therapy Today*, 19(10): 34–7.

Hawkins, P. and Shohet, R. (2000) *Supervision in the Helping Professions* (2nd edn). Milton Keynes, UK: Open University Press.

Hawkins, P. and Shohet, R. (2007) *Supervision in the Helping Professions: An Individual, Group and Organizational Approach.* Milton Keynes/Maidenhead, UK: Open University Press.

Hayes, S.C., Strosahl, K.D. and Wilson, K.D. (1999) *Acceptance and Commitment Therapy: An Experiential Approach to Behaviour Change.* New York: Guilford Press.

Haynes, R., Corey, G. and Moulton, P. (2003) *Clinical Supervision in the Helping Professions: A Practical Guide.* Pacific Grove, CA: Brooks Cole.

Hazan, C. and Shaver, P. (1987) 'Romantic love conceptualized as an attachment process', *Journal of Personality and Social Psychology*, 52(3): 511–24.

Heidegger, M. (1962) *Being and Time*. Trans. J. Macquarrie and E. Robinson. London: SCM Press.

Helms, J.E. (ed.) (1990) *Black and White Racial Identity: Theory, Research Practice*. Westport, CT: Greenwood Press.

Helms, J.E. (1995) 'An update of Helms' white and people of colour racial identity models', in J.G. Ponterotto, J.M. Casas, L.A. Suzuki and C.M. Alexander (eds), *Handbook of Multicultural Counselling*. Thousand Oaks, CA: Sage.

Helms, J.E. and Piper, J.E. (1994) 'Implications of racial identity theory for vocational psychology', *Journal of Vocational Behaviour*, 44: 124–36.

Herman, J. (1992) *Trauma and Recovery: The Aftermath of Violence – from Domestic Abuse to Political Terror*. New York: Basic Books.

Higgins, R. (2004) 'Balance is the key: coping with secondary traumatic stress'. Unpublished MA Dissertation, St John College, York.

Hollan, D.W. (2012) 'Emerging issues in the cross-cultural study of empathy', *Emotion Review*, 4(70): 79–80.

Holmes, P., Paul, S. and Pelham, G. (1996) 'A relational model of counselling', *Counselling*, August: 229–40.

Horvath, A.O. and Bedi, R.P. (2002) 'The alliance', in J. Norcross (ed.), *Psychotherapy Relationships that Work: Therapist Contributions and Responsiveness to Patients*. New York: Oxford University Press. pp. 37–70.

Horvath, A.O., Del Re, A.C., Fluckiger, C. and Symonds, D. (2011) 'Alliance in adult psychotherapy', in J.C. Norcross (ed.), *Psychotherapy Relationships that Work* (2nd edn). New York: Oxford University Press. pp. 25–69.

Horvath, A.O. and Greenberg, L.S. (eds) (1994) *The Working Alliance: Theory, Research, and Practice*. New York: Wiley & Sons.

Horvath, A.O. and Symonds, R.D. (1991) 'Relation between working alliance and outcome in psychotherapy: a meta-analysis', *Journal of Counselling Psychology*, 38: 139–49.

Horwitz, A.V. and Wakefield, J.C. (2007) *The Loss of Sadness: How Psychiatry Transformed Normal Sorrow into Depressive Disorder*. Oxford: Oxford University Press.

House, R. and Loewenthal, D. (eds) (2008) *Against and For CBT: Towards a Constructive Dialogue?* Ross-on-Wye: PCCS Books.

Howard, A. (2000) *Philosophy for Counselling & Psychotherapy*. London: Palgrave.

Howard, P. (2008) 'The therapeutic relationship in psychoanalytic psychotherapy', in S. Haugh and S. Paul (eds), *The Therapeutic Relationship: Perspectives and Themes*. Ross-on-Wye: PCSS Books.

Hyatt, J. (2014) 'Psychotherapy 2.0: for better or for worse? Commentator one', in P. Weitz (ed.), *Psychotherapy 2.0: Where Psychotherapy and Technology Meet* (Vol. 1). London: Karnac.

Hycner, R. (1993) *Between Person and Person: Toward a Dialogical Psychotherapy*. New York: The Gestalt Journal Press.

Hycner, R. and Jacobs, L. (1995) *The Healing Relationship in Gestalt Therapy*. New York: The Gestalt Journal Press.

Ibrahim, F.A. (1991) 'Contribution of cultural worldview to generic counselling and development', *Journal of Counselling and Development*, 70: 13.

Imel, Z. and Wampold, B. (2008) 'The importance of treatment and the science of common factors in psychotherapy', in S. Brown and R. Lent (eds), *Handbook of Counseling Psychology*. Hoboken, NJ: Wiley. pp. 249–62.

Ivey, E.A., D'Andrea, J.M. and Ivey, B.M. (2012) *Theories of Counselling and Psychotherapy: A Multicultural Perspective* (7th edn). London: Sage.

Ivey, A.E., Ivey, M.B., Zalaquett, C. and Quirk, K. (2009) 'Counseling and neuroscience: the cutting edge of the coming decade', *Counseling Today*, 52: 44–55.

Jacobs, L. (2005) 'For whites only', in T.L. Bar-Joseph (ed.), *The Bridge: Dialogues across Cultures*. New Orleans, LA: The Gestalt Institute Press.

Jenkins, P. (2007) *Counselling, Psychotherapy and the Law* (2nd edn). London: Sage.

Johnson, J. (2008) 'Using research-supported group treatments', *Journal of Clinical Psychology: In Session*, 64(11): 1206–24.

Jordan, J.V. (1991) 'The Development of Women's Sense of Self', in J.V. Jordan, A. Kaplan, J.B Miller, I. Stiver and Surrey, J. (eds), *Women's Growth in Connection: Writings from the Stone Center*. New York: Guilford Press. pp. 81–96.

Joseph, R. (1999) 'Environmental influences on neural plasticity, the limbic system, emotional development and attachment: a review', *Child Psychiatry and Human Development Journal*, 29(3): 189–208.

Kabat-Zinn, J. (2001) *Full Catastrophe Living: How to Cope with Stress, Pain and Illness Using Mindfulness Meditation*. London: Piatkus.

Kabat-Zinn, J. (2004) *Wherever You Go, There You Are*. London: Piatkus.

Kahill, S. (1988) 'Symptoms of professional burnout: a review of the empirical evidence', *Canadian Psychology*, 59: 284–97.

Kahn, M. (1991) *Between Therapist and Client*. New York: W.H. Freeman.

Kahn, M. (1997) *Between Therapist and Client* (2nd edn). New York: W.H. Freeman.

Katzow, A.W. and Safran, J.D. (2007) 'Recognizing and resolving ruptures in the therapeutic alliance', in P. Gilbert and R.L. Leahy (eds), *The Therapeutic Relationship in Cognitive Behavioral Psychotherapies*. Abingdon, UK: Psychology Press. pp. 90–105.

Kearney, R. (1986) *Modern Movements in European Philosophy*. Manchester: Manchester University Press.

Kerwin, C. and Ponterotto, J. (1995) 'Biracial identity development', in J.G. Ponterotto, J.M. Casas, L.A. Suzuki and C.M. Alexander (eds), *Handbook of Multicultural Counseling*. Thousand Oaks, CA: Sage. pp. 199–217.

Keys, S. (2003) *Idiosyncratic Person-Centred Therapy: From the Personal to the Universal*. Ross-on-Wye: PCCS Books.

Kivlighan, D.M. and Arthur, E.G. (2000) 'Convergence in client and counselor recall of important session events', *Journal of Counselling Psychology*, 47: 79–84.

King, M., Marston, L. and Bower, P. (2013) 'Comparison of non-directive counselling and cognitive behaviour therapy for patients presenting in general practice with an ICD-10 depressive episode: a randomized control trial', *Psychological Medicine*, 44(9): 1835–44.

Kirk, K. (1998) 'The impact on professional workers', in Z. Bear (ed.), *Good Practice in Counselling People Who Have Been Abused*. London: Jessica Kingsley.

Kogler, H.H. and Stueber, K.R. (eds) (2000) *Empathy and Agency: The Problem of Understanding in the Human Sciences*. Boulder, CO: Westview Press.

Kohler, W. (1947/1970) *Gestalt Psychology*. New York: Liveright.

Kohut, H. (1959) 'Introspection, empathy, and psychoanalysis', *Journal of the American Psychoanalytic Association*, 7: 459–83.

Kohut, H. (1971) *The Analysis of the Self*. New York: International Universities Press.

Kohut, H. (1977) *The Restoration of the Self*. New York: International Universities Press.

Kohut, H. (1978) 'The psychoanalyst in the community of scholars', in P.H. Ornstein (ed.), *The Search for Self: Selected Writings of H. Kohut (Vols. 1–3)*. New York: International Universities.

Kohut, H. (1982) 'Introspection, empathy, and the semicircle of mental health', *International Journal of Psychoanalysis*, 63: 395–408.

Kohut, H. (1984) *How Does Analysis Cure?* Ed. A. Goldberg and P.E. Stepansky. Chicago, IL: University of Chicago Press.

Kohut, H. (1991) 'The technique of psychoanalytic psychotherapy', in E. Rowe and D. Isaac (eds), *Empathic Attunement*. Northvale, NJ: Jason Tournier.

Kolden, G.G., Klein, M.H., Wang, C.C. and Austin, S.B. (2011) 'Congruence/genuineness', *Psychotherapy*, 48(1): 65.

Kottler, J. (1986) *On Being a Therapist*. San Francisco: Jossey-Bass.

Kroenke, K., Spitzer, R.L. and Williams, J.B. (2001) 'The PHQ-9: validity of a brief depression severity measure', *Journal of General and Internal Medicine*, 16: 606–13.

Kuhn, T.S. (1962) *The Structure of Scientific Revolutions*. Chicago, IL: University of Chicago Press.

Lago, C. (ed.) (2011) *The Handbook of Transcultural Counselling & Psychotherapy*. Maidenhead, UK: Open University Press.

Lago, C. and Haugh, S. (2006) 'White counsellor racial identity: the unacknowledged, unknown, unaware aspect of self in relationship', in G. Proctor, M. Cooper, P. Sanders and B. Malcom (eds), *Politicizing the Person Centred Approach*. Ross-on-Wye: PCCS Books. pp. 198–214.

Lago, C. and Smith, B. (eds) (2010) *Anti-Discriminatory Practice in Counselling and Psychotherapy* (2nd edn). London: Sage.

Lago, C.S. and Wright, J.K. (2006) 'Email supervision', in K. Tudor and M. Worral (eds), *Freedom to Practice (11): Person-Centred Perspectives on Supervision*. Ross-on-Wye: PCCS Books.

Laing, R.D. (1960) *The Divided Self*. London: Tavistock.

Laing, R.D. (1971) *The Divided Self: An Existential Study in Sanity and Madness*. London: Penguin Books.

Laing, R.D. and Esterson, A. (1964) *Sanity, Madness and the Family. Volume 1: Families of Schizophrenics*. London: Tavistock.

Lajoie, D. and Shapiro, S. (1992) 'Definitions of transpersonal psychology: the first twenty-three years', *Journal of Transpersonal Psychology*, 24(1), 79–98.

Lambers, E. (2000) 'Supervision in person-centered therapy: facilitating congruence', in D. Mearns and B. Thorne (eds), *Person-Centered Therapy Today: New Frontiers in Theory and Practice*. London: Sage. pp. 196–211.

Lambert, M.J. (1992) 'Implications of outcome research for psychotherapy integration', in J.C. Norcross and M.R. Goldfried (eds), *Handbook of Psychotherapy Integration*. New York: Basic Books. pp. 94–129.

Lambert, M.J. (2002) 'Research summary on the therapeutic relationship and psychotherapy outcome', in J.C. Norcross (ed.), *Psychotherapy Relationships that Work: Therapist Contributions and Responsiveness to Patients*. Oxford: Oxford University Press. pp. 17–32.

Lambert, M.J. (ed.) (2004) *Handbook of Psychotherapy and Behavior Change* (5th edn). New York: John Wiley & Sons.

Lambert, M.J. (ed.) (2013) *Handbook of Psychotherapy and Behavior Change* (6th edn). New York: John Wiley & Sons.

Lambert, M.J., Bergin, A.E. and Garfield, S.J. (2004) 'Introduction and historical overview', in M.J. Lambert (ed.), *Handbook of Psychotherapy and Behavior Change* (5th edn). New York: John Wiley & Sons. pp. 509–39.

Lambert, M.J. and Ogles B.M. (2004) 'The efficacy and effectiveness of psychotherapy', in M.J. Lambert (ed.), *Handbook of Psychotherapy and Behavior Change* (5th edn). New York: John Wiley & Sons. pp. 139–93.

Langs, R. (1976) *The Bipersonal Field*. New York: Jason Aronson.

Latner, J. (2000) 'The theory of Gestalt therapy', in E. Vevis (ed.), *Gestalt Therapy: Perspectives and Applications*. Cambridge, MA: The Gestalt Press.

Layard, R., Clark, D., Knapp, M. and Mayraz, G. (2007) 'Cost–benefit analysis of psychological therapy', *National Institute Economic Review*, 202: 90–98.

Lazarus, A.A. (2005) 'Multimodal therapy', in J.C. Norcross and M.R. Goldfried (eds), *Handbook of Psychotherapy Integration* (2nd edn). New York: Oxford University Press. pp. 105–20.

Leahy, R.L. (2008) 'The therapeutic relationship in cognitive-behavioral therapy', *Behavioural and Cognitive Psychotherapy*, 36: 769–77 (doi:10.1017/S1352465808004852).

Lee, C.C. and Na GoEun (2011) 'Identity development and its impact on the therapy relationship', in C. Lago (ed.), *The Handbook of Transcultural Counselling & Psychotherapy*. Maidenhead, UK: Open University Press. pp. 54–63.

Leichsenring, F. and Rabung, S. (2007) 'The role of efficacy versus effectiveness research in evaluating psychotherapy', *Mental Health and Learning Disabilities Research and Practice*, 4(2): 125–43.

Levenson, E. (1991) *The Purloined Self*. New York: William Alanson White Institute.

Liddle, H.A. and Rowe, C.L. (2004) 'Advances in family therapy research', in M. Nichols and R. Schwartz (eds), *Family Therapy: Concepts and Methods* (6th edn). Boston, MA: Allyn & Bacon. pp. 395–435.

Lietaer, G. (1984) 'Unconditional positive regard: a controversial basic attitude in client-centered therapy', in R.F. Levant and J.M. Shlien (eds), *Client-Centered Therapy and the Person-Centered Approach: New Directions in Theory, Research and Practice*. New York: Praeger. pp. 59–75.

Lietaer, G. (1993) 'Authenticity, congruence and transparency', in D. Brazier (ed.), *Beyond Carl Rogers*. London: Constable. pp. 17–46.

Linehan, M.M. (1993) *Cognitive-Behavioural Treatment of Borderline Personality Disorder*. New York: Guilford Press.

Loner, W.J. (1985) 'Issues in testing and assessment in cross-cultural counselling', *The Counselling Psychologists*, 13: 599–614.

Lorenz, K. (1935) 'Der Kumpan in der Umwelt des Vogels', *Journal für Ornithologie*, 83: 137–213, 289–413.

Luborsky, L., Diguer, L., Seligman, D.A., Rosenthal, R., Krause, E.D., Johnson, S., et al. (1999) 'The researcher's own therapy allegiances: A "wild card" in comparisons of treatment efficacy', *Clinical Psychology: Science and Practice*, 6: 95–106.

Luborsky, L., Rosenthal, R., Diguer, L., Andrusyna, T.P., Berman, J.S., Levitt, J.T., Seligman, D. and Krause, E.D. (2002) 'The dodo bird verdict is alive and well – mostly', *Clinical Psychology: Science and Practice*, 9(1): 2–12.

Luborsky, L., Singer, B. and Luborsky, E. (1975) 'Comparative studies of psychotherapies: is it true that "Everybody has won and all must have prizes"?', *Archives of General Psychiatry*, 32: 995–1008.

Mace, C. and Moorey, S. (2001) 'Evidence in psychotherapy: a difficult balance', in C. Mace, S. Moorey and B. Roberts (eds), *Evidence in the Psychological Therapies*. Hove: Brunner- Routledge. pp. 1–11.

Mackenzie-Mavinga, I. (2009) *Black Issues in the Therapeutic Process*. Basingstoke: Palgrave Macmillan.

MacKewn, J. (1997) *Developing Gestalt Counselling*. London: Sage.

Main, M. and Hesse, E. (1990) 'Parents' unresolved traumatic experiences are related to infant disorganized attachment status', in M.T. Greenberg, D. Ciccehetti and E.M. Cummings (eds), *Attachment in the Preschool Years: Theory, Research and Intervention*. Chicago, IL: University of Chicago. pp. 161–84.

Main, M. and Solomon, J. (1986) 'Discovery of an insecure-disorganized/disoriented attachment pattern: procedures, findings and implications for the classification of behavior', in T.B. Brazelton and M. Yogman (eds), *Affective Development in Infancy*. Norwood, NJ: Ablex. pp. 95–124.

Main, M. and Solomon, J. (1990) 'Procedures for identifying infants as disorganized/disoriented during the Ainsworth Strange Situation', in M.T. Greenberg, D. Cicchetti and E.M. Cummings (eds), *Attachment in the Preschool Years: Theory, Research and Intervention*. Chicago: University of Chicago. pp. 121–60

Malik, M.L., Beutler, L.E., Gallagher-Thompson, D., Thompson, L. and Alimohamed, S. (2003) 'Are all cognitive therapies alike? A comparison of cognitive and non-cognitive therapy process and implications for the application of empirically supported treatments (ESTs)', *Journal of Consulting and Clinical Psychology*, 71: 150–58.

Margison, F.R., Barkham, M., Evans, C., McGrath, G., Mellor-Clark, J., Audin, K. and Connell, J. (2000) 'Measurement and psychotherapy: evidence-based practice and practice-based evidence', *British Journal of Psychiatry*, 177(August): 123–30.

Maris, J.A. (2009) 'The impact of a mind/body medicine class on counselor training: a personal journey', *Journal of Humanistic Psychology*, 49: 229.

Marszalek, J.F. and Cashwell, C.S. (1999) 'The gay and lesbian affirmative development (GLAD) model: facilitating positive gay identity development', *Adultspan Journal*, 1: 13–31.

Martell, C.R., Addis, M.E. and Jacobson, N.S. (2001) *Depression in Context: Strategies for Guided Action*. New York: W.W. Norton.

Martin, D.J., Graske, J.P. and Davis, M.K. (2000) 'Relation of the therapeutic alliance with outcome and other variables: a meta-analytic review', *Journal of Consulting and Clinical Psychology*, 68: 438–50.

Maslach, C. (1978) 'The client role in staff burn-out', *Journal of Social Issues*, 34: 111–24.

Masterson, J.F. (1985) *The Real Self: A Developmental, Self, and Object Relations Approach*. New York: Brunner/Mazel.

Marzillier, J. and Hall, J. (2009) 'The challenge of the Layard initiative', *The Psychologist*, 22(5): 396–9.

McCarn, S.R. and Fassinger, R.E. (1996) 'Revisioning sexual minority identity formation: a new model of lesbian identity and its implications for counseling and research', *The Counseling Psychologist*, 24: 508–34.

McLeod, S. (2007) *Bowlby's Attachment Theory*. Available at: www.simplypsychology.org/bowlby.html (accessed 21 January 2014).

McLuhan, M. (1964) *Understanding Media: The Extensions of Man*. New York: McGraw-Hill.

Mearns, D. (1994) 'The dance of psychotherapy', *Person-Centred Practice*, 2(2): 5–13.

Mearns, D. (1997) *Person-centred Counselling Training*. London: Sage.

Mearns, D. (2003) *Developing Person-Centred Counselling* (2nd edn). London: Sage.

Mearns, D. and Cooper, M. (2005) *Working at Relational Depth in Counselling and Psychotherapy*. London: Sage.

Mearns, D. and Thorne, B. (1988) *Person-Centred Counselling in Action*. London: Sage.

Mearns, D. and Thorne, B. (2000) *Person-Centered Therapy Today: New Frontiers in Theory and Practice*. London: Sage.

Merwin, M.R. and Smith-Kurtz, B. (1988) 'Healing of the whole person', in F.M. Ochberg (ed.), *Post-Traumatic Therapy and Victims of Violence*. New York: Brunner/Mazel.

Mikulincer, M. and Shaver, P.R. (2004) 'Security-based self-representations in adulthood: contents and processes', in W.S. Rholes and J.A. Simpson (eds), *Adult Attachment: Theory, Research, and Clinical Implications*. New York: Guilford Press. pp. 159–95.

Miller, J.B. and Stiver, I.P. (1995) *Relational Images and their Meanings in Psychotherapy*. Work in Progress No. 74. Wellesley, MA: Stone Center Working Paper Series.

Miller, J.B. and Stiver, I.P. (1997) *The Healing Connection: How Women form Relationships in Therapy and in Life*. Boston, MA: Beacon Press.

Miller, S., Wampold, B., and Varhely, K. (2008) 'Direct comparisons of treatment modalities for youth disorders: a meta-analysis', *Psychotherapy Research*, 18(1): 5–14.

Miller, S.D., Duncan, B.L. and Hubbard, M.A. (2004) 'Beyond integration: the triumph of outcome over process in clinical practice', *Psychotherapy in Australia*, 10(2): 2–19.

Mitchell, S. (1988) *Relational Concepts in Psychoanalysis: An Integration*. Cambridge, MA: Harvard University Press.

Mitchell, S. (2000) *Relationality*. Hillsdale, NJ: The Analytic Press.

Moodley, R. (2005) 'Diversity matrix revisited: criss-crossing multiple identities in clinical practice'. Keynote paper at Multicultural and Counseling symposium. Ithaca, NY: Cornell University.

Mudakiri, M.M. (2003) 'Working with interpreters in adult mental health', in R. Tribe and H. Raval (eds), *Working with Interpreters in Mental Health*. London and New York: Routledge.

National Health Services (2013) *Improving Access to Psychological Therapies*. Available at: www.iapt.nhs.uk/ (accessed 27 May 2013).

National Institute of Clinical Excellence (NICE) (2004) *Depression: Management of Depression in Primary and Secondary Care*. London: NICE.

NICE (2009) *Depression: Treatment and Management of Depression in Adults*. Clinical Guideline 90. London: National Institute for Health and Clinical Excellence. Available at: www.nice.org.uk (accessed 28 November 2013).

NICE (2011) *Common Mental Health Disorders: Identification and Pathways to Care*. Clinical Guideline 123. London: National Institute for Health and Clinical Excellence. Available at www.nice.org.uk (accessed 28 November 2013).

Nicholson, R.A. and Berman, J.S. (1983) 'Is follow up necessary in evaluating psychotherapy?', *Psychological Bulletin*, 93: 261–78.

Nolan, P. (2012) *Therapist and Client: A Relational Approach to Psychotherapy*. Chichester: Wiley & Sons.

Norcross, J.C. (2005) 'A primer on psychotherapy integration', in J.C. Norcross and M.R. Goldfried (eds), *Handbook of Psychotherapy Integration*. (2nd edn). New York: Oxford University. pp. 3–23.

Norcross, J.C. and Lambert, M.J. (2011) 'Evidence-based therapy relationships', in J.C. Norcross (ed.), *Psychotherapy Relationships that Work*. New York: Oxford University Press. pp. 3–21.

Orlinsky, D.E., Grawe, K. and Parks, B.K. (1994) 'Process and outcome in psychotherapy: noch einmal', in A.E. Bergin and S.L. Garfield (eds), *Handbook of Psychotherapy and Behavior Change* (4th edn). New York: John Wiley & Sons. pp. 270–376.

Orlinsky, D.E. and Howard, K.I. (1978) 'The relation of process to outcome in psychotherapy', in S. Garfield and A. Bergin (eds), *Handbook of Psychotherapy and Behavior Change* (2nd edn). New York: John Wiley & Sons. pp. 283–330.

Orlinksy, D.E., Rønnestad, M.H. and Willutzki, U. (2004) 'Fifty years of psychotherapy process – outcome research: continuity and change', in M.J. Lambert (ed.), *Bergin & Garfield's Handbook of Psychotherapy and Behavior Change* (5th edn). New York: Wiley & Sons. pp. 307–90.

Ossana, S.M., Helms, J.E. and Leonard, M.M. (1992) 'Do "womanist" identity attitudes influence college women's self-esteem and perceptions of environmental bias?', *Journal of Counseling and Development*, 70: 402–8.

Parlett, M. and Page, F. (1990) 'Gestalt therapy', in W. Dryden (ed.), *Individual Therapy: A Handbook*. Maidenhead, UK: Open University Press.

Parsons, F. (1909) *Choosing a Vocation*. Boston, MA: Houghton Mifflin.

Patterson, C.H. (1974) *Relationship Counseling and Psychotherapy*. New York: Harper & Row.

Paul, S. (2008) 'The relationship in group therapy', in S. Haugh and S. Paul (eds), *The Therapeutic Relationship: Themes and Perspectives*. Ross-on-Wye: PCCS Books.

Paul, S. and Charura, D. (2012) 'Accepting the therapeutic relationship as love', *The Psychotherapist*, 52: 22–3.

Paul, S. and Haugh, S. (2008) 'The relationship not the therapy? What the research tells us', in Haugh, S. and Paul, S. (eds), *The Therapeutic Relationship: Perspectives and Themes*. Ross-on-Wye: PCCS Books. pp. 8–22.

Paul, S. and Pelham, G. (2000) 'A relational approach to therapy', in S. Palmer and R. Woolfe (eds), *Integrative and Eclectic Counselling and Psychotherapy*. London: Sage. pp. 110–26.

Paus, T., Zijdenbos, A., Worsley, K., Collins, D.L., Blumenthal, J., Giedd, J.N. ... and Evans, A.C. (1999) 'Structural maturation of neural pathways in children and adolescents: *in vivo* study', *Science*, 283(5409): 1908–11.

Pearlman, L.A., Saakvitne, K.W. et al. (1995) *Vicarious Traumatization I: The Cost of Empathy*. Ukiah, CA: Cavalcade Productions.

Pedersen, P.B. (1999a) *Culture-Centred Counselling Interventions: Striving for Accuracy*. Thousand Oaks, CA: Sage.

Pedersen, P.B. (1999b) *Multiculturalism as a Fourth Force*. Philadelphia, PA: Taylor & Francis.

Pedersen, P.B. (2000) 'Cross-cultural counselling', in A.E. Kazdin (ed.), *Encyclopaedia of Psychology* (Vol. 2). Washington, DC: American Psychological Association. pp. 359–61.

Pelham, G. (2008) 'The relational approach', in S. Haugh and S. Paul (eds), *The Therapeutic Relationship: Perspectives and Themes*. Ross-on Wye: PCCS Books.

Pelham, G. and Stacey, J. (1999) *Counselling Skills for Creative Arts Therapists.* Richmond, UK: Worth.

Perls, F. and Baumgartner, P. (1975) *Gifts from Lake Cowichan/Legacy from Fritz*. Palo Alto, CA: Science & Behavior Books.

Perls, F., Hefferline, R. and Goodman, P. (1951) *Gestalt Therapy: Excitement and Growth in the Human Personality*. New York: Julian.

Phinney, J. (1989) 'Stages of ethnic identity development in minority group adolescents', *Journal of Early Adolescence*, 9: 34–49.

Phinney, J.S. and Ong, A.D. (2007) 'Conceptualization and measurement of ethnic identity: current status and future directions', *Journal of Counseling Psychology*, 54: 271–81.

Pilgrim, D. (2005) *Key Concepts in Mental Health*. London: Sage.

Pinsof, W.M. (1994) 'An overview of integrative problem-centered therapy: a synthesis of family and individual psychotherapies', *Journal of Family Therapy*, 16: 103–20.

Polster, E. and Polster, M. (1973) *Gestalt Therapy Integrated: Contours of Theory and Practice*. New York: Brunner/Mazel.

Ponterotto, J.G. and Park-Taylor, J. (2007) 'Racial and ethnic identity theory, measurement, and research in counseling psychology: present status and future directions', *Journal of Counseling Psychology*, 54: 282–94.

Poston, W.S.C. (1990) 'The biracial identity development model: a needed addition', *Journal of Counseling and Development*, 69: 152–5.

Proctor, G. (2002) *The Dynamics of Power in Counselling and Psychotherapy: Ethics, Politics and Practice*. Ross-on-Wye: PCCS Books.

Prouty, G. (1990) 'Therapy: a theoretical evolution in the person-centered experiential psychotherapy of the psychotherapy of schizophrenia and retardation', in G. Lietaer, J. Rombauts and R. Van Balen (eds), *Client-Centered and Experiential Psychotherapy in the Nineties*. Leuven, Belgium: Leuven University Press.

Prouty, G., Van Werde, D. and Pörtner, M. (2002) *Pre-Therapy: Reaching Contact-Impaired Clients*. Ross-on-Wye: PCCS Books.

Public Sector Equality Duties (2011) www.equalityhumanrights.com/advice-and-guidance/public-sector-equality-duty/ (accessed 27 October 2013).

Purton, C. (2004) 'Differential response, diagnosis, and the philosophy of the implicit', *Person-Centered and Experiential Psychotherapies*, 3(4): 245–55.

Raval, H. and Smith, J. (2003) 'Therapist's experiences of working with language and interpreters', *International Journal of Mental Health*, 32(2): 6–31.

Reik, T. (1948) *Listening with the Third Ear: The Inner Experience of a Psychoanalyst*. New York: Grove Press.

Richards, D.A. (2010) 'Behavioural activation', in J. Bennet-Levy, D. Richards, P. Farrand, H. Chrisensen, K. Griffiths, D. Kavanagh, B. Klein, M.A. Lau, J. Proudfoot, L. Ritterband, J. White and C. Williams (eds), *Oxford Guide to Low Intensity CBT Interventions*. Oxford: Oxford University Press. pp. 141–50.

Rogers, C.R. (1942) *Counselling and Psychotherapy: Newer Concepts in Practice*. Boston, MA: Houghton Mifflin.

Rogers, C. (1951) *Client-Centred Therapy: Its Current Practice, Implications and Theory*. London: Constable; Boston, MA: Houghton Mifflin.

Rogers, C. (1957) 'The necessary and sufficient conditions of therapeutic personality change', *Journal of Consulting Psychology*, 21(2): 95–103.

Rogers, C.R. (1959) 'A theory of therapy, personality and interpersonal relationships as developed in the client-centred framework', in S. Koch (ed.), *Psychology: A Study of Science* (Vol. 3). New York: McGraw-Hill. pp. 184–256.

Rogers, C.R. (1961) *On Becoming a Person: A Therapist's View of Psychotherapy*. London: Constable; Boston, MA: Houghton Mifflin.

Rogers, C.R. (1962) 'The interpersonal relationship: the core of guidance', in C.R. Rogers and B. Stevens (eds), *Person to Person: The Problem of Being Human*. Moab, UT: Real People Press. pp. 89–104.

Rogers, C.R. (1966) 'Client centred therapy', in S. Arieti (ed.), *American Handbook of Psychiatry* (Vol. 3). New York: Basic Books. pp. 183–200.

Rogers, C.R. (1980) *A Way of Being*. Boston, MA: Houghton Mifflin.

Rogers, C.R. (1986) 'Client-centered approach to therapy', in I.L. Kutash and A. Wolf (eds), *Psychotherapist's Casebook: Theory and Technique in Practice*. San Francisco: Jossey Bass. pp. 197–208.

Rosenhan, D.L. (1973) 'On being sane in insane places', *Science*, 179: 250–58.

Roth, A. and Fonagy, P. (1996) *What Works for Whom? A Critical Review of Psychotherapy Research*. New York: Guilford Press.

Roth, A. and Fonagy, P. (2004) *What Works for Whom? A Critical Review of Psychotherapy Research* (2nd edn). New York: Guilford Press.

Roth, A., Hill, A. and Pilling, S. (2009) *The Competencies Required to Deliver Effective Humanistic Psychological Therapies*. London: University College of London.

Roth, A.D. and Pilling, S. (2008) 'Using an evidence-based methodology to identify the competencies required to deliver effective cognitive and behavioural therapy for depression and anxiety disorders', *Behavioural and Cognitive Psychotherapy*, 36: 129–47.

Rothschild, B. (2006) *Help for the Helper.* London and New York: W.W. Norton.

Rucker, N.G. and Lombardi, K.L. (1998) *Subject Relations: Unconscious Experience and Relational Psychoanalysis*. New York: Routledge.

Ryde, J. (2011) 'Issues for white therapists', in C. Lago (ed.), *The Handbook of Transcultural Counselling & Psychotherapy*. Maidenhead, UK: Open University Press.

Saakvitne, K.W., Gamble, S., Pearlman, L.A. and Lev, B.T. (2000) *Risking Connection: A Training Curriculum for Working with Survivors of Childhood Abuse*. Lutherville, MD: The Sidran Press.

Safran, J.D., Muran, J.C., Wallner Samstag, L. and Stevens, C. (2001) 'Repairing therapeutic alliance ruptures', *Psychotherapy*, 38: 406–12.

Sand, S. (2007) 'Future considerations: interactive identities and the interactive self', *The Psychoanalytic Review*, 94: 83–97.

Sanders, P. and Cooper, M. (2006) 'Research into person-centred counselling', in P. Sanders (ed.), *The Person-Centred Counselling Primer.* Ross-on-Wye: PCCS Books.

Sarkar, S.P. (2004) 'Boundary violation and sexual exploitation in psychiatry and psychotherapy: a review', *Advances in Psychiatric Treatment*, 10(4): 312–20.

Schauben, L.J. and Frazier, P.A. (1995) 'Vicarious trauma: the effects on female counsellors of working with sexual violence survivors', *Psychology of Women Quarterly*, 19(1): 49–64.

Schechter, R.A. (1992) 'Voice of a hidden minority: identification and countertransference in the cross-cultural working alliance', *The American Journal of Psychoanalysis*, 52(4): 339–49.

Schmid, P.F. (1998) '"Face to face": the art of encounter', in B. Thorne and E. Lambers (eds), *Person-Centred Therapy: A European Perspective*. London: Sage. pp. 74–90.

Schmid, P.F. (2001) 'Authenticity: the person as his or her own author. Dialogical and ethical perspectives on therapy as an encounter relationship, and beyond', in G. Wyatt (ed.), *Rogers' Therapeutic Conditions: Evolution, Theory and Practice. Volume 1: Congruence*. Ross-on-Wye: PCCS Books. pp. 217–32.

Schmid, P.F. (2004) '"In the beginning there is community": implications and challenges of the belief in a triune God and a person-centred approach. Invited lecture given at the International Conference 'The Spiritual Dimension in Therapy and Experiential Exploration: a conference for those counsellors, psychotherapists and other practitioners concerned to explore the significance of spirituality to their life and practice', Norwich, 18–22 July 2004, 20 July.

Segal, Z., Williams, M. and Teasdale, J. (2002) *Mindfulness-Based Cognitive Therapy for Depression: A New Approach to Preventing Relapse*. New York: Guilford Press.

Sexton, L. (1999) 'Vicarious traumatisation of counsellors and effects on their workplaces', *British Journal of Guidance and Counselling*, 27(3): 393–403.

Shapiro, S., Shapiro, D. and Schwartz, G. (2000) 'Stress management in medical education: a review of the literature', *Academic Medicine*, 75: 748–59.

Shiers, J. and Paul, S. (2008) 'Transpersonal dimensions of the therapeutic relationship', in S. Haugh and S. Paul (eds), *The Therapeutic Relationship: Perspectives and Themes*. Ross-on-Wye: PCCS Books.

Shirk, S.R. and Karver, M. (2003) 'Prediction of treatment outcome from relationship variables in child and adolescent therapy: a meta-analytic review', *Journal of Consulting and Clinical Psychology*, 71(3): 462–71.

Shirk, S.R. and Karver, M. (2011) 'Alliance in child and adolescent therapy', in J.C. Norcross (ed.), *Psychotherapy Relationships that Work* (2nd edn). New York and Oxford: Oxford University Press.

Shorter, E. (1997) *A History of Psychiatry: From the Era of the Asylum to the Age of Prozac*. New York: John Wiley & Sons.

Shostrom, E.L. (1965) *Three Approaches to Psychotherapy: 'Gloria'*. Corona Del Mar, CA: Psychological & Educational Films.

Siegel, D.J. (1999) *The Developing Mind: How Relationships and the Brain Interact to Shape Who We Are*. New York: Guilford.

Siegel, D. (2003) *Parenting from the Inside Out*. New York: Penguin.

Siegel, D.J. (2007) *The Mindful Brain: Reflection and Attunement in the Cultivation of Wellbeing*. New York: W.W. Norton & Co.

Sills, C. (ed.) (2006) *Contracts in Counselling and Psychotherapy* (2nd edn). London: Sage.

Simon, R.I. (1995) 'The natural history of therapist sexual misconduct: identification and prevention', *Psychiatric Annals*, 25, 90–94.

Singh, J. and Tudor, K. (1997) 'Cultural conditions of therapy', *The Person-Centred Journal*, 4(3): 32–46.

Singleton, N., Bumpstead, R., O'Brien, M. et al. (2001) *Psychiatric Morbidity among Adults Living in Private Households, 2000*. London: The Stationery Office.

Sotsky, S.M. et al. (1991) 'Patient predictors of response to psychotherapy and pharmacotherapy – findings in the NIMH Treatment of Depression Collaborative Research-Program', *American Journal of Psychiatry*, 148(8): 997–1008.

Speight, S.L., Myers, L.J., Cox, C.I. and Highlen, R.S. (1991) 'A redefinition of multicultural counselling', *Journal of Counselling and Development*, 70: 29–36.

Spinelli, E. (2008) 'The existential approach', in S. Haugh and S. Paul (eds), *The Therapeutic Relationship: Perspectives and Themes*. Ross-on-Wye: PCCS Books. pp. 51–64.

Spitzer, R.L., Kroenke, R., Williams, J.B. and Lowe, B. (2006) 'A brief measure for assessing generalized anxiety disorder: the GAD-7', *Archives of Internal Medicine*, 166: 1092–7.

Stamm, B.H. (ed.) (1999) *Secondary Traumatic Stress: Self-Care Issues for Clinicians, Researchers & Educators* (2nd edn). Lutherville, MD: The Sidran Press.

Steed, L.G. and Downing, R. (1998) 'Vicarious traumatisation amongst psychologists and professional counsellors working in the field of sexual abuse/assault', *The Australasian Journal of Disaster and Trauma Studies*, 2: Electronic Journal: www.massey.ac.nz/~trauma/issues/1998–2/steed.htm (accessed 11 June 2014).

Steering Committee of the American Psychological Association's Division 29 Task Force on Empirically Supported Therapy Relationships (2002) 'Conclusions and recommendations on the Division 29 task force', in J.C. Norcross (ed.), *Psychotherapy Relationships that Work: Therapist Contributions and Responsiveness to Patients*. Oxford: Oxford University Press. pp. 441–3.

Stern, D.N. (1985) *The Interpersonal World of the Infant*. New York: Basic Books.

Stern, D.N. (2004) *The Present Moment in Psychotherapy and Everyday Life*. New York: W.W. Norton and Company.

Stern, D.N., Sander, L.W., Nahum, J.P., Harrison, A.M., Lyons-Ruth, K., Morgan, A.C., et al. (1998) 'Non-interpretive mechanisms in psychoanalytic therapy: The "something more" than interpretation', *International Journal of Psycho-Analysis*, 79: 903–21.

Stiles, W.B., Barkham, M., Mellor-Clark, J. and Connell, J. (2008) 'Effectiveness of cognitive behavioural, person-centred, and psychodynamic therapies in UK primary care routine practice: replication in a larger sample', *Psychological Medicine*, 38(5): 677–88.

Stiles, W.B., Barkham, M., Twigg, E., Mellor-Clark, J. and Cooper, M. (2006) 'Effectiveness of cognitive-behavioural, person-centred and psychodynamic therapies as practised in UK National Health Service settings', *Psychological Medicine*, 36: 555–66.

Stolorow, R. (1994) 'The nature and therapeutic action of psychoanalytic interpretation', in R. Stolorow, G. Atwood and B. Brandchaft (eds), *The Intersubjective Perspective*. Northvale, NJ: Jason Aronson.

Stolorow, R. and Atwood, G. (1992) *Contexts of Being: The Intersubjective Foundations of Psychological Life*. Hillsdale, NJ: The Analytic Press.

Stolorow, R., Atwood, G., Brandchaft, B. and Atwood, G. (1987) *Psychoanalytic Treatment: An Intersubjective Approach*. Hillsdale, NJ: The Analytic Press.

Sue, D.W., Arredondo, P. and McDavis, R.J. (1992) 'Multicultural counselling competencies and standards: a call to the profession', *Journal of Counseling and Development*, 70: 477–86.

Sue, D.W., Carter, R.T., Casas, J.M., Ivey, A.E., Jensen, M. et al. (1998) *Multicultural Counselling Competencies: Individual and Organizational Development*. Thousand Oaks, CA: Sage.

Sue, D.W. and Sue, D. (1990) *Counselling the Culturally Different: Theory and Practice* (2nd edn). New York: Wiley.

Sue, D.W. and Sue, D. (2003) *Counselling the Culturally Diverse: Theory and Practice* (4th edn). New York: Wiley.

Sullivan, H.S. (1953) *The Interpersonal Theory of Psychiatry*. New York: Basic Books.

Syed, I.B. (2002) 'Islamic medicine: 1000 years ahead of its times', *Journal of the International Society for the History of Islamic Medicine*, 1(2): 2–8.

Thomas, L.K. (1992) 'Psychotherapy in the context of race and culture: An intercultural therapeutic approach', in S. Fernando (ed.), *Mental Health in a Multi-ethnic Society*. London: Routledge. pp. 172–90.

Thomas, L.K. (1999) 'Communicating with a black child: Overcoming obstacles of difference', in B. Carolin and P. Milner (ed.), *Time to Listen to Children: Personal and Professional Communication*. London: Routledge. pp. 65–78.

Thomas, M. (2008) 'Cognitive behavioural dimensions of the therapeutic relationship', in S. Haugh and S. Paul (eds), *The Therapeutic Relationship: Perspectives and Themes*. Ross-on-Wye: PCCS Books.

Tribe, R. and Raval, H. (eds) (2003) *Working with Interpreters in Mental Health*. Hove, UK: Brunner-Routledge.

Troiden, R. (1988) 'Homosexual identity development', *Journal of Adolescent Health Care*, 9: 105–13.

Truax, C. and Carkhuff, R. (1967) *Toward Effective Counselling and Psychotherapy*. Chicago, IL: Aldine.

Tryon, G.S. and Winograd, G. (2002) 'Goal consensus and collaboration', in J.C. Norcross (ed.), *Psychotherapy Relationships that Work*. New York: Oxford University Press. pp. 106–22.

Tsai, M., Kohlenburg, R.J., Kanter, J.W., Kolenburg, B., Folette, W.C. and Callaghan, G.M. (2009) *A Guide to Functional Analytic Psychotherapy: Awareness, Courage, Love and Behaviourism*. New York: Springer.

Tuckman, B.W. (1996) *Theories and Applications of Educational Psychology*. New York: McGraw Hill (3rd edn, with D. Moneth, published 2001).

Van Belle, H.A. (1980) *Basic Intent and Therapeutic Approach of Carl R. Rogers*. Toronto: Wedge.

Van der Kolk, B.A. (2005) 'Developmental trauma disorder: towards a rational diagnosis for chronically traumatized children', *Psychiatric Annals*, 35(5): 401–8.

Vash, C.L. (1981) *The Psychology of Disability* (Vol. 1). Springer Series on Rehabilitation. New York: Springer.

Vontress, C.E. (1988) 'An existential approach to cross-cultural counselling', *Journal of Multicultural Counselling and Development*, 16: 73–83.

Vontress, C.E. (2012a) 'Social class influences on counselling', in R. Moodley, L. Epp and H. Yusuf (eds), *Counseling across the Cultural Divide*. Ross On Wye: PCCS Books. pp. 42–62.

Vontress, C.E. (2012b) 'Counselling across the cultural divide', in R. Moodley, L. Epp and H. Yusaf (eds), *Counseling across the Cultural Divide: A Clemmont Vontress Reader*. Ross-on-Wye: PCCS Books.

Vredenburgh, L.D., Carlozzi, A.F. and Stein, L.B. (1999) 'Burnout in counseling psychologists: type of practice setting and pertinent demographics', *Counselling Psychology Quarterly*, 12(3): 295–304.

Walford, J. and Walford, R. (2008) 'Transactional analysis: a diversity of relationships', in S. Haugh and S. Paul (eds), *The Therapeutic Relationship: Perspectives and Themes*. Ross-on-Wye: PCCS Books.

Walsh, R. and Vaughan, F. (eds) (1993) *Paths Beyond Ego*. New York: J.P. Tarcher/Putnam.

Wampold, B.E. (2001) *The Great Psychotherapy Debate*. Englewood Cliffs, NJ: Lawrence Erlbaum Associates.

Warner, M. (1991) 'Fragile process', in L. Fusek (ed.), *New Directions in Client-Centered Therapy: Practice with Difficult Client Populations*. Monograph Series I. Chicago, IL: Chicago Counseling Center.

Weerasekera, P., Linder, B., Greenberg, L. and Watson, J. (2001) 'The working alliance in client-centered and process-experiential therapy of depression', *Psychotherapy Research*, 11: 221–33.

Weiss, D.S. and Marmar, C.R. (1997) 'The impact of event scale revised', in J.P. Wilson and T.M. Keane (eds), *Assessing Psychological Trauma and PTSD*. New York: Guilford Press. pp. 399–411.

Weiss, E. (1950) *Principles of Psychodynamics*. New York: Grune & Stratton.

Weitz, P. (2014) 'Psychotherapy 2.0: for better or for worse?', in P. Weitz (ed.), *Psychotherapy 2.0: Where Psychotherapy and Technology Meet* (Vol. 1). London: Karnac.

Wessely, S. (2001) 'Randomised goal trials: the gold standard', in C. Mace, S. Moorey and B. Roberts (eds), *Evidence in the Psychological Therapies*. Hove, UK: Brunner-Routledge. pp. 46–60.

Westen, D., Novotny, C.M. and Thompson-Brenner, H. (2004) 'The empirical status of empirically supported psychotherapies: assumptions, findings, and reporting in controlled clinical trials', *Psychological Bulletin*, 130(4): 631.

Wilde McCormick, E. (2000) 'The therapeutic relationship', in N. Wellings and E. McCormick (eds), *Transpersonal Psychotherapy*. London and New York: Continuum. pp. 20–51.

Wills, F. and Sanders, D. (2013) *Cognitive Behaviour Therapy: Foundations for Practice*. London: Sage.

Wilson, J.E. and Syme, G. (2006) *Objectives and Outcomes: Questioning the Practice of Therapy*. Maidenhead, UK: Open University Press.

Winnicott, D. (1965) *The Maturational Process and the Facilitating Environment*. New York: International Universities Press.

Wittine, B. (1993) 'Assumptions of transpersonal psychotherapy', in R. Walsh and F. Vaughan (eds), *Paths Beyond Ego*. New York: J.P. Tarcher/Putnam.

Wolpe, J. (1959) *Psychotherapy by Reciprocal Inhibition*. Stanford, CA: Stanford University Press.

Wolpe, J. (1973) *The Practice of Behavior Therapy*. Oxford: Pergamon.

Worsley, R. (2002) *Process Work in Person-Centred Therapy: Phenomenological and Existential Perspectives*. Ross-on-Wye: PCCS Books.

Worsley, R. (2008) 'The ground of our relating, Martin Buber's *I and Thou*', in S. Haugh and S. Paul (eds), *The Therapeutic Relationship: Perspectives and Themes*. Ross-on-Wye: PCCS Books.

Wosket, V. (2009) 'Relational ethics in supervision', in L. Gabriel and R. Casemore (eds), *Relational Ethics in Practice: Narratives from Counselling and Psychotherapy*. Hoboken, NY: Routledge. pp. 44–57.

Wright, J.K. (2002) 'Online counselling: learning from writing therapy', *British Journal of Guidance and Counselling*, 30: 285–98.

Wright, K.M. (2010) 'Therapeutic relationship: developing a new understanding for nurses and care workers within an eating disorder unit', *International Journal of Mental Health Nursing*, 19: 154–61 (doi: 10.1111/j.1447–0349.2009.00657).

Wundt, W. (1896) *Grundriss der Psychologie*. Leipzig: Engelmann.

Yalom, I.D. (1975) *The Theory and Practice of Group Psychotherapy*. New York: Basic Books.

Yalom, I.D. (1980) *Existential Psychotherapy*. New York: Basic Books.

Yalom, I.D. (1985) *The Theory and Practice of Group Psychotherapy* (3rd edn). New York: Basic Books.

Yalom, I.D. and Lescz, M. (2005) *The Theory and Practice of Group Psychotherapy*. (5th edn). New York: Basic Books.

Yontef, G.M. (2005) 'Gestalt therapy theory of change', in A. Woldt and S. Toman (eds), *Gestalt Therapy: History, Theory and Practice*. New York: Sage.

Index

Terms in the glossary are in **bold**